CHILD and YOUTH CARE
across SECTORS

CHILD and YOUTH CARE across SECTORS

Canadian Perspectives | Volume 2

Edited by Kiaras Gharabaghi and Grant Charles

Toronto | Vancouver

Child and Youth Care across Sectors: Canadian Perspectives, Volume 2
Edited by Kiaras Gharabaghi and Grant Charles

First published in 2020 by
Canadian Scholars, an imprint of CSP Books Inc.
425 Adelaide Street West, Suite 200
Toronto, Ontario
M5V 3C1

www.canadianscholars.ca

Copyright © 2020 Kiaras Gharabaghi, Grant Charles, the contributing authors, and Canadian Scholars.

All rights reserved. No part of this publication may be reproduced, stored in a retrieval system, or transmitted, in any form or by any means, without the prior written permission of Canadian Scholars, under licence or terms from the appropriate reproduction rights organization, or as expressly permitted by law.

Every reasonable effort has been made to identify copyright holders. Canadian Scholars would be pleased to have any errors or omissions brought to its attention.

Library and Archives Canada Cataloguing in Publication

Title: Child and youth care across sectors : Canadian perspectives / edited by Kiaras Gharabaghi and Grant Charles.
Names: Gharabaghi, Kiaras, editor. | Charles, Grant, 1953- editor.
Description: Includes bibliographical references.
Identifiers: Canadiana (print) 20190055383 | Canadiana (ebook) 20190055448 | ISBN 9781773381954 (v. 2 ; softcover) | ISBN 9781773381961 (v. 2 ; PDF) | ISBN 9781773381978 (v. 2 ; EPUB)
Subjects: LCSH: Child care—Canada. | LCSH: Child care services—Canada. | LCSH: Children—Institutional care—Canada.
Classification: LCC HQ778.7.C3 C55 2019 | DDC 362.70971—dc23

Text and cover design by Elisabeth Springate
Page layout by S4Carlisle Publishing Services

Printed and bound in Ontario, Canada

Canadä

CONTENTS

Introduction   Moving beyond Child and Youth Care Orthodoxies   1
Kiaras Gharabaghi and Grant Charles

Chapter 1   Being Indigenous Is Not a Risk Factor: A Sisters Rising Story of Resurgence and Sovereignty   6
Sandrina de Finney, Anna Chadwick, Chantal Adams, Shantelle Moreno, Angela Scott, and Shezell-Rae Sam

Chapter 2   Mino-Bimaadiziwin Wiidookodaadiwag (Helping Each Other through the Good Life): Implications for Research and Practice with Indigenous Communities   24
Nicole Ineese-Nash

Chapter 3   Towards a Framework of African-Centred Child and Youth Care Praxis   43
Julian Hasford, Peter Amponsah, Travonne Edwards, and Juanita Stephen

Chapter 4   Newcomer, Immigration, and Settlement Sectors   60
Francis Hare

Chapter 5   Youth Homelessness and Shelter Settings   74
Hans Skott-Myhre

Chapter 6   Child and Youth Care in the North   88
Heather Modlin, Kelly Shaw, Sheldon Lane, and Jennifer Oliver

Chapter 7   Child and Youth Care Practice in Hospital Settings   105
Agnes Quittard and Grant Charles

Chapter 8   School-Based Child and Youth Care Practice: A Case Study of Ontario   116
Saira Batasar-Johnie and Kiaras Gharabaghi

Chapter 9 Child and Youth Care Practice in Day Treatment Settings 130
Jessica Carriere and Kiaras Gharabaghi

Chapter 10 Child and Youth Care and the Youth Criminal Justice System 148
Grant Charles and Ashley Quinn

Chapter 11 The Other, Forgotten, Hidden, Current, and Future Settings of Child and Youth Care Practice 164
Kiaras Gharabaghi and Grant Charles

Conclusion Expansion and Consolidation: Where to from Here? 189
Kiaras Gharabaghi and Grant Charles

About the Contributors 195

INTRODUCTION

Moving beyond Child and Youth Care Orthodoxies

Kiaras Gharabaghi and Grant Charles

In the first volume of this two-volume series, we were able to present the reader with 12 "sectors" or contexts in which the field of child and youth care is active. Some of these sectors reflected the traditional work settings of child and youth care practitioners, such as residential care settings, foster care, and in-home family support programs. Others were reflective of changing times, both politically and socially. To this end, we were able to include chapters on child and youth care activity in the Trans youth sector, outdoor adventure programs, and autism services. And we even included chapters that present the reader with perhaps less familiar territory, such as a chapter on the post-secondary education setting as practice site, and another chapter on cyberspace as a child and youth care setting. We tried to be as inclusive as possible in the first volume, and included a chapter on child and youth care practice within Deaf communities, and another that tackled gender and sexuality dynamics in our field. Finally, we wanted to make sure that child and youth care practice in Canada is not limited to English Canada, and therefore included perhaps the most comprehensive chapter written in the past decade on child and youth care in Quebec. We were intentional in seeking out a range of authors who could present their sector or context from multiple positions of lived experience, scholarly study, and professional practice. Some of our authors are world-renowned scholars, such as Varda Mann-Feder, Doug Magnuson, Jennifer Martin, Ben Anderson-Nathe, Julie James, and Carol

Stuart. Others are emerging scholars who are also activists and practitioners in their chosen sectors or contexts, such as Nancy Marshall and Shay Erlich. And others mix their scholarship with professional leadership, or focus entirely on professional leadership, such as Kelly Shaw, Heather Modlin, and Andy Leggett. We think the first volume of *Child and Youth Care across Sectors* turned out to be a wonderfully diverse collection of deep and meaningful analyses of our field in multiple sectors and contexts.

It was clear from the beginning, however, that one volume, in which all authors had to abide by specific time frames, was never going to capture the richness of our field, nor the diversity of themes, issues, sectors, and contexts in which our field plays a role. In spite of our best efforts, the first volume of this series is written almost entirely by people who identify as white, who are voluntary settlers in Canada on Indigenous lands, and who reflect, at least in many cases, a history of our field that has not been particularly inclusive. Our field is changing, and as co-editors of these two volumes, we can only cheer on these changes and do our part to ensure that we don't move to perpetuate our lack of inclusiveness through yet more writing that exclusively reflects a particular set of lived experiences. With volume 2 of the series, we were able to wait for contributions that took longer, or that had to wait in line while the contributor completed other projects. Credit must go to our publisher, Canadian Scholars, who waited patiently for the manuscript for volume 2 to materialize. Well, here it is, and it was worth waiting for.

In this volume, we continue with the presentation of sectors and contexts that are familiar to child and youth care–involved people, but we also give space and voice to different ways of thinking about and describing our field, and to different ways of articulating the future directions our field ought to take. To this end, we have two chapters that centre Indigenous ways of being and thinking, both written by Indigenous scholars, in one case with co-authorship by a number of emerging scholars of varying identities. One of these chapters is based on the Indigenous context in British Columbia, the other in Ontario, both of which are, of course, settler-constructed geographic jurisdictions. We also have a chapter that contemplates child and youth care as a field that is African-centred—one that acknowledges the anti-Back racism in which it is complicit but moves towards a field embedded in a commitment to social justice. We confront issues of homelessness, of immigration and settlement, and of working in Canada's North, specifically in Labrador and Nunavut, areas that are rarely acknowledged in our literature. Finally, we also ensure that more traditional settings that didn't make it into volume 1 are represented in this volume: hospitals, schools, day treatment programs, and, of course, the always complicated and messy youth criminal justice sector.

Between the two volumes in the series, we cover enormous ground. It is fair to say that most child and youth care practice does indeed unfold in the sectors and contexts we have covered. Still, there are additional areas for which we were unable to curate authors but that nevertheless deserve chapters of their own. Perhaps there will eventually be a third volume in the series, but until such time, we engage these sectors and contexts in chapter 11 of this volume. As editors, we took the lead in identifying the specific sectors and contexts we wished to address, but we worked with many colleagues in the field to ensure that each of these sectors and contexts is addressed by someone actively involved or directly associated. We have identified 10 such sectors and contexts: private practice, advocacy, policy and government, transition work, AfroFuturism, rehabilitation and brain injury, secure treatment, addictions, management and leadership, and international practice. It is quite something to pause and think about: between the two volumes and this chapter, we have identified over 30 sectors and contexts in which our field has come to play a role, sometimes a leading role and other times a supporting role, but relevant in all cases.

FOCUSING ON ANTI-RACISM AND INDIGENOUS WAYS OF BEING

While we reserve a more thorough discussion of these themes for the concluding chapter of this volume, it is worthwhile to reflect for a moment on why we deemed it important to start volume 2 with two chapters on Indigenous ways of being and a chapter on African-centred perspectives and approaches. For too long, our field considered itself to be an extension of its early roots in residential care settings (see chapter 1, Gharabaghi & Charles, volume 1). It is, of course, true that residential settings provided the foundations for the development of the field in Canada. However, within that truth, we must acknowledge the damage this has done. Residential care itself cannot meaningfully be untied from the Indian Residential School System in Canada that was an instrument of a state-sanctioned cultural genocide. It also set the foundations for harmful experiences directly associated with current child and youth care practice, especially for Black Youth and Indigenous communities. While we celebrate the expansion of our field into so many different service sectors and contexts, we are conscious that we have not made significant strides in ensuring our field expands in resistance to the perpetuation of the racism and social injustice committed against many peoples. A great deal of child and youth care practice today still unfolds in institutional settings that are directly and very seriously implicated in anti-Black racism and anti-Indigenous racism and violence. Schools, residential programs of varying types, and even hospitals continue to marginalize and actively harm people, and our practices are not beyond the perpetration of such harm. For this reason, we wanted to make sure that we get started in this volume with a different frame. The two Indigenous-focused chapters are clear in their critique of settler colonialism, but also provide extremely valuable and extensive reference points for how things can be different. And similarly, the chapter on Black Youth is a constructive chapter—one that pulls no punches about what has gone wrong, but one that provides a clear and meaningful roadmap for healing and moving forward. Our hope is that these three chapters provide a frame for reading the rest of the book, and ideally for rereading volume 1 in our series.

MOVING BEYOND ORTHODOXIES

Congruent with our position above, we are anxious to ensure that child and youth care practice is recognized as multi-faceted, flexible, fluid, and not limited to universal concepts of relationship, caring, love, and others. We are offering these two volumes, and chapter 11 in this volume, as an attempt to ensure that we continue to focus on sectors, contexts, and settings where, for better or for worse, we have been active for a long time; but we are also interested in pushing further and recognizing that child and youth care practice has been a feature of many activities, connections, communities, and grassroots initiatives, even if such contexts have sometimes been discounted as "other." Whether it is AfroFuturism, the unpaid labour of Indigenous women providing care for children and communities or Elders caring for youth, or advocacy work in the context of community mobilization and resisting systemic oppressions—all of these are unfolding, congruent with the core of our field's values and ambitions. These are all ways of connecting, ways of ensuring young people know they matter, and ways of seeking change that centres the many ways in which young people find themselves positioned through their multiple identities, their lived experiences, and their community allegiances.

With these points in mind, let us move forward. But before we do, a few notes of gratitude. Natalie Garriga has been our main contact at Canadian Scholars, and she has been a joy to work with. Patient but persistent, open to new ideas and always graceful in response to delays, Natalie is a professional through and through, albeit one who quite on her own manages to be relational, in the true spirit of our field.

We have been working together, talking together, and contemplating together for quite some time. We are grateful for the opportunity to have continued this process through the editing of these two volumes. But, ultimately, we are grateful to the contributors, all of whom worked hard to meet deadlines, reissued deadlines, and final deadlines, and in the true spirit of great writers, they all submitted their excellent work at times that were quite unrelated to those deadlines. We are grateful to be able to display this work here, and we hope it will resonate with you, the reader.

Finally, it always falls on family members and close friends to listen to and pretend to care about the pitfalls of editing books. We are grateful for their very convincing performances, which helped us carry on.

CHAPTER 1

Being Indigenous Is Not a Risk Factor: A Sisters Rising Story of Resurgence and Sovereignty[1]

Sandrina de Finney, Anna Chadwick, Chantal Adams, Shantelle Moreno, Angela Scott, and Shezell-Rae Sam

> My dream is that First Nations girls can walk home alone without fear.
> —Jenny, 12, Sisters Rising participant

THE SISTERS RISING STORY: DIGNITY, SPIRIT, SOVEREIGNTY

We are writing this chapter together as part of our collective work on Sisters Rising, an Indigenous-led, land- and arts-based research project with Indigenous youth of all genders in Indigenous communities on the west coast of Turtle Island (British Columbia, Canada). The vision of Sisters Rising (see sistersrising.uvic.ca) is to support young people's dignity, healing, and strengths in relation to historical and ongoing sexualized and gender-based violence. For the past two years, we have been working through arts- and land-based workshops with young people (ages 13–26) who self-identify as Native, Aboriginal, on- and off-reserve First Nations, mixed, Métis, Indigenous, and/or Inuit. Community and family members, including service providers and knowledge holders such as Elders, are also welcomed to participate. Our workshops include a range of multimedia activities, including circles with Elders; walks on the land; working with water; art and collage making; tanning hides; working with wool, stone, hide, and cedar; digital storytelling; spoken word; painting; making masks and image collages; and traditional felt and beading work. We have had the great honour and privilege of hosting workshops with numerous youth, communities, and organizations in both urban and remote rural communities across British Columbia, including in Lax Kw'alaams, Prince Rupert, Kitamaat, Haida Gwaii, Tsawwassen, Greater Victoria, Lekwungen, W̱SÁNEĆ and T'souke territories, and Duncan, Cowichan Tribes territory. Central to our ethics is that we only work with communities and organizations that have invited us and/or where we have family roots and existing connections.

A primary focus of our work is to re-centre Indigenous sacred teachings regarding gender and sexual wellness and well-being. Our participants and research staff (primarily Indigenous young adults) have worked alongside Elders and Knowledge Keepers, presented at local and international conferences, co-authored academic journal articles, produced videos and numerous individual and collective art pieces, and facilitated dozens of public presentations and workshops. Our Sisters Rising website shows the artwork, digital media, and images created in our workshops, exploring topics such as self-love, dignity, sovereignty, intergenerational trauma, consent, decolonization, land-based healing, racism, cis- and heteronormativity, 2Spirit-phobia, and the colonial roots of violence.

Sisters Rising is one of many responses to the critical need for innovative interventions to support Indigenous girls, young women, and 2Spirit youth who face the highest rates of gendered and sexualized violence. Our work focuses on challenging the victim-blaming and criminalizing climate of racialized violence by re-centring Indigenous values and teachings and linking body sovereignty to questions of decolonization and land sovereignty.

Our approach to co-writing this chapter and to our Sisters Rising work is rooted in our teachings from our diverse communities and nations: Haida, Nuu-chah-nulth, Maliseet, Anishinaabe, Indian, Irish, French, Cree, Métis, British, Indian-Fijian, Chilean, Mapuche, Zambian, and South African. This is no essentialized listing of ethnic backgrounds but rather a reclaiming of our connections to our ancestral legacies and homelands—connections that have been muted, for ourselves and generations of our families, through hundreds of years of transnational European invasion, colonial assimilation, and forced relocation. We draw on our work with youth, families, and communities as front-line workers, community-based researchers, counsellors, advocates, artists, and activists, as well as undergraduate and graduate students and faculty in the School of Child and Youth Care (CYC) at the University of Victoria, located on Lekwungen and W̱SÁNEĆ territories in western Canada.

We open this chapter with context and statistics related to enduring colonial pathways to violence that have contributed to the drastic overrepresentation of Indigenous children and families in child welfare and social services contexts. This analysis is not to abstract or quantify trauma, but rather to insist that statistics matter, because they represent the lived realities of young Indigenous people who face indefensible structural and systemic inequities within settler states.

SETTLER STATE STATISTICS AND CONTEXT

Being Indigenous is not a risk factor—colonialism is the risk factor:

> They tell me it's lateral, lateral, OK. Lateral, side-ways, all around, top down. Yeah, it's a bad circle, a very bad cycle. It doesn't matter how it happens, though, it all came from the same place, it all came from what they did to us in residential schools and all that. Open your eyes. Stop blaming the victims. (Sisters Rising participant)

Countries like Canada, the United States, Aotearoa (New Zealand), and Australia are colonial settler states, meaning that colonialism cannot be thought of as an event in the past that is over and done with. In settler states, the settlers never left (Tuck & Yang, 2012). White settler states are states in which settlers now constitute the demographic and political majority while Indigenous people who once represented 100% of the population have been reduced to a significant minority (5% currently in Canada). In a settler state, colonial violence is constantly reasserted, and Euro-Western languages, laws, values, and policies are forcefully imposed on Indigenous peoples (Tuck & Yang, 2012). Settler states have always seen Indigenous children as prime targets for cultural, spiritual, physical, and gender-based genocide (Truth and Reconciliation Commission of Canada, 2015; National Inquiry into Murdered and Missing Indigenous Women and Girls, 2019).

One of Canada's most significant child-targeting policies has been residential schools, which served as internment camps (Richardson & Reynolds, 2014) from 1883 to 1996. Children in residential schools had a higher chance of dying than Canadian soldiers did during World War II (Canadian Broadcasting Corporation, 2015). Residential schools are often presented as a shameful past from which we are now recovering through generously funded reconciliation initiatives. The reality is that we are currently in the midst of the worst epidemic of Indigenous children being removed from their homes by government workers in what has become known as the "Millennium Scoop" (Beaucage, as cited in Canadian Broadcasting Corporation, 2011). Per capita, more Indigenous children are in government "care" today than at any other point in history (Truth and Reconciliation Commission of Canada, 2015), while Indigenous education and social services chronically receive 20 to 40% less than mainstream services (First Nations Child and Family Caring Society, 2016). Those of us who work in social systems understand the enormous harm that 20 to 40 percent less funding produces: systemic policing and tracking of our families, higher caseloads, lack of follow-up, an absence of culturally grounded, community-led care, systemic gaps that compound harm, trauma that remains unresolved across generations, and children who continue to slip through pervasive cracks. This funding inequity helps explain why we see disproportionate numbers of Indigenous families return to the services we provide as CYC workers.

PATHWAYS TO SEXUALIZED AND GENDER-BASED VIOLENCE

> Holding back tears inside I say no, I am worth it. Ask for help, hope and heal.
> —Jakie, 17, Sisters Rising participant

The pathways to sexualized and gender-based violence are carved into this same colonial landscape. As shared by a Sisters Rising participant, "this violence does not simply happen." Sarah Deer (2009) stresses that rape and sexual violence "are deeply embedded in the colonial mindset. Rape is more than a metaphor for colonization—it is part and parcel of colonization" (p. 150). Through centuries of dehumanization and overt sexualization, Indigenous girls, women, and 2Spirit people in particular have been targeted for centuries by colonial institutions, stripped of their tribal rights and leadership roles (de Finney, 2015; Dhillon, 2015). Kim Anderson (2000) and Ruth Pierson (2005), among others, discuss how Indigenous girls and women have been degraded and sexualized to justify colonial violence. Historically, for example, government agents often exploited their authority and withheld food supplies "unless Aboriginal women were made available to them" (Razack, 2002, p. 131). Following hundreds of years of targeted colonial violence, Indigenous girls and women today experience the highest rates, compared to other groups, of sexual and racialized violence and exploitation, sex trafficking, incarceration, murder, poverty, under-housing, homelessness, and under-servicing in health and education (Dhillon, 2015; Hunt, 2015; Ontario Native Women's Association, 2016). Indigenous girls apprehended by the child welfare system are the victims of sexual violence more than twice as often as other girls in care (Turpel-Lafond, 2016).

In addition to sexual exploitation and systemic degradation of Indigenous girls and women, the damaging legacy of the Euro-Western gender binary muted Indigenous gender and sexuality systems. The gender binary (male/female), as enacted in residential schools, created shame and propagated gender violence that persists today. As Sam McKegney (2016) writes: "The systematic assault on Indigenous cosmologies of gender and Indigenous kinship structures enacted through the separation of boys and girls, the shaming of the body, and the corrosion of empathy creates conditions in which ... cyclical violence ... proliferate[s]" (pp. 206–207). Evidence abounds that Indigenous 2Spirit, gender-fluid, queer, and Trans youth face isolation, stigmatization, and increased victimization across social services (Lyons et al., 2016; National Aboriginal Health Organization, 2012; Toomey, Ryan, Diaz, Card, & Russell, 2013). LGBTQ+ youth transitioning out of government care are particularly vulnerable to exploitation and survival sex work due to a lack of basic supports, housing, and employment (Turpel-Lafond, 2016), as well as intersecting forms of discrimination and violence. With the weight of colonial history on their backs and current gaps in support and systemic inequities, Indigenous 2Spirit and LGBTQ+ youth are exposed to risk factors that impinge on their capacity to live in dignity and safety. Compounding these erasures, our communities are too often the focal point of evidence-based, risk-, and deficit-focused investigations that pathologize and criminalize us and prolong a cycle of damaging colonial assessments and interventions.

By all accounts, we have reached a crisis. The release of the federal inquiry into stolen, missing, and murdered Indigenous women, girls, and 2Spirit people (National Inquiry into Murdered and Missing Indigenous Women and Girls, 2019) identified systemic failures by law enforcement and legal, social, health, and educational services across Canada as a failure to uphold the basic rights and well-being of Indigenous women and girls and Trans, non-binary, and 2Spirit people. The inquiry found that these systems have generated outright gender-based genocide—conditions that precipitate death for Indigenous girls, women, and 2Spirit people (National Inquiry into Murdered and Missing Indigenous Women and Girls, 2019).

We often ask ourselves, what is our responsibility as CYC workers to these realities? We see our own families and communities overrepresented in practically every context in which we work. We grapple with what it means to be practitioners and CYC academics working in systems premised on genocide, on the deliberate erasure of centuries of knowledge held by Indigenous, Brown, and Black communities. We seek tools and information to understand and disrupt how—while it is rarely even spoken about in CYC circles—it is colonialism in our midst that *produces* the risk factors we seek to address in our practice. How do we enact our responsibilities to these realities? This difficult, vital question is the starting place for Sisters Rising.

SISTERS RISING STORIES

> They most often tell me "I am native, but I don't practice my culture." Lost to the urban community of a colonized nation, where there is no Indigenous sovereignty of the body, of the land, of culture. I see that Indigenous girls and women living in urban communities, like myself, are ghosts: not seen or heard. Pain is forgotten and ignored. There are no increases in services or programs that provide cultural intervention or spirit-nourishing guidance.
> —Angela Scott, Ojibwe/Métis/Danish/English, CYC MA, Sisters Rising clinical counsellor

Stories matter, Leanne Betasamosake Simpson (2014) says, because they have been used for centuries to affirm "ancient codes of ethics" (p. 8). These are stories where tears, dreams, words, objects, spirit, and wonder all comingle, screaming unequivocally: "[We] are supposed to be here" (p. 8).

One story about resilient, adaptive fungi reminds us about the need for resurgence in the face of colonial genocide. Apparently, the melting permafrost in the Mackenzie Delta, a sacred waterway that criss-crosses several First Nations in the Far North, is releasing an ancient native fungus that has lain dormant for thousands of years (Canadian Broadcasting Corporation, 2017). This fungus is extremely adaptive and resilient, and it might be able to nourish and sustain the roots of trees and plants stressed out by rapid climate change (Canadian Broadcasting Corporation, 2017). This story reminds us that settler state violence helps the settler state make room for itself—it severs us from our kin relations, from roots, soil, air, and water. Working in all directions, it seeks to contain, dispirit, and immobilize us in shame and self-blame. But, like ancient fungi, we are adaptive, creative spirits with stories that cannot be contained, even across time and under shifting, stressful conditions. Our ancestors lie underground but are never dormant; they sustain the pathways over which new generations will walk (de Finney, Moreno, et al., 2018).

Our main purpose in coming together to work on Sisters Rising is to engage intercessions that extricate Indigenous girls, youth, and their bodies from exploitive and dehumanizing colonial relations (de Finney, Palacios, Mucina, & Chadwick, 2018). Our commitment is informed by our experiences as mothers, aunties, siblings, cousins, community members, kin, and children of our homelands. As CYC practitioners, we work with communities—including our own—that have experienced compounded racialized, gendered, sexualized, and ableist violence in countless state-run, government-funded colonial systems, including the criminal, legal, education, immigration, health care, and child welfare systems. We see Indigenous children and families routinely victim-blamed and criminalized by authority figures such as child welfare and social workers, police officers, and judges (de Finney, Moreno, et al., 2018; Dhillon, 2015; Hunt, 2015). They are told the intergenerational trauma they and their families experienced simply put them at higher risk and justifies the damaging state interventions to which they are exposed without consent (de Finney, Palacios, Mucina, & Chadwick, 2019; Hunt, 2015; Toomey, Ryan, Diaz, Card, & Russell, 2013). In turn, because so few interventions centre their diverse strengths and knowledge systems, too many Indigenous children, youth, and families turn their shame and self-blame inwards, towards their own bodies and communities (de Finney, 2017).

Having sustained themselves for centuries in the face of violent attack, Indigenous communities have demonstrated the most impressive courage, self-determination, dignity, and creativity (de Finney, 2017). These strengths are what should be centred in practice and inquiries into sexualized and gender-based violence. These strengths guide our work with Sisters Rising.

Research and programs on sexualized violence in our communities tend to focus on risk and the impact of trauma, and on the legal, social, and psychological costs of interventions. Sisters Rising, in contrast, focuses on blanketing and honouring those who have experienced sexualized and gender-based violence. Centring our own teachings and perspectives, we seek to retrace our circles of relation with our lands, waterways, and bodies and to re-story and re-body colonial violence. Our workshops focus on land- and water-based Indigenous art methods across mediums such as sculpture, storytelling, audio, video, painting, beading, collages, photography, song, and poetry. We tend to work in collaboration and in circle, and participants choose whatever approach suits their needs, pursuing individual projects (e.g., cedar weaving or painting) and/or group activities (e.g., creating a mural of stereotypes Indigenous girls encounter). We use multimedia tools to produce and document stories for knowledge sharing. For example, many of the participants used project iPads to take pictures, audio, or video of what they produced.[2]

A number of questions drive our workshops: How do we challenge the persistent construction of Indigenous bodies as dispensable "damaged goods"? What do youth of all genders need to create safe, honouring spaces in which to address gendered and sexualized violence? What do they need from their homelands, ancestors, relations, peers, families, schools, and communities to support their well-being and self-determination? What teachings do their communities hold about sexuality and gender roles and relations? What do dignity and body and land sovereignty look like, and how do we enact it in our daily lives? What systemic and structural transformations are required to support the decolonization of our bodies and homelands?

Participants have shared that fear, stigma, and lack of effective responses all perpetuate the silence and isolation that surround violence. In turn, they experience silence and denial as rooted in persistent, intersecting systemic barriers, including high rates of gendered, sexualized, and racialized poverty, lack of services and infrastructure, colonial policies such as the *Indian Act* and land appropriation, and continued colonial violence. In workshop after workshop, participants have shared one important vision: the need to honour community- and youth-generated responses that support intergenerational connections, the resurgence of Indigenous teachings (particularly those that relate to gender and sexual well-being), and self-determination over their bodies and homelands.

In the rest of this chapter, we focus on two kinds of knowledge that guide our work: Indigenous gender teachings and land- and water-based teachings. This knowledge provides the framework for Sisters Rising and informs our CYC practice.

RE-CENTRING INDIGENOUS GENDER TEACHINGS: RETHINKING THE GENDER BINARY

> My power is greater than what I have been through.
> —Sisters Rising participant

Rather than reproducing damage-centred stories, Sisters Rising seeks to honour creative, community-generated interventions rooted in dignity, kinship, and land

and body well-being. By re-centring cultural teachings, arts-based stories help retrace kinship trails that link girls' and youths' body sovereignty to Indigenous self-determination (de Finney, 2018a). In looking back to our gender teachings, we have been inspired to think about the ways our communities are reimagining and rewriting narratives of reclamation, resurgence, and love. Although the funding for this project is focused on promoting the necessary engagement of girls and young women, we have also committed to troubling the categories of "girl" and "young woman" beyond strict colonial gender binaries. Unsettling cis-heteronormativity in our work is a constant challenge, but we could not envision exploring gender and sexualized violence without disrupting these binaries. Gender fluid, gender nonconforming, Trans, 2Spirit, lesbian, gay, bisexual, and queer young people face unique issues and barriers that produce distinct risks for gender-based and sexualized violence (Hunt, 2015; Saramo, 2016; Toomey, Ryan, Diaz, Card, & Russell, 2013). The high risk is due in part to their invisibility and stigmatization under colonial gender formations. A strict gender binary and unequal gender roles are damaging tenets of colonialism and residential schools (Filice, 2015). Eurocentric definitions of girlhood create "marginalized others whose lives, bodies, relationships, and selves do not conform" to white privileged norms (Aapola, Gonick, & Harris, 2005, p. 3). In contrast, Indigenous nations have always had their own diverse gender concepts and roles, and re-centring these is an important aspect of anti-colonial violence prevention. Our communities hold sacred healing practices and distinct concepts of gender and sexual well-being that need to be amplified in our discussions about colonial violence. Such a movement reasserts flexibility for Indigenous children and youth to live genders and sexualities outside of prescriptive Euro-Western norms that prioritize cis- and heteronormativity and the primacy of men over women (de Finney, Moreno, et al., 2018).

As examples, Indigenous-led projects such as 2spirits (www.2spirits.com), Continuous Series, Two Spirit Nation (https://www.facebook.com/TwoSpiritNation), and the Native Youth Sexual Health Network (http://www.nativeyouthsexualhealth.com) are shifting conversations to honour diverse Indigenous teachings about gender, bodies, relationships, and consent. At the heart of these initiatives is the importance of supporting young Indigenous people to self-identify and build community using terminology and concepts that fit best for them and their communities. We want to highlight the importance of directly including Indigenous children and youth of all genders and sexualities in developing and leading research, practice, and policy around sexual violence and settler violence initiatives that reflect their unique experiences (de Finney, Moreno, et al., 2018).

LAND-BASED TEACHINGS THAT RECONNECT US TO OUR KIN

> Sisters Rising is not a story where colonialism is the centrefold. Power comes from our ancestors, our homelands and waters, our cultures, our spirits, and all things surrounding who we are as people. Power is there. It has always been there.
> —Chantal Adams, Haida and European ancestry, BCYC, Sisters Rising facilitator

Land and water are central to shaping body and sexual sovereignty. As Indigenous peoples were removed from our homelands to make lands/waters and resources accessible to white settlers, our communities were dismembered and dispirited from the places that hold our knowledges, languages, and worldviews. Too often in our work, we import interventions, programs, and materials created outside our communities—another form of diluting local knowledge systems and reproducing the message that Indigenous ways of being are "not good enough," unscientific, not rooted in evidence, and so on. For this reason, in many of our workshops, Elders share stories and teachings related to gender well-being and to their specific cultural heritage, such as taking part in coming-of-age ceremonies, making family and clan crests, weaving cedar, canoeing, and gathering traditional medicines. This is not to say that Indigenous youth are bound to using only land- and water-based materials and approaches in our workshops. Participants use whatever methods and materials they choose, including diverse digital and new media. However, we have always been taught that Indigenous youth—regardless of where and how they live—are citizens of sovereign Indigenous nations who are intimately linked to their tribal and kinship networks, lands, and ancestors. Our approach, following Segalo, Manoff, and Fine (2015), rejects "imported and borrowed knowledges" (p. 343). We are guided by the strong drumbeat of our collective communities and homelands that blanket us in "relational and intimate spaces of witnessing" (Clark, 2016, p. 56).

A politicized and deeply situated approach to witnessing highlights the vitality of kinship models. Indigenous scholar Leroy Little Bear (2000) describes Indigenous notions of kinship as a "spider-web of relations" (p. 79) that includes humans and the natural world. Such a concept of kinship clearly exceeds the boundaries of Western notions of relational practice, life-space interventions, professional boundaries, and developmental theories. Working with medicines and teachers from our kinship networks helped us avoid both reductive anxieties about "reclaiming" unrecoverable Indigenous pasts and romanticized Western ideas about land and kinship (de Finney, Moreno, et al., 2018). We know our approach is imperfect: It does not resolve substantial issues about the colonial histories of practice and research, about working across multiple academic and land-based communities and in unceded Indigenous territories, or about re/claiming mixed, urbanized, diasporic Indigenous ontologies and methodologies. However, instead of being constrained by these limitations, we seek to enact practices that support self-determination, complexity, consent, and dignity at every step (Ormiston, 2010; Wilson, 2008). These objectives are particularly important given that our team often partners with our own communities, with relatives, and/or in communities where we work as counselling professionals.

A HOPEFUL VISION FOR CYC PRACTICE

> My traditional teachings on resurgence and decolonization consist of acknowledging that strength-based practice has been embedded in our ways of life as Indigenous people since the beginning of time. We always embraced everyone and held them up, acknowledging their gifts to this world and encouraging them to walk their path. This supports our sovereignty because it gives us courage and strength to continue walking.
> —Shezell-Rae Sam, Ahousat (Nuu-chah-nulth), BCYC, Sisters Rising research facilitator

As front-line workers and members of this research team, approaching the topic of sexualized violence has felt precarious and always imperfect. We are witnesses to how settler colonial ontologies of what is right and normal create lateral violence in our communities by imparting practices that jeopardize Indigenous ways of knowing, doing, and being and turn us against each other. Under this regime, colonial violence is constantly reproduced through social services, and Indigenous families become perpetual clients of services that do not fix what is wrong. Families are thus further burdened with psychosocial labels of PTSD, intergenerational neglect, substance use, complex trauma, and self-harm (de Finney, Moreno, et al., 2018). These labels serve to hide the systemic fault lines of racialized poverty and colonial heteropatriarchy while ignoring that trauma is a deliberate strategy of the colonial state (de Finney, Moreno, et al., 2018). Thus, the harm imposed by colonial systems is reduced to individualized mental health diagnoses that trap Indigenous families in endless social services interventions.

So how do we support the well-being, gender and sexual health, decolonization, dignity, and respect of Indigenous bodies and spirits?

In terms of translating these learned lessons into our CYC praxis framework, our biggest learning thus far is that we need to politicize taken-for-granted concepts such as relationship, engagement, advocacy, competencies, and professional boundaries. As front-line workers in social systems, we become justified in using individualized approaches to treat harm—relational practice, developmental interventions, trauma-informed care, and life-space interventions. These approaches are not without merit, and we use these skills every day in our practice, but they do not address the depth of the issues at hand; they simply delay, obscure, and do little to disrupt and transform the colonial systems and ideologies that produce harm in the first place.

Decolonizing CYC practice includes radically redefining and reclaiming what constitutes care, relationships, and well-being, and understanding how all these principles are inextricably linked to land and body sovereignty.

We acknowledge with great humility that none of what we are saying is new. Indigenous communities identified these urgent needs decades if not centuries ago. The work of Sisters Rising is part of a broader movement aimed at ensuring that Indigenous children and youth have meaningful connections with their bodies, spirits, communities, and ancestral lands and waterways, and that they understand there is another way to live in a settler state that does not include being a vessel for racialized colonial violence.

For Sisters Rising, these responses may take a myriad of shapes: creating art, writing our stories, voicing the roots of trauma, calling out settler colonialism, speaking our languages, practicing our cultural traditions in public and private spaces, honouring our Elders, taking part in activism and advocacy, and creating resurgent practices and scholarship. Resistance may not stop the ongoing colonization and violence against the sovereignty of Indigenous bodies and land, but it is an essential element in restoring dignity and respect—for self and for the communities to which our spirits are intricately connected. This project is a journey of remaking our kin, of rehoming and re-presencing, of materializing bodied reconnections with our many teachers—all our relations (de Finney, 2018b). Practices of kinship making, place interconnectedness, and self-determination contribute a much-needed ethical framework for Indigenous human service work, and we place these unapologetically in the landscape of CYC.

We extend our deepest gratitude to all of the participants, collaborators, and partners who have stepped forward to participate in Sisters Rising. We raise our hands to our ancestors and all our relations, to all of those who have survived, and to those who were stolen from us. We raise our hands to all who grieve, resist, create, love, and walk in dignity through pain and beautiful resurgence.

The following poem, featured in one of our videos (https://onlineacademic community.uvic.ca/sistersrising/), contains our collective stories and reflections from the Sisters Rising project (previously published in de Finney, Moreno, et al., 2018):

Sisters Rising

sisters

rising

we shape shift

intergenerational pain
intergenerational healing

liminal tensions
to be seen and heard

we did not consent

your saviour complex
we don't need your investigation
we don't need your intervention
we are not the problem

blow this up small scale
this amazing project
recreates
retraces
retells
our art transcends colonial time and language

blow this up large scale
challenge the very systems that uphold
this violence—

child welfare
education
the injustice system
black holes into which our children disappear

pull them back out
retrace worn pathways
back to home

we shape shift

we are not broken

we did not consent

we are calling out white supremacy
we understand what is going on in our communities
we grieve, respect, and celebrate
hidden (but not forgotten)
gift givers

we are not the problem

we did not consent

reopen pathways
our ceremonies
gatherings
rhythms of our ancestors
slowly retracing
holding up our children
praising the teachings of our Elders
sharing space with others
educating settlers

vital breath
love flows

we walk with friends, mentors, family, kin
across generations
into relationship
touching our kinship
communities of care blanket us with love

connections restitch
one
by one
by one

resurgence
subversion
dignity appears
out of submersion
it was always there

Sisters Rising
we
shape
shift
community
kinship
circles
friendship
care
love

Sisters
Rising

NOTES

1. We are incredibly thankful for the support of our research partners: Canadian Institutes of Health Research (FRN: 158385); the SSHRC/IDRC-funded international partnership of Canadian and South African researchers and community groups entitled *Networks for Change and Well-Being: Girl-Led "From the Ground Up" Policy-Making to Address Sexual*

Violence in Canada and South Africa (see http://www.n4c.co.za); the Northwest Inter-Nation Family and Community Services Society (NIFCS); the Canet Foundation; and the Siem Smun'eem Indigenous Child Well-Being Research Network (ICWRN), a provincial research and advocacy network.

2. Participants keep all their original artwork and provide explicit consent throughout the workshops. We follow strict Indigenous research protocols for consent, participation, ownership, and engaging with cultural knowledge and teachings.

REFERENCES

Aapola, S., Gonick, M., & Harris, A. (2005). *Young femininity: Girlhood, power, and social change*. New York, NY: Palgrave Macmillan.

Anderson, Kim. 2000. *A recognition of being: Reconstructing Native womanhood*. Toronto, ON: Sumach Press.

Canadian Broadcasting Corporation. (2011, August 2). First Nations children still taken from parents. *CBC News*. Retrieved from https://www.cbc.ca/news/politics/first-nations-children-still-taken-from-parents-1.1065255

Canadian Broadcasting Corporation. (2015, June 2). Truth and Reconciliation Commission: By the numbers. *CBC News*. Retrieved from https://www.cbc.ca/news/indigenous/truth-and-reconciliation-commission-by-the-numbers-1.3096185

Canadian Broadcasting Corporation. (2017, July 7). Dormant ancient fungi could help trees adapt to climate change, study says. *CBC News British Columbia*. Retrieved from http://www.cbc.ca/news/canada/british-columbia/dormant-ancient-fungi-could-help-trees-adapt-to-climate-change-study-says-1.4194399

Clark, N. (2016). Red intersectionality and violence-informed witnessing praxis with Indigenous girls. *Girlhood Studies, 9*(2), 46–64.

Deer, S. (2009). Decolonizing rape law: A Native feminist synthesis of safety and sovereignty. *Wicazo Sa Review, Fall*, 149–167. Retrieved from https://turtletalk.files.wordpress.com/2009/10/deer-decolonizing-rape-law.pdf

de Finney, S. (2015). Playing Indian and other settler stories: Disrupting Western narratives of Indigenous girlhood. *Continuum: Journal of Media and Cultural Studies, 29*(2), 169–181.

de Finney, S. (2017). Indigenous girls' resilience in settler states: Honouring body and land sovereignty. *Agenda, 31*(2), 10–21.

de Finney, S. (2018a, June 27). Sisters Rising: Indigenous resurgence and kinship. *Culturally Modified, 3*. Retrieved from https://culturallymodified.org/sisters-rising-indigenous-resurgence-and-kinship/

de Finney, S. (2018b). *Kinship trails: De-settling trauma-informed practice in Indigenous child welfare*. Paper presented to Critical Ethnic Studies Association, June 21–24, 2018, University of British Columbia, Vancouver, British Columbia.

de Finney, S., Moreno, S., Chadwick, A., Adams, C., Sam, S., Scott, A., & Land, N. (2018). Sisters Rising: Shape shifting settler violence through art and land retellings. In C. Mitchell & R. Moletsane (Eds.), *Disrupting shameful legacies* (pp. 21–46). Boston, MA: Brill Sense.

de Finney, S., Palacios, L., Mucina, M., & Chadwick, A. (2018, September). Refusing band-aids: Unsettling "care" under the carceral settler state. *CYC-Online, 235*. Retrieved from https://www.cyc-net.org/cyc-online/sep2018.pdf

Dhillon, J. (2015). Indigenous girls and the violence of settler colonial policing. *Decolonization: Indigeneity, Education, & Society, 4*(2), 1–31.

Filice, M. (2015). Two-Spirit. *The Canadian Encyclopedia*. Retrieved from http://www.thecanadianencyclopedia.ca/en/article/two-spirit/

First Nations Child and Family Caring Society. (2016). *Canadian Human Rights Tribunal decisions on First Nations child welfare and Jordan's Principle*. Retrieved from https://fncaringsociety.com/sites/default/files/Info%20sheet%20Oct%2031.pdf

Hunt, S. (2015). Representing colonial violence: Trafficking, sex work, and the violence of law. *Atlantis, 27*(2), 25–39.

Little Bear, L. (2000). Jagged worlds colliding. In M. Battiste (Ed.), *Reclaiming Indigenous voice and vision* (pp. 77–85). Vancouver: University of British Columbia Press.

Lyons, T., Krusi, A., Pierre, L., Smith, A., Small, W., & Shannon, K. (2016). Experiences of Trans women and Two-Spirit persons accessing women-specific health and housing services in a downtown neighborhood of Vancouver, Canada. *LGBT Health, 1*(3), 373–378. doi: 10.1089/lgbt.2016.0060

McKegney, S. (2016). "Pain, pleasure, shame. Shame": Masculine embodiment, kinship, and reterritorialization. In D. Robinson & K. Martin (Eds.), *Arts of engagement: Taking aesthetic action in and beyond the truth and reconciliation commission of Canada* (pp. 193–214). Waterloo, ON: Wilfrid Laurier University Press.

National Aboriginal Health Organization. (2012). *Suicide prevention and two-spirited people*. Retrieved from https://ruor.uottawa.ca/bitstream/10393/30544/1/Suicide_Prevention_2Spirited_People_Guide_2012.pdf

National Inquiry into Murdered and Missing Indigenous Women and Girls. (2019). *Reclaiming power and place, final report*. Retrieved from https://www.mmiwg-ffada.ca/wp-content/uploads/2019/06/Final_Report_Vol_1a-1.pdf

Ontario Native Women's Association. (2016, February). *Sex trafficking of Indigenous women in Ontario*. Retrieved from http://www.onwa.ca/upload/documents/report-sex-trafficking-of-indigenous-wom.pdf

Ormiston, T. (2010). Reconceptualizing research: An Indigenous perspective. *First Peoples Child and Family Review, 5*(1), 50–56.

Pierson, R. (2005). Nation, empire, colony: Historicizing gender and race. In L. Biggs & P. Downe (Eds.), *Gendered intersections: An introduction to women's and gender studies* (pp. 42–47). Halifax, NS: Fernwood.

Razack, S. (2002). *Race, space, and the law: Unmapping a white settler society.* Toronto, ON: Between the Lines.

Richardson, C., & Reynolds, V. (2014). Structuring safety in therapeutic work alongside Indigenous survivors of residential schools. *Canadian Journal of Native Studies, 34*(2), 147–164.

Saramo, S. (2016). Unsettling spaces: Grassroots responses to Canada's missing and murdered Indigenous women during the Harper government years. *Comparative American Studies An International Journal, 14*(3–4), 204–220.

Segalo, P., Manoff, E., & Fine, M. (2015). Working with embroideries and counter-maps: Engaging memory and imagination within decolonizing frameworks. *Journal of Social and Political Psychology, 3*(1), 342–364.

Simpson, L. B. (2014). Land as pedagogy: Nishnaabeg intelligence and rebellious transformation. *Decolonization: Indigeneity, Education, & Society, 3*(3), 1–25.

Toomey, R. B., Ryan, C., Diaz, R. M., Card, N. A., & Russell, S. T. (2013). Gender-nonconforming lesbian, gay, bisexual, and transgender youth: School victimization and young adult psychosocial adjustment. *Psychology of Sexual Orientation and Gender Diversity, 1*(S), 71–80.

Truth and Reconciliation Commission of Canada. (2015). *Honouring the truth, reconciling for the future: Summary of the final report of the Truth and Reconciliation Commission of Canada.* Retrieved from http://www.trc.ca/websites/trcinstitution/File/2015/Honouring_the_Truth_Reconciling_for_the_Future_July_23_2015.pdf

Tuck, E., & Yang, K. W. (2012). Decolonization is not a metaphor. *Decolonization: Indigeneity, Education & Society, 1*(1), 1–40. Retrieved from http://decolonization.org/index.php/des/article/view/18630/15554

Turpel-Lafond, M. E. (2016). *Too many victims: Sexualized violence in the lives of children and youth in care.* Victoria, BC: Representative for Children and Youth. Retrieved from https://www.rcybc.ca/toomanyvictims

Wilson, S. (2008). *Research is ceremony: Indigenous research methods.* Winnipeg, MB: Fernwood.

CHAPTER 2

Mino-Bimaadiziwin Wiidookodaadiwag (Helping Each Other through the Good Life): Implications for Research and Practice with Indigenous Communities

Nicole Ineese-Nash

INTRODUCTION

This chapter explores the ways in which practitioners and researchers may enter into good relations with Indigenous communities and individuals. Centring Anishinaabe perspectives, this chapter seeks to offer a set of frameworks to enable non-Indigenous practitioners and community visitors to reframe their roles from "benevolent helpers" to partners in self-determination through culturally informed practices. In this way, community practitioners and researchers are regarded as working within non-hierarchical relationships with Indigenous peoples, in which they are able to mutually walk together in a good way. Understanding and engaging the colonial context of helping professions is essential to this work and offers the basis for decolonizing practice and research in Indigenous communities. The chapter offers both cautions and suggestions for professionals involved in practice and/or research in Indigenous communities.

AUTHOR'S STATEMENT

Nanaboozhoo, waciye. Songe Winnishe Wabigwanikwe niindishinikaas. Mamamattawa nindojiba, mukwa nindodem, Anishnaabekwe nindow. I am an able-bodied cisgender mixed Anishinaabe (Oji-Cree) and European woman whose lineage comes from the place where three rivers meet (Mamamattawa) near Constance Lake First Nation in Treaty 9 territory, where I am a registered member. I am writing this as an Indigenous scholar, writer, and thinker who has been gifted with knowledge from the academy, from my community, from Elders, and from my ancestral wisdom held within my genetic memory. I am also writing this as an auntie and community member. It is for my family and community that I write, so that those who may cross their paths may do so in a better way.

I am beginning in this manner as an acknowledgement of my identity, but also as a measure of personal accountability. Knowing who I am is important in understanding the value (or lack thereof) of my perspective, but it is also a way that I honour the gifts that I have come to receive. My name to Creation is Songe Winnishe Wabigwanikwe, which roughly translates to Strong Beautiful Flower Woman. When I was a child, I believed this name to be a reflection of my resiliency, in that I was able to thrive in the many environments I was raised, in and out of the foster care system. As I came into adulthood, I sought clarification from traditional people and asked for guidance on how to best honour this name. A spirit name is not only a reflection of your identity; it also represents the gifts you are to share with your people (Willmott, 2016). Through conversations with multiple people and Elders, I have come to know that I have a responsibility to share the strengths of our communities with those who may not see them. Although my botanical knowledge is limited, I have come to understand that flowers are holders of medicine and grow in communities of other plants and beings in mutually beneficial ways. I see it as my responsibility to share ways that I have come to know to support the growth of our young people in this same manner. I encourage you to also see your roles in helping young people to discover their own gifts in any work you may do.

IDEOLOGICAL UNDERPINNINGS

This chapter is entitled *Mino-Bimaadiziwin Wiidookodaadiwag*, which, interpreted from Ojibway (a language of the Anishinaabe people), means "they help each other through the good life." This title was chosen to reflect the overall ideology of this chapter, and to conceptualize the role of practitioners working with Indigenous peoples. In this way, outside peoples can be seen as helpers who work by centring reciprocal relationships and supporting community members towards their self-determined destiny. In the realm of child and youth care (CYC), both young person and practitioner are independent agents, mutually helping each other to realize their individual and shared goals. This is a critical perspective that underlies ethical relationships from an Indigenous perspective, which are furthermore embedded in the following two frameworks: Indigenous knowledge systems and cultural safety frameworks.

Indigenous Knowledge

Indigenous knowledge is fundamental to understanding what it means to support Indigenous futurity, both at the individual and community levels (Corntassel, 2012). Indigenous knowledge is about learning through and about Indigenous ontologies, epistemologies, and relational models in tangible ways (more on this later). Indigenous knowledge is a complex empirical system with structures and processes as rigorous to that of scientific study (Kovach, 2010). Knowledge, from an Indigenous perspective, is held in shared meanings that cannot be separated from the relational context in which they occur (Haig-Brown, 2008). Indigenous knowledge is uncovered, rather than constructed, through empirical observation, traditional teachings, and revelation (Brant-Castellano, 2000). It is important to note, however, that Indigenous cultures across Turtle Island are diverse and have varying understandings of the world. I am writing this from an Anishinaabe perspective, which is land-appropriate for much of the Great Lakes region but may not be generalizable to other Indigenous cultures.

Cultural Safety Framework

Cultural safety is a concept that has recently been popularized in social sciences as a means to critically examine practices when working with culturally diverse populations (Gerlach, 2012). Although there are many interpretations of the term, cultural safety is generally understood as a set of practices and attitudes that enable workers to engage with clients in ways that are mutually respectful, non-hierarchical, and responsive to each individual's unique ideologies and cultural perspectives (Lenette, 2014). Cultural safety is a framework designed specifically to address the systemic inequalities faced by Indigenous populations (originally in New Zealand), who continue to experience racism and poorer care in social services (Wepa, 2015). Cultural safety seeks to hold practitioners accountable by honouring the client as the one to determine whether or not a relationship is culturally safe (De & Richardson, 2008). In this way, cultural safety is more than a checklist of practices, but rather an ethic of engagement that acknowledges cultural difference and strives for mutual understanding and reciprocal relationships (Lenette, 2014).

RESEARCH AND PRACTICE WITH INDIGENOUS COMMUNITIES

Indigenous communities have endured mixed experiences with non-Indigenous practitioners and researchers. To many communities, research is synonymous with exploitation and harm (Deloria, 1969). Knowledge, as it is conceived by Eurocentric ideals, is something that is measurable, commodifiable, and replicable (Battiste, 2009). From this ideological position, research is a method of inquiry based on the assumption that everything can and should be known (Kuper, Reeves, & Levinson, 2008). It operates from the premise that there exists an absolute truth that can be simplified and understood by humans, and that it is humans' (largely conceived as man's) right to know that truth (Radford, 2008). This anthropocentric perspective asserts itself on the social world through the lens of research, positioning its gaze on life's workings to tell of something not yet known, or rather not yet packaged (Braidotti, 2016). The packaging of knowledge is the business of research, which allows for particular understandings to be socially reproduced as reality (Kincheloe & McLaren, 2002).

Many social service fields working in relationship with Indigenous peoples have been informed by the research done with and about Indigenous communities. While there has been an increased shift towards more ethical research relationships and Indigenous-led community practices, much of the dominant discourse about Indigenous peoples remains unquestioned and reproductive of negative presumptions of Indigenous peoples. Under the guise of benevolence, information about Indigenous peoples has been operationalized to monitor and marginalize Indigenous communities (Smith, 2012). Entering into Indigenous territory, regardless of positionality, necessitates an understanding of the legacy of external influence that has extracted lands and resources, erased Indigenous histories, and undermined Indigenous self-determination (Tuck & Yang, 2012). If you are a non-Indigenous person, you are walking into communities in the footsteps of all those outsiders before you; you are a representation of every researcher, community worker, government official, and religious leader that has come to the community to take up some form of "work." I employ the term *work* here as a means to capture the wide array of projects taken up in Indigenous communities by non-Indigenous peoples, which may include research, intervention, education, and other professions deemed to be outside of everyday community life. From a community perspective, these roles are often arbitrary. It is up to you to walk a path that defines your role as a community helper—one that does less harm and contributes to community well-being rather than to its undoing.

WORKING AGAINST INDIGENOUS KNOWLEDGE

Community-based research and practice are cultural and political activities that are laden with power, privilege, and responsibility (Chilisa, 2011). From an Indigenous perspective, research is a ceremonial practice that occurs through generational encounters with knowledge (Wilson, 2008). Yet, research from Euro-Western frameworks has negated these epistemologies (Smith, 2012). Interactions with researchers and clinicians have and continue to do harm to many pathologized groups in North America, particularly Indigenous (Smith, 2012), Black (Tuck & Guishard, 2013), and disabled communities (Barton, 2005). One of the ways this harm has been operationalized against Indigenous peoples, in particular, is through the attempted erasure of Indigenous knowledge systems (Smith, 2012). Indigenous peoples in North America have held complex systems of social order since time immemorial (Battiste & Barman, 1995; Simpson, 2008a). Through settler influence, these systems have been disrupted and demonized as threats to colonial progress. Indigenous practices of education (Battiste, 2005), governance (Simpson, 2008a), economy (Willow, 2013), spirituality (Lavallee & Poole, 2010), and child-rearing (Sinclair, 2016) have been criminalized and made illegitimate through colonial policy. Within the project of settler colonialism, it is easier to subjugate those you can name "savage" than to comply with protocols you do not care to understand.

Research and pathology have been used as tools against Indigenous sovereignty (Deloria, 1969; Tuck & Yang, 2012). Indigenous peoples have been studied in ways that have reduced their vast and diverse cultures into anthropological snippets that position white researchers as experts (Deloria, 1969). These representations of Indigenous peoples have reproduced the cultural assumptions that Indigenous peoples are primitive, less than human, and unwilling to cooperate with colonial and capitalistic projects (Absolon & Willett, 2004). It is in these retellings that Indigenous peoples are problematized and pathologized; they are debilitated in such ways that they are framed as dependent on colonial intervention (Deloria, 1969; Manuel & Derrickson, 2017). The infantilization of Indigenous communities is reproduced through research projects, such as those that measure outcomes of colonial interventions as necessary for Indigenous well-being (de Leeuw, Greenwood, & Cameron, 2010).

Colonial interventions in Canada have historically done devastating harm in the name of assimilation and charity (McKenzie, Varcoe, Browne, & Day, 2016). Settler-colonial tactics of Indigenous erasure (which will not be discussed in detail here) have come to be known as genocidal and have forever changed the course of Indigenous futurity (MacDonald, 2015). With this recognition, many research institutions are working within reconciliation frameworks that seek to engage research as a tool to expose and mitigate harm (McGregor, 2018). However, this often materializes as a disassociation with culpability that further hinders Indigenous self-determination (Tuck & Yang, 2012).

WORKING FOR INDIGENOUS KNOWLEDGE

As long as there have been peoples who wish to erase Indigenous ways of knowing and being, there have also been those who wish to cultivate it (Wilson, 2008). Indigenous peoples hold auspicious knowledge for applications outside of Indigenous contexts. Understanding the natural world is a scholarly pursuit practised by many Indigenous communities globally (Ohmagari & Berkes, 1997). The understanding of the earth and our relationship to it informs the ethic of living in harmony—in *bimaadiziwin*—with Creation (Manitowabi, 2014). Knowledge of the natural world is valued in mainstream institutions insomuch as it can be commodified and profitable. Settlers have appropriated Indigenous medicines and marketed them for mass consumption (Barsh, 2001). Work in this realm is done for the extraction of Indigenous knowledge that may be appropriated for capitalistic gain (Trotti, 2001).

In the current era of social rupture and natural disorder, Indigenous knowledge holders are now seen as pivotal players in combatting climate change (Huntington, 2000; Riedlinger & Berkes, 2001). Understanding the depth of ecological knowledge held by Indigenous peoples, researchers wish to apply traditional methods to understand current trends and develop innovations to protect the environment (Huntington, 2000). While this may be an altruistic occupation, it is also one that fails to examine structures that maintain Indigenous subjugation. The mechanism of commodifying Indigenous knowledge of the natural world disallows for relationality that is central to this understanding. Indigenous peoples engage in processes of peer review over generations that build a body of knowledge through oral traditions and blood memory (Smith, 2012). Rather than seeking ways to honour those knowledge systems, settlers have created something else entirely. Two-eyed seeing is applied loosely to translate to fact-checking Indigenous understandings held for millennia, so that Indigenous knowledge can be packaged, mass produced, and sold for profit (Bartlett, Marshall, & Marshall, 2012; Posey, 2002).

Indigenous knowledge is not for public consumption in the way that research institutions have presented it, and it is not something that can be arbitrarily applied to de-contextualized circumstances as a metaphor. Our medicines are not for sale and our cultural practices are not meant to be tried on. Prevalent practices in research and community intervention remove Indigenous knowledge from the hands of Indigenous people and place it in other contexts to be used as a tool for progress, usually against Indigenous sovereignty (Smith, 2000). Indigenous research methodologies are mechanisms to protect Indigenous knowledge and hold relational accountability at the forefront (Wilson, 2008). Research on Indigenous worldviews that does not explicitly acknowledge or attempt to redress colonial practices that remove Indigenous peoples from their lands, cultures, and communities is work that perpetuates colonial innocence and fails Indigenous peoples (Tuck & Yang, 2012).

WORKING WITH INDIGENOUS KNOWLEDGE

The pursuit of knowledge is not limited to scientific or academic institutions. Indigenous peoples have always looked for meaning in the world around them. We are scientists, scholars, and clinicians in our communities. Indigenous research has emerged as a scholarly field over the course of the last several decades, as Indigenous peoples have come to assert these methods as an empirical system of research (Alfred, 2005; Battiste, 2011; Smith, 2012; Wilson, 2008). Their work is influential in positioning Indigenous studies as a body of knowledge that operates with a set standard of methodologies and epistemologies tied to language, land, and cultural practices (Chilisa, 2011). Doing "work" with Indigenous knowledge means centring these knowledge systems as the basis for inquiry and engaging in methods that honour connection to land, ancestry, story, and spirit (Wilson, 2008) in culturally appropriate ways.

Community practice from an Indigenous paradigm is always focused on ways to promote collective well-being through relationship building and mutual understanding (Simpson, 2004). Nationhood is at the centre of Indigenous ontologies, which means the value of relational mutuality in both theory and practice are of utmost importance (Kovach, 2010). Work by and with Indigenous peoples cannot operate within a de-contextual vacuum. There is no interpretation of Indigenous perspectives that does not also require an analysis of colonial processes that continue to obstruct Indigenous reclamation and resurgence (Corntassel, 2012). There is no relationship with Indigenous peoples that does not necessitate critical conversations of land, culture, and self-determination. For Indigenous peoples, these are woven into our ethics of being in relationship with one another and Creation; *research* is just a colonial term for the ways that we have sustained our knowledge systems for generations and will continue to for generations to come.

ETHICAL CONSIDERATIONS

In the wake of the Truth and Reconciliation Commission of Canada's (TRC) report (2015), there is renewed interest in engaging Indigenous communities in many aspects of Canada's social order (McGregor, 2018). The TRC has particular implications for educational, governmental, judicial, and social service fields operating with Indigenous peoples in Canada (TRC, 2015). While Canadians may believe this to be a step in the right direction (Denis & Bailey, 2016), many Indigenous communities and scholars caution against the expeditious approach taken by many institutions and governments in the pursuit of reconciliation (Manuel & Derrickson, 2017). As Manuel and Derrickson (2017) remind us, "the overriding objective in all of the government's dealing with Indigenous peoples is to have continued unfettered access and control over Indigenous lands" (p. 204). Reconciliation is therefore just another mechanism for colonial governments to render its supremacy over Indigenous lands and life more covert and pertinacious through policy. Tuck and Yang (2012) have titled the process of evasion towards formidable decolonization "settler moves to innocence" (p. 1), which in effect further conceal colonial processes and undermine Indigenous sovereignty.

Collaborations between Indigenous and non-Indigenous peoples offer promising practices in working towards a place of reconciliation, however impossible that place may be to arrive at. Indigenous peoples have been willing to engage in respectful relationships with non-Indigenous peoples since Europeans arrived on Turtle Island (Simpson, 2008a). Although many Indigenous peoples have articulated the nature of the relationships they expect from visitors to their communities (Battiste, 2016; Kovach, 2015; First Nations Information Governance Centre, 2014; TRC, 2015), relationships between Indigenous communities and mainstream Canadians remain contentious. With an increasing number of research projects, philanthropic initiatives, and drop-in intervention programs, there is a need to evaluate ethical engagement processes with Indigenous communities to ensure past mistakes are not replicated.

Ethics from an Indigenous perspective are not static practices and procedures; ethics are ways of being in the world that hold value, belief, and relational positioning (Simpson, 2008b). While professional ethics provide protocols to mitigate risk, these protocols are predominantly in place to protect liability rather than support community priorities (Tuck & Guishard, 2013). These differing operational understandings of ethics create dichotomous perspectives of relationships, which may result in problematic outcomes (Smith, 2012). Being in good relation with Indigenous peoples occurs at each stage in the engagement process and cannot be separated from measurable outcomes (Battiste, 2005; Smith, 2012). Engaging in a good way means ensuring that communities determine and benefit from any work involving them (Smith, 2012; Wilson, 2008).

REIMAGINING WORK AND COMMUNITY PRACTICE

As an Anishinaabe person, I see research within the everyday transmissions of cultural knowledge. Research is the process we engage in when we seek out cultural knowledge from our Elders. Dissemination happens when we tell our children traditional stories. Peer review happens when we have tea together and retell what we have learned. Our analysis starts when we put our tobacco down and ask for permission to seek understanding. Research for us is not for profit or for acclaim; it is for survival. Reclaiming our knowledges, histories, and languages is a mechanism to restore our futurities (Simpson, 2008b). In attempting to decolonize our practices, we must be careful to do so with an understanding of the precarity and urgency that Indigenous self-determination work necessitates.

Relationships with Indigenous communities do not end when the project is completed, when the contract ends, when the funds run out, or when the reports are written. Relationships are key components to supporting Indigenous futurity in colonial contexts and must be sustained in ways that are responsive to community needs. Engaging in extractive processes reiterates colonial harm that will only further marginalize Indigenous communities. It is therefore important that mechanisms are put into place to have long-lasting community impact and sustainability once project deadlines are complete. Participatory action research (PAR) is a method of inquiry that operates from a community engagement model to empower community members to become co-researchers and develop ownership over research findings (Johnston-Goodstar, 2013); this serves as an example of engaging in ethical research and community support relationships with Indigenous communities. Regardless of orientation, be it research, education, intervention, or something else, working in Indigenous communities and with their members in ethical ways means allowing them to be integral parts of the work from the outset, enabling them to inform, determine, and take up outcomes of said work with or without your support.

"HELPING" PROFESSIONS WITH A COLONIAL STRUCTURE

Helping professions, like social work and child and youth care, serve as mechanisms for addressing social conditions hindering self-determination, which can be a means to improve overall health outcomes for Indigenous populations (Czyzewski, 2011; Moniz, 2010). Child and youth care, in particular, can be understood as a social justice field dedicated to ameliorating the well-being of children and youth (Mattingly, Stuart, & VanderVen, 2002). While the goals and approaches of many helping professions have been criticized (Czyzewski & Tester, 2014), others operate from wholistic relational models that may be more aligned with Indigenous community structures (Carriere & Richardson, 2012). What constitutes normative expressions of well-being are culturally determined. There is therefore a need for practitioners and researchers to understand Indigenous perspectives of well-being, as well as the historical and continuing impact of colonization on Indigenous health (Czyzewski & Tester, 2014).

Indigenous populations across Turtle Island (North America) experience a disproportionately high rate of social inequality as compared to non-Indigenous peoples (Adelson, 2005). Indigenous peoples are generally considered to be at higher risk of experiencing chronic disease and illness (Gracey & King, 2009), disability (Durst, South, & Bluechardt, 2006), and infant mortality (Smylie & Anderson, 2006), and have a shorter life expectancy (NCCAH, 2013). While efforts to close these gaps have increased over the last few decades, systemic barriers continue to maintain social inequalities for Indigenous populations in Canada (Browne et al., 2012). Organizations both locally (see TRC, 2015) and internationally (see Jackson Pulver et al., 2010) have called for significant commitments on the part of governments to address the ongoing health and educational disparities affecting Indigenous peoples, with little observable progress.

In Canada, Indigenous populations continue to face systemic barriers within health, education, and social service systems. This is largely due to the conflict these institutions pose to Indigenous ways of being. Social and educational fields are implicated in colonial violence as vehicles of assimilation (Hill & Wilkinson, 2014). The residential school system, 60s scoop, and ongoing mass apprehension of Indigenous children through the child welfare system are just a few examples of colonial policies that have impacted Indigenous lives in Canada (Sinclair, 2004) While there has been a shift towards a "decolonization" of the field, social programs across the country are still largely failing to provide students with a strong foundation of Indigenous ontologies of social service delivery, which inevitably leads to poorer professional relationships with Indigenous clients (Hill & Wilkinson, 2014).

CAUTIONS FOR WORK IN INDIGENOUS COMMUNITIES

Every community is different, with variable experiences with colonialism and outside influence. The following represents some of the most tangible points of contention that I have seen in working in many Indigenous communities, including my own. This is by no means an exhaustive list but serves as a place of conversation when entering into community work.

There Is No Such Thing as Best Practices

What is the right way to support Indigenous communities? The simplest answer to this is: There is none. That is not to say that there is no harm from any approach taken, but that there cannot be a set standard of practices for such a culturally and geographically diverse population. Indigenous peoples across Turtle Island are incredibly diverse, with varying experiences, perspectives, and cultures. It is therefore impossible for one individual to represent the entirety of that experience, and even more impossible to quantify a set of practices that would apply to all contexts. It is also bad relations to assume the answers before having the opportunity to learn from local knowledge and experience. The best practices are the ones that are determined by the community and individuals who are most impacted. It is important to respect the rights of Indigenous communities to determine their own relationships and futurities, even if that does not involve settler support.

Doing Something Is Not Always Better than Doing Nothing

In many helping professions, intervention is regarded as the primary vehicle of support. Intervention in the lives of Indigenous peoples is often a mechanism of assimilation. That is not to say that Indigenous peoples do not want or need support, but the manner in which Indigenous lives are acted upon matters in terms of supporting Indigenous self-determination. When we do something upon Indigenous lives, we must ask ourselves who that action serves. Oftentimes, we assume our benevolence is appreciated and warranted, but in many cases, these actions conflict with Indigenous ways of being. Sometimes, intervention is not what is required; rather, being in proximity allows that person to find their way to the good path on their own.

Relationship Is Everything

There is a common saying in Indigenous communities (in many different languages) that speaks to the concept of interconnectedness. "All my relations" is a phrase that honours the connections individuals have with each other, with land, with ancestry, and with spirit. It is an ethic of being in the world that acknowledges the web of influence each individual has on collective well-being and futurity. There is an understanding that the actions of this generation hold significance for the following seven generations to come (Lavallee & Poole, 2010). Being in good relations requires an understanding that our work is not decentred from who we are as individuals and who we represent institutionally, but rather that our relationships span across generations. These relationships not only are anthropocentrically based, but also include land, water, and non-human beings. Entering into research and practice with Indigenous communities necessitates responsive and reciprocal relationships with all of these members of the community.

Honouring All Gifts

As I began this chapter, I spoke about my spirit name and gifts. I did this for you to understand who I am, but also as an example of the attention that should be paid to understanding individuals for who they are. Not every Indigenous person has come to know their name to Creation, and many have yet to realize their gifts from spirit world. As a community partner, it is important that we help individuals to cultivate their gifts to walk along the good path. Anishinaabe stories and traditions tell of the origins of our peoples as gifts from the sky world brought to earth to serve the community in their own ways (Johnston, 2010). It is important to foster inclusive spaces where all community members are able to offer their unique abilities and knowledges. Sometimes that requires thoughtful strategies of engagement that allow for those "hard to reach" individuals to participate.

When in Doubt, Look to the Elders

Elders are our Knowledge Keepers in our communities. Their knowledge and wisdom is essential to the transmission of cultural knowledge. Traditionally, Elders were foundational to the governance of Anishinaabe community structures (Simpson, 2008b). When entering into relationships with Indigenous communities, we must honour Elders as the holders of knowledge of both the past and future. Research and community practice with youth, for instance, needs to be grounded in connection to community Elders, as these relationships have been severed through colonial interventions (Iseke & Moore, 2011). From an Anishinaabe perspective, youth sit in the southern doorway, where they are focused on learning about the world and their place within it. Elders sit in the north, in direct juxtaposition to youth, where they are to pass on their knowledge before travelling back to the spirit world. Through the many harms of colonization, this reciprocal relationship has been disrupted, leaving Elders with few outlets to bestow their teachings, and youth feeling disconnected from their culture. It is important that we honour their experience and wisdom by seeking their involvement in matters that affect their community.

CONCLUSION

Institutional interaction through research, education, and various interventions have done harm to Indigenous communities through extractive, exploitative, and paternalistic approaches and practices (Smith, 2012). Indigenous research as a burgeoning field of scholarship offers a counterculture of sorts, finding shared meanings of our beliefs, values, and ways of being in the world that should be centralized in work with Indigenous communities (Wilson, 2008). This chapter discussed three approaches to working with Indigenous peoples: (1) work *against* Indigenous knowledge; (2) work *for* Indigenous knowledge; and (3) work *with* Indigenous knowledge. The first of these approaches categorizes projects that seek to use knowledge of Indigenous peoples in order to silence Indigenous voices and reaffirm settler-colonial knowledge systems as authoritative of Indigenous life. Although there are perhaps very explicit examples of harmful practices (such as genetic testing of Indigenous peoples without consent; see Arbour & Cook, 2006), the silencing of Indigenous perspectives and assumption of colonial ideals is prevalent in nearly all fields of research and community "work."

Work *for* Indigenous knowledge can be just as harmful, as it assumes that Indigenous knowledge is procurable and for the consumption of all. This can be seen by those who wish to quantify Indigenous knowledge in ways that do not benefit communities (Marinova & Raven, 2006) or in cases where Indigenous knowledge is "proven" with imperialistic mechanisms (Castleden et al., 2016). While integrating Indigenous perspectives into mainstream frameworks can be a useful decolonizing strategy, there also needs to be consideration of the appropriateness and authenticity of this engagement. Engaging in cultural practices may be important to ethical relationships with Indigenous communities, but the recording of cultural knowledge for later dissemination out of context is cultural appropriation and intellectual property theft. Cultural safety is a mechanism to do less harm in this respect, which enables non-Indigenous and Indigenous peoples to continuously negotiate relationships.

Doing work *with* Indigenous knowledge is ceremonial in nature and necessitates connection to culture, ancestry, and spirit (Wilson, 2008). It is this approach that will contribute to Indigenous resurgence. Yet, this is not always the space of non-Indigenous researchers or practitioners. We must be careful to engage Indigenous communities in ways that allow for resurgence work, without presuming to know what that looks like, and avoid busying communities with projects that are not beneficial to them. Thus, we need to reconsider: What are the roles of non-Indigenous peoples in this work? What are the priorities of Indigenous communities that would be best supported by non-Indigenous professionals? Largely, this space requires the exposure and dismantling of colonial policies, practices, and systemic barriers that hinder Indigenous sovereignty and self-determination over land and life (Tuck & Yang, 2012)—though this is much less fun than playing Indian (Deloria, 1969).

Research and community practice are interwoven as institutional intervention on Indigenous lives. Entering into relationships with Indigenous communities, particularly those who are geographically remote, is not a self-discovery tour or an anthropological quest. Engaging in community work with Indigenous communities necessitates a team-oriented approach that allows for institutions, individuals, and communities to mobilize resources in response to community needs. There is no set standard for what community work will look like with Indigenous communities, as each community has particular dynamics that require different approaches. The key aspect of being in good relations is seeing communities as reciprocal partners and drivers of the work, but not expecting those approaches or priorities to match one's own.

One way to understand *Mino-Bimaadiziwin Wiidookodaadiwag* is perhaps looking to the Two-Row Wampum Belt (Hallenbeck, 2015). Although not an Anishinaabe-specific treaty, the Two-Row Wampum Belt offers a Haudenosaunee perspective of settler-Indigenous relationships. The Two-Row Wampum Belt Covenant is a living treaty between the Iroquois Confederacy and European settlers, which articulated their relationships to one another as distinct peoples coexisting in peace with one another. The two rows represent their distinct paths as separate, but proximate, parallel lines. There is an understanding that these lines are not to cross, meaning that Indigenous peoples were to continue living their lives as they wished (Hallenbeck, 2015). Colonization has interfered in that path, and it is important that we enable Indigenous people to walk their own path again. We can walk beside them in partnership and solidarity when we walk the good path ourselves.

REFERENCES

Absolon, K., & Willett, C. (2004). Aboriginal research: Berry picking and hunting in the 21st century. *First Peoples Child & Family Review*, *1*(1), 5–17.

Adelson, N. (2005). The embodiment of inequity: Health disparities in Aboriginal Canada. *Canadian Journal of Public Health/Revue Canadienne de Sante'e Publique*, S45–S61.

Alfred, T. (2005). *Wasase: Indigenous pathways of action and freedom*. Toronto, ON: University of Toronto Press.

Arbour, L., & Cook, D. (2006). DNA on loan: Issues to consider when carrying out genetic research with Aboriginal families and communities. *Community Genet, 9*, 153–160.

Barsh, R. L. (2001). Who steals Indigenous knowledge? In *Proceedings of the ASIL Annual Meeting* (Vol. 95, pp. 153–161). Cambridge, UK: Cambridge University Press.

Bartlett, C., Marshall, M., & Marshall, A. (2012). Two-Eyed Seeing and other lessons learned within a co-learning journey of bringing together Indigenous and mainstream knowledges and ways of knowing. *Journal of Environmental Studies and Sciences, 2*, 331–340.

Barton, L. (2005). Emancipatory research and disabled people: Some observations and questions. *Educational Review*, *57*(3), 317–327.

Battiste, M. (2005). Indigenous knowledge: Foundations for First Nations. *World Indigenous Nations Higher Education Consortium—WINHEC Journal*, *1*(1), 1–12.

Battiste, M. (2009). Naturalizing Indigenous knowledge in Eurocentric education. *Canadian Journal of Native Education*, *32*(1), 5.

Battiste, M. (2011). *Reclaiming Indigenous voice and vision*. Vancouver, BC: UBC Press.

Battiste, M. (2016). Research ethics for chapter protecting Indigenous knowledge and heritage. In N. K. Denzin and M. D. Giardina (Eds.), *Ethical futures in qualitative research: Decolonizing the politics of knowledge* (pp. 111–132). New York: Routledge.

Battiste, M. A., & Barman, J. (Eds.). (1995). *First Nations education in Canada: The circle unfolds*. Vancouver, BC: UBC Press.

Braidotti, R. (2016). Posthuman critical theory. In D. Banerji & M. R. Paranjape (Eds.), *Critical posthumanism and planetary futures* (pp. 13–32). New Delhi: Springer.

Brant-Castellano, M. (2000). Updating Aboriginal traditions of knowledge. In G. Dei, B. Hall, & D. Rosenberg (Eds.), *Indigenous knowledges in global contexts* (pp. 21–36). Toronto, ON: University of Toronto Press.

Browne, A. J., Varcoe, C. M., Wong, S. T., Smye, V. L., Lavoie, J., Littlejohn, D., ... & Fridkin, A. (2012). Closing the health equity gap: Evidence-based strategies for primary health care organizations. *International Journal for Equity in Health*, *11*(1), 59.

Carriere, J., & Richardson, C. (2012). Relationship is everything: Holistic approaches to Aboriginal child and youth mental health. *First Peoples Child & Family Review, 7*(2), 8–26.

Castleden, H., Lewis, D., Jamieson, R., Gibson, M., Rainham, D., Russell, R., ... & Hart, C. (2016). "Our ancestors are in our land, water, and air": A two-eyed seeing approach to researching environmental health concerns with Pictou Landing First Nation. Final Report.

Chilisa, B. (2011). *Indigenous research methodologies*. Thousand Oaks, CA: Sage Publications.

Corntassel, J. (2012). Re-envisioning resurgence: Indigenous pathways to decolonization and sustainable self-determination. *Decolonization: Indigeneity, Education & Society, 1*(1).

Czyzewski, K. (2011). Colonialism as a broader social determinant of health. *The International Indigenous Policy Journal, 2*(1/5), 1–14.

Czyzewski, K., & Tester, F. (2014). Social work, colonial history and engaging Indigenous self-determination. *Canadian Social Work Review / Revue canadienne de service social, 31*(2), 211–226.

De, D., & Richardson, J. (2008). Cultural safety: An introduction. *Paediatric Nursing, 20*(2), 39–43.

de Leeuw, S., Greenwood, M., & Cameron, E. (2010). Deviant constructions: How governments preserve colonial narratives of addictions and poor mental health to intervene into the lives of Indigenous children and families in Canada. *International Journal of Mental Health and Addictions, 8*, 282–295.

Deloria, V. (1969). *Custer died for your sins: An Indian manifesto*. New York: Macmillan Publishing Company.

Denis, J. S., & Bailey, K. A. (2016). "You can't have reconciliation without justice": How non-Indigenous participants in Canada's truth and reconciliation process understand their roles and goals. In S. Maddison, T. Clark, & R. de Costa (Eds.), *The limits of settler colonial reconciliation* (pp. 137–158). Singapore: Springer.

Durst, D., South, S. M., & Bluechardt, M. (2006). Urban First Nations people with disabilities speak out. *Journal of Aboriginal Health, 3*(1), 34–43.

First Nations Information Governance Centre. (2014). Ownership, control, access and possession (OCAP): The path to First Nations information governance. Retrieved from https://fnigc.ca/sites/default/files/docs/ocap_path_to_fn_information_governance_en_final.pdf

Gerlach, A. J. (2012). A critical reflection on the concept of cultural safety. *The Canadian Journal of Occupational Therapy, 79*(3), 151–158.

Gracey, M., & King, M. (2009). Indigenous health part 1: Determinants and disease patterns. *The Lancet, 374*(9683), 65–75.

Haig-Brown, C. (2008). Working a third space: Indigenous knowledge in the post/colonial university. *Canadian Journal of Native Education, 31*(1), 253–267, 319–320.

Hallenbeck, J. (2015). Returning to the water to enact a treaty relationship: The Two Row Wampum Renewal Campaign, *Settler Colonial Studies, 5*(4), 350–362.

Hill, G., & Wilkinson, A. (2014). INDIGEGOGY: A transformative Indigenous educational process. *Canadian Social Work Review / Revue Canadienne De Service Social, 31*(2), 175–193.

Huntington, H. P. (2000). Using traditional ecological knowledge in science: Methods and applications. *Ecological Applications, 10*(5), 1270–1274.

Iseke, J., & Moore, S. (2011) Community-based Indigenous digital storytelling with Elders and youth. *American Indian Culture and Research Journal, 35*(4), 19–38.

Jackson Pulver, L.R.; Haswell, M.R.; Ring, I.; Waldon, J., … et al. (2010). *Indigenous health: Australia, Canada, Aotearoa, New Zealand and the United States—Laying claim to a future that embraces health for us all.* Retrieved from https://www.researchgate.net/publication/281774474_Indigenous_Health_-_Australia_Canada_Aotearoa_New_Zealand_and_the_United_States_-_Laying_claim_to_a_future_that_embraces_health_for_us_all

Johnston, B. (2010). *The gift of the stars.* Wiarton, ON: Kegedonce Press.

Johnston-Goodstar, K. (2013). Indigenous youth participatory action research: Re-visioning social justice for socialwork with Indigenous youths. *Social Work (United States), 58*(4), 314–320.

Kincheloe, J. L., & McLaren, P. (2002). Rethinking critical theory and qualitative research. In Y. Zou & E. T. Trueba (Eds.), *Ethnography and schools: Qualitative approaches to the study of education* (pp. 87–138). Lanham, MD: Rowman and Littlefield.

Kovach, M. (2010). *Indigenous methodologies: Characteristics, conversations, and contexts.* Toronto, ON: University of Toronto Press.

Kovach, M. (2015). Emerging from the margins: Indigenous methodologies. In S. Strega & L. Brown (Eds.), *Research as resistance: Revisiting critical, Indigenous, and anti-oppressive approaches*, Second Edition (pp. 43–64). Toronto: Canadian Scholars' Press.

Kuper, A., Reeves, S., & Levinson, W. (2008). An introduction to reading and appraising qualitative research. *BMJ, 337*(7666), 404–407.

Lavallee, L. F., & Poole, J. M. (2010). Beyond recovery: Colonization, health and healing for Indigenous people in Canada. *International Journal of Mental Health and Addiction, 8*(2), 271–281.

Lenette, C. (2014). Teaching cultural diversity in first year human services and social work: The impetus for embedding a cultural safety framework. A practice report. *The International Journal of the First Year in Higher Education, 5*(1), 117–123.

MacDonald, D. B. (2015). Canada's history wars: Indigenous genocide and public memory in the United States, Australia and Canada. *Journal of Genocide Research, 17*(4), 411–431.

Manitowabi, D. (2014). *Living with animals: Ojibwe spirit powers.* Toronto, ON: University of Toronto Press.

Manuel, A., & Derrickson, G. C. R. (2017). *The reconciliation manifesto: Recovering the land, rebuilding the economy.* Toronto, ON: James Lorimer & Company.

Marinova, D., & Raven, M. (2006). Indigenous knowledge and intellectual property: A sustainability agenda. *Journal of Economic Surveys, 20*(4), 587–605.

Mattingly, M., Stuart, C., & VanderVen, K. (2002). North American Certification Project (NACP) competencies for professional child and youth work practitioners. *Journal of Child and Youth Care Work, 17,* 16–49.

McGregor, D. (2018). From "decolonized" to reconciliation research in Canada: Drawing from Indigenous research paradigms. *ACME: An International Journal for Critical Geographies, 17*(3), 810–831.

McKenzie, H. A., Varcoe, C., Browne, A. J., & Day, L. (2016). Disrupting the continuities among residential schools, the sixties scoop, and child welfare: An analysis of colonial and neocolonial discourses. *The International Indigenous Policy Journal, 7*(2), 4.

Moniz, C. (2010). Social work and the social determinants of health perspective: A good fit. *Health and Social Work, 35*(4), 310–313.

NCCAH. (2013, July). *An overview of Aboriginal health in Canada.* Report. Prince George, BC: National Collaborating Centre for Aboriginal Health.

Ohmagari, K., & Berkes, F. (1997). Transmission of Indigenous knowledge and bush skills among the Western James Bay Cree women of subarctic Canada. *Human Ecology, 25*(2), 197–222.

Posey, D. A. (2002). Commodification of the sacred through intellectual property rights. *Journal of Ethnopharmacology, 83*(1–2), 3–12.

Radford, M. (2008). Complexity and truth in educational research. *Educational Philosophy and Theory, 40*(1), 144–157.

Riedlinger, D., & Berkes, F. (2001). Contributions of traditional knowledge to understanding climate change in the Canadian Arctic. *Polar Record, 37*(203), 315–328.

Simpson, L. R. (2004). Anticolonial strategies for the recovery and maintenance of Indigenous knowledge. *American Indian Quarterly, 28*(3/4), 373–384.

Simpson, L. (2008a). Looking after Gdoo-naaganinaa: Precolonial Nishnaabeg diplomatic and treaty relationships. *Wicazo Sa Review, 23*(2), 29–42.

Simpson, L. (2008b). Our elder brothers: The lifeblood of resurgence. In L. B. Simpson (Ed.), *Lighting the eighth fire: The liberation, resurgence, and protection of Indigenous nations* (pp. 73–87). Winnipeg, MB: ARP Books.

Sinclair, R. (2004). Aboriginal social work education in Canada: Decolonizing pedagogy for the seventh generation. *First Peoples Child & Family Review, 1*(1), 49–62.

Sinclair, R. (2016). The Indigenous child removal system in Canada: An examination of legal decision-making and racial bias. *First Peoples Child & Family Review, 11*(2), 8–18.

Smith, G. H. (2000). Protecting and respecting Indigenous knowledge. In M. Battiste (Ed.), *Reclaiming Indigenous voice and vision* (pp. 209–224). Vancouver: UBC Press.

Smith, L. T. (2012). *Decolonizing methodologies: Research and Indigenous peoples*, 2nd ed. London, UK: Zed Books.

Smylie, J., & Anderson, M. (2006). Understanding the health of Indigenous peoples in Canada: Key methodological and conceptual challenges. *CMAJ: Canadian Medical Association Journal, 175*(6), 602.

Trotti, J. L. (2001). Compensation versus colonization: A common heritage approach to the use of Indigenous medicine in developing Western pharmaceuticals. *Food & Drug Law Journal, 56*, 351.

Truth and Reconciliation Commission of Canada. (2015). *Honouring the truth, reconciling for the future: Summary of the final report of the Truth and Reconciliation Commission of Canada*. Retrieved from http://www.trc.ca/assets/pdf/Honouring_the_Truth_Reconciling_for_the_Future_July_23_2015.pdf

Tuck, E., & Guishard, M. (2013). Uncollapsing ethics: Racialized sciencism, settler coloniality, and an ethical framework of decolonial participatory action research. In T. M. Kress, C. Malott, & B. J. Porfilio (Eds.). *Challenging status quo retrenchment: New directions in critical research* (pp. 3–28). Charlotte, NC: Information Age Publishing.

Tuck, E., & Yang, K. W. (2012). Decolonization is not a metaphor. *Decolonization: Indigeneity, Education & Society, 1*(1), 1–40.

Wepa, D. (Ed.). (2015). *Cultural safety in Aotearoa New Zealand*. Cambridge, UK: Cambridge University Press.

Willmott, C. A. (2016). Toward language in action: Agency-oriented application of the GRASAC database for Anishinaabe language revitalization. *Museum Anthropology Review, 10*(2), 91–116.

Willow, A. J. (2013). Doing sovereignty in Native North America: Anishinaabe countermapping and the struggle for land-based self-determination. *Human Ecology, 41*(6), 871–884.

Wilson, S. (2008). *Research is ceremony: Indigenous research methods*. Winnipeg, MB: Fernwood.

CHAPTER 3

Towards a Framework of African-Centred Child and Youth Care Praxis

Julian Hasford, Peter Amponsah, Travonne Edwards, and Juanita Stephen[1]

INTRODUCTION

Long ago, when the world was young and people suffered from terrible ignorance, Nyame, the sky god, decided to send wisdom to the Earth to help alleviate humanities' suffering. Anansi, the human-spider trickster god, overheard Nyame's plan and offered to take the wisdom down to the people on the sky god's behalf.

Nyame trusted Anansi, so he poured his wisdom into a big clay pot and allowed the trickster to take it to Earth. When he arrived, Anansi eagerly peered inside, and was so moved by the wonderful knowledge and skills, he decided to use the wisdom for himself before giving it to the people. As each day passed, Anansi's greed grew with his knowledge, and he decided that the wisdom was too valuable to share. He decided, therefore, to hide the pot in the top of a tall tree that could not be climbed by any human. However, there was a problem: How could he carry such a heavy pot up such a huge tree? Anansi had an idea: He made a strong rope and tied one end around the pot and the other end around his waist, so he could climb the tree with the pot dangling from his body. However, as he started to climb, the dangling pot kept getting caught in the branches, making his ascent impossible.

Anansi's young son saw his father's struggle, and said, "Father, if you tie the pot to your back, it will be much easier for you to climb!" Anansi followed his son's advice, and was able to complete the climb much easier. When he got to the top, he looked down at his son and thought, "What a fool I am! I have the pot of wisdom, yet a little boy had more common sense than I did! What use is all of this wisdom to me?" Anansi angrily threw the pot to the ground, where it smashed into millions of pieces, and scattered the wisdom all over the world, where it became the foundation for the diverse traditions, knowledge, and practices of today's societies. That is why no one person has all of the wisdom in the world and why we share wisdom with each other when we exchange ideas. (Adapted from http://www.readingspots.org/site/wp-content/uploads/2017/09/50_Anansi_and_the_Pot_of_Wisdom.pdf)

···

Child and youth care (CYC) is a field that has ostensibly grown from the collective wisdom of adults and young people from diverse cultures of the world. In actuality, however, much of our field's wisdom—its theories, values, literature, and leading voices—is based largely upon European and North American traditions that prescribe a relatively narrow and White conceptualization of CYC as a field of practice. In spite of claims of diversity, multiculturalism, or cultural competency, the mainstream orthodoxy of our field continues to police the boundaries of "authentic" CYC theory and practice, which subtly and invisibly reinforce colonial, White, Euro-American ways of knowing, doing, and being, and idealize colour-blind liberal ideologies and depoliticized, professionalized relational practice. Disappointingly, efforts to disturb the White elephant in our classrooms, conferences, workplaces, and other shared spaces are often met with deflection, denial, despair, and anger—especially when the issues pertain to anti-Black racism.

To be fair, there have been increasing calls for CYC to contend with its Whiteness and coloniality (Gharabaghi, 2017; Saraceno, 2012) and to adopt more anti-oppressive orientations to its pedagogy and practice (Garfat, Freeman, Gharabaghi, & Fulcher, 2018; Kouri, 2015; Munroe, 2017; Skott-Myhre & Skott-Myhre, 2011). Although this emerging scholarship and growing diversity amongst the field's leading voices has exciting possibilities, it is not without constraints, including (a) a continued reliance on the Eurocentric theory and voices; (b) an often global orientation to oppression that lacks an explicit focus on anti-Black or anti-Indigenous racism; and (c) (somewhat paradoxically) an over-emphasis on oppression. Although structural oppression is undoubtedly the root of many of problems that justify the need for CYC, oppression is not the sole defining aspect of the lived experience or wisdom of historically marginalized peoples.

What might it mean to engage in CYC praxis from a place that centres the knowledge, experience, and values of young people and practitioners of African descent? We hope to explore this question in this chapter by putting forward a tentative and exploratory framework for African-Centred Child and Youth Care Practice (ACYCP), which is grounded in the literature and experiential knowledge of people of African descent, including the authors—four African Canadian CYC educators, activists, and practitioners. We recognize the complexities of our status as settlers on Indigenous lands (Amadahy & Lawrence, 2009), and write this chapter in a spirit of solidarity with Indigenous peoples.

CONTEXT

Most historical accounts suggest that the presence of African people in Canada began in the early 17th century, with the arrival of Mathieu da Costa, a native of Benin, who arrived in (present-day) Nova Scotia as a translator employed by Portuguese colonizers. Over subsequent centuries, African peoples settled in Canada following a number of routes, including as enslaved peoples of British and French colonizers during the 17th and 18th centuries, as Black Loyalists who fought for the British during the American Revolutionary War and settled largely in Nova Scotia in the late 18th century, and as refugees who fled to Canada from the US through the Underground Railroad following the War of 1812 (Blackett, 2013; Whitehead, 2013).

The vast majority of today's African Canadian population arrived as migrants from the Caribbean and Africa following the gradual liberalization of immigration policies during the mid- to late 20th century. According to the 2016 census, African Canadians comprise the third largest visible minority group in Canada, accounting for 3.5 percent of the general population (numbering approximately 1.2 million) (Statistics Canada, 2017). Most African Canadians (over 90 percent) reside in the five provinces of Ontario (52.4 percent), Quebec (26.6 percent), Alberta (10.8 percent), Manitoba (2.4 percent), and Nova Scotia (1.8 percent), and are heavily concentrated in the urban areas (94.3 percent compared to 71.2 percent for the general population).

ANTI-BLACK RACISM IN CANADA

Since their arrival in Canada, the lived experience of African Canadians has been over-determined by anti-Black racism (a particular form of racism that emerged from European colonization and enslavement, and consists of a specific set of institutional structures and practices, social myths, beliefs, and outcomes concerning Black peoples) (Benjamin, 2003). Anti-Black racism is embedded within Canadian child and youth serving sectors, as reflected by persistent and pernicious racial inequities in sectors such as child welfare (Ontario Association of Children's Aid Societies [OACAS], 2016), education (James & Turner, 2017; Gray, Bailey, Brady, & Tecle, 2016), justice (Gharabaghi, Trocme, & Newman, 2016), and academia (Munroe, 2016). Although there have been several efforts to address anti-Black racism in Canadian child and youth serving sectors through publicly funded strategic planning, community-based youth programs, youth employment initiatives, workforce diversification, and anti-racism training (Lewis, 1992; For Youth Initiative, 2018; McMurtry & Curling, 2008; Government of Ontario, 2017; OACAS, 2016), nothing has significantly mitigated the impacts of anti-Black racism.

AFRICAN CANADIAN RESISTANCE AND RESILIENCE

The identities and lived experiences of African Canadians are not defined by anti-Black racism, in spite of its pervasiveness. People of African descent across the globe have rich traditions of youth empowerment and engagement that cut across cultural, political, and economic domains. Although it is beyond the scope of this chapter to discuss here, some notable Canadian examples are the establishment of Africentric schools in Toronto (Dei & Kempf, 2013), community-based child welfare advocacy of the One Vision, One Voice project (OACAS, 2016), youth-led advocacy of HairStory (Ontario Child Advocate, 2018), faith-based youth leadership development in Black churches (Este, 2007), youth-led urban agriculture (Hasford & Boye, 2008), political activism of Black Lives Matter (Furman, Singh, Darko, & Wilson, 2018), and innovative support of young fathers with the Black Daddies Club (Bagnall et al., 2014).

AFRICAN-CENTRED CHILD AND YOUTH CARE PRAXIS

The concept of praxis has become a principal framework for conceptualizing the integrative nature of CYC work (Kouri, 2015). White (2007), in a seminal paper on CYC praxis, defined it as "ethical, self-aware, responsive and accountable action, which reflects dimensions of knowing, doing and being" (p. 226). More recently, scholars such as Kouri (2015), Skott-Myhre and Skott-Myhre (2011), and Saraceno (2012) have called for more critical orientations to CYC praxis that foreground social justice and structural analyses, while decentring Euro-American hegemony of theory and practice.

Of course, the integration of knowledge, ethics, and action is not a uniquely European problem. Such issues have been at the crux of political, moral, and spiritual discourse in numerous non-Western regions, including Africa, where it is embedded within the deep philosophies expressed through proverbs, literature, religions, and arts (Asante, Miike, & Yin, 2013). Since at least the 15th century, the integration of knowledge, ethics, and action has been a driving force of various African liberation struggles, often with young people at the helm. This exploration is reflected in the praxes of emancipation and faith in slave narratives (Washington, 1901), political and psychological liberation in African anti-colonial and pan-Africanist social movements (Biko, 1978; Fanon, 1963), radical pedagogy within Black civil rights movements (Carmichael & Hamilton, 1992; Seale, 1991), intersectional intellectual activism in Black feminism (Combahee River Collective, 1973), and cultural politics through hip hop (Watkins, 2001).

To our knowledge, little literature has explicitly examined CYC praxis from an African-centred perspective. Perhaps the most notable body of work stems from the Isibindi model from South Africa, which embodies a praxis of love and caring in the context of poverty and the AIDS pandemic (Thumbadoo, 2011). Much of the literature about Isibindi, however, has been produced by non-Black (albeit racialized, in some cases) peoples, and thus may not be grounded within Black South African worldviews. There is nonetheless a significant body of related scholarship on African-centred praxis in other disciplines, such as social work (Bernard & Smith, 2018; Gilbert, Harvey, & Belgrave, 2009; Harvey & Hill, 2004), education (Dei, 2018; Durden, 2007), psychology (Akbar, 1984), public health (Ford & Airhihenbuwa, 2010), and youth mental health (Hatcher, King, Barnett, & Burley, 2017).

We define African-Centred Child and Youth Care Practice (ACYCP) as a quality of thought and action that places at the centre of analysis and practice the worldviews, voices, histories, and cultures of young people of African descent, and that explicitly focuses on their well-being and liberation (Asante, Miike, & Yin, 2013; Goggins, 1996). In Figure 3.1, we present a visual model of our ACYCP framework, which is based on the Adinkra symbol,[2] referred to as *Ananse Ntontan* (the spider's web), representing wisdom, creativity, and the complexities of life. The web in the model involves an interweaving of two main domains: (a) African worldviews (and its four domains of cosmology, ontology, epistemology, and axiology); and (b) action (in three domains of relational, spiritual, and political praxis). Much like the spider's web, we believe that ACYCP is characterized by fluidity, complexity, adaptability, creativity, beauty, and strength.

We recognize that there are a number of limitations inherent in any attempt to articulate a framework for ACYCP. This includes the risk of such efforts becoming reductionist or prescriptive, given the insufficient room to explore the full breadth or depth of perspectives. Second, we recognize that the ideas and values espoused in this chapter do not reflect those of all (or most) Black Youth or CYC practitioners, who vary substantially in cultural, religious, or political orientations. Third, there is a risk of essentializing and romanticizing African-ness and of reproducing colonial gazes that fetishize and dehumanize Black peoples. We hope to mitigate these issues by ensuring that the goal of the chapter is not to prescribe a recipe for CYC practice with Black Youth, nor to make any claims about the homogeneity of African worldviews and practices. Instead, we view this as an aspirational undertaking to explore and encourage a wider range of theory and practice in the field.

Figure 3.1: Ananse Ntontan

AFRICAN-CENTRED WORLDVIEWS

We use the concept of worldview to frame the underlying paradigm that informs ACYCP, as it is commonly used in African-centred scholarship (Carroll, 2010; Thabede, 2008). *Worldview* refers to the culturally and historically influenced lens through which people make sense of their lived experiences (Carroll, 2014). Carroll (2014) suggests that worldview is composed of four main sets of philosophical assumptions: ontology (nature of reality and being), cosmology (nature and origins of the universe), epistemology (nature of knowledge), and axiology (nature of values, ethics, and morals).

Ontology

Many African ontologies are based on a view of reality as consisting of inseparable spiritual and material realms, with reality having an essentially spiritual nature that manifests materially (Carroll, 2014). The nature of the human being is based on a relational ontology, which views the Self as interdependent with its social and environmental relationships, with its humanity arising through these relationships (Airoboman & Asekhauno, 2012; Nwoye, 2017). The inseparability of spirit from physical matter suggests that what is experienced in the flesh also resonates in the spiritual realm and vice versa (Doumbia & Doumbia, 2004), and also recognizes the spiritual agency of non-human actors (Datta, 2015).

Cosmology

African cosmologies are often based on a belief that the universe's interconnected material and spiritual components are governed and guided by a hierarchy of spiritual entities (Carroll, 2014). The universe is typically believed to have been created by an eternal, omnipotent supreme being (God) that governs the affairs of subordinate entities. These entities may consist of various divinities or demi-gods that personify various natural and social forces, ancestral spirits, human beings and their immortal souls, and spirits of animal, plants, and other earthly forms. Divinities and other spiritual beings may influence human affairs (either of their own volition or by human invocation), and may be good or evil.

Epistemology

Common epistemological perspectives in African contexts suppose that knowledge is multi-faceted, including and transcending both reason and empirical sense experience (Carroll, 2014). Valid forms of knowledge in African epistemologies may include emotion, intuition, and insight received through spirits or ancestors. Moreover, the value of knowledge is not necessarily based upon its neutrality or objectivity, but rather its experiential, place-based, ethical, and social utility (Airoboman & Asekhauno, 2012; Udefi, 2014). Stories, proverbs, myths, and arts provide powerful sources of knowledge attainment and transmission across generations and contexts.

Axiology

The axiological strands of African worldviews emphasize character and moral personhood as a central existential imperative for human beings, the elevation of duty over rights, an emphasis on social over individual ethics, and beauty (Ikuenobe, 2016; Mangena, 2016).

AFRICAN-CENTRED CYC PRAXIS IN ACTION

The following sub-sections explore some of the practices and problems that can arise when engaging in ACYCP as Black CYC practitioners. Although we focus on the three domains of relational, spiritual, and political action, these are not intended to be definitive, as there are many other realms of action or lenses used to conceptualize them. Broadly speaking, however, action from an African-centred perspective often places value on the qualities of spontaneity, orality, creativity, authenticity, and rhythmicity (Goggins, 1996).

African-Centred Relational Praxis

We propose that African-centred relational praxis involves the cultivation of holistic relationships between young people, kin, kith, Elders, ancestors, spirits, and the natural world, which are characterized by harmony, interdependence, reciprocity, and respect. This differs from the conceptualization of relationality in orthodox CYC, which typically focuses primarily on relationships between practitioners and young people (and their families or communities).

Forms of African-centred relational praxis vary tremendously based on personal and local contexts, and have included a range of approaches such as mentorship programs, storytelling, elder mediation, and kin/kith care. Historically, relationships with land have also played an important role in the development of African youth and communities; however, this relationship has been weakened in contemporary times (Behrens, 2014; Engel-Di Mauro & Carroll, 2014). I (Hasford) discovered the power of land as a space for transformative holistic relationality when I began working as a youth worker for a program that used urban agriculture as a tool for Black Youth leadership development, employment, mentorship, and environmental stewardship. It was a program that some might refer to as a counter-space, enabling the formation of renewed or expanded identities, including narratives that often narrowly define Black Youth in terms of sports and music. I too grew considerably through the experience, deepening my connection to land and young people through the shared rhythmicity of cultivation throughout the seasons and direct interdependency of community and land, as well as the importance of humility and respect for dynamic ecosystems and non-human worlds.

Although my experience in urban agriculture was transformative for me and other Black Youth, it wasn't without its challenges. As with many Black-focused undertakings in Western contexts, we had to contend with multiple manifestations of institutional racism and white supremacy. Moreover, we also had to learn to engage with resistance among some young people who associated farming with slavery and menial labour, internalizing narratives about land that some suggest are responsible for an underrepresentation of Black peoples in environmental initiatives (Hasford & Boye, 2008).

African-Centred Spiritual Praxis

African-centred spiritual praxis involves the cultivation of spiritual knowledge and energy towards personal and community growth. Studies have found that spirituality can play a protective role in the lives of Black Youth (Sink & Simpson, 2013). Although the spiritual traditions of African peoples span an array of Indigenous, Christian, and Islamic forms, some common themes include the significance of rituals; rhythm and ceremonies as resistance to dominance (Asante, Miike, & Yin, 2013); prayer; and love and accountability for self and community (Karenga, 2010), to name a few. For CYC practitioners practising from an African-centred perspective, such themes can offer reference points for deeper connections with youth.

There are no codified spiritual practices for African-centred youth work; however, some common strategies include drumming (Watson, Washington, & Stepteau-Watson, 2015), dance (Banks, 2014), and rites of passage (Harvey & Hill, 2004). Drumming and dance, for example, can have powerful spiritual aspects of communication and healing. Dor (2014) reminds us of the varied ways in which drumming and dance was supressed during slavery in North America, and notes that West African drumming and dance classes can be both challenging and stimulating, thereby providing access to "different kinds of energies with which students are familiar" (p. 216).

There are a number of challenges with spiritual praxis. Foremost, perhaps, is the general fear of engaging with spirituality in our professional work regardless of personal orientation. We also cannot be naive to the negative connotations associated with African spirituality, which often evoke colonial images of evil, savagery, and witchcraft. However, as Doumbia and Doumbia (2004) acknowledge, "Little is known about the important function of the energy of Spirit . . . and its crucial role in the very fabric of daily existence. Many misuse labels such as possession, juju, or fetish to describe African sacred practices. These are all misunderstandings of the deep and powerful expressions of love and devotion for Spirit, humanity, and creation within African cultures" (p. xiii). Unfortunately, the misapplication of practices like traditional drumming and dance in some contemporary mainstream child and youth programming may reflect a misunderstanding of their historical or spiritual significance.

African-Centred Political Praxis

African-centred political praxis involves the analysis and mobilization of power (psychologically, relationally, and structurally) towards the liberation of people of African descent from Imperialist-White-Supremacist-Capitalist-Patriarchy (hooks, 2003). It recognizes that the personal is political, and thus does not neatly demarcate between professional and non-professional contexts, and extends to realms of action that may extend from the home to community, electoral politics, and the economy (Combahee River Collective, 1973; Collins, 2002). The history of African-centred political praxis can be traced through liberation movements in Africa and throughout its diaspora, which have often included an emphasis on youth engagement. Notable examples from North America include the Black Power movements such as the Student Nonviolent Coordinating Committee and Black Panther Party (Williams, 1997), Nation of Islam (Akom, 2003), and Black Lives Matter (Walcott & Abdillahi, 2019).

Although there is significant variety in strategies and philosophies used, African-centred political praxis with youth often centres *critical civic praxis*, the development of critical consciousness, social networks, and experiences that enhance young people's ability to influence oppressive conditions (Edwards, 2018; Ginwright & Cammarota, 2007). Socio-political consciousness-raising is a particularly important element that integrates a greater understanding of sociopolitical contexts with young peoples' racial identity (Watts, Williams, & Jagers, 2003). Strategies may also include youth-led initiatives, formal civic engagement, social action, political arts (particularly hip hop), collective economics, and tackling of everyday issues. In order to effectively engage youth in political praxis, practitioners should adopt a *critical youth work* orientation (Bamber & Murphy, 1999), ensuring they are informed about issues related to power, race, and social justice in ways that can support young people in connecting their personal issues to the political level and in being agents of change within their own lives (Ginwright & Cammarota, 2007).

Although there is great potential in African-centred political praxis, there are numerous challenges to its effectiveness. The lack of race-based data in our child and youth serving systems is a major structural barrier, as it maintains a lack of evidence regarding systemic anti-Black racism, which is a critical resource for effective advocacy and structural change. There are also challenges in bridging intergenerational gaps between elders and young people engaged in anti-racist politics. Although Elders possess vast knowledge and experience that can support Black Youth in navigating political spaces, there can be tensions between the traditional approaches and values of Elders and the more contemporary perspectives and needs of young people.

African-Centred Allyship

Allyship is a certain expression in CYC (and social services more generally) that is associated with good practice and the intent to engage with contemporary issues within the field. However, the term has been diluted over time, becoming the stand-in signifier for anything resembling support of a person or group experiencing oppression. This is particularly true as it relates to "allyship" with Black Youth and families that amounts to little more than an expression of empathy, outrage, or (quite popularly) a declared position of "standing in solidarity with the Black community." Multicultural and colour-blind ideologies mask the reality of racial dominance and privilege (Bonilla-Silva, 2013), giving rise to the development of well-meaning helpers who, despite good intentions, have difficulty either acknowledging the contemporary climate of anti-Blackness or recognizing when their attempts at *standing in solidarity* with Black folks are misguided, counterproductive, or even injurious. In order to do meaningful solidarity work with people of African descent, we offer the notion of African-centred allyship in child and youth care practice.

African-centred allyship is conceptualized as non-African peoples engaging in authentic and congruent practice that supports the empowerment, liberation, and well-being of people of African descent. This definition highlights two key aspects of this work: first, it centres the needs, values, and voices of African-descendant peoples; and second, it emphasizes the requirement of *action* on the part of non-African peoples. African-centred allyship requires more than simply *standing* in solidarity. Rather, it requires non-African peoples to leverage their privilege in tangible ways and on multiple levels—personal, relational, and structural—to redirect human, financial, and material resources into a commitment to equity and justice. This notion of allyship asks non-African peoples to persist in their action of centring the perspectives and welfare of Black people in spite of risks, fear, or ignorance. For example, a public call to stop the use of a racist exam as the certification standard for practitioners may present a risk to your personal reputation or your opportunity for professional advancement. You may find it uncomfortable to challenge a colleague who has put forth a policy that disadvantages the Black young people and families accessing services at your organization. The word *ally* is so widely contested as a term (Leonard & Misumi, 2016) that it isn't actually necessary to link the solidarity action that we are proposing to a specific language. What is necessary is *action* that centres Black well-being.

CONCLUSION

In this chapter we have briefly examined the theoretical and practical implications of ACYCP, based upon a review of the literature and critical reflection on the lived experiences of people of African descent. Notwithstanding the many limitations highlighted earlier, we hope this work will contribute to a deeper exploration of the ways in which CYC praxis, particularly with Black Youth, can be enriched through an examination of African lived experiences of being with young people across time and space, and a centring of spirit in our journey onwards.

NOTES

1. Julian Hasford is the lead author. Peter Amponsah, Travonne Edwards, and Juanita Stephen contributed equally to this chapter.
2. Adinkra symbols are those that represent concepts and proverbs from the traditions of the Akan peoples of modern-day Ghana.

REFERENCES

Airoboman, F. A., & Asekhauno, A. A. (2012). Is there an "African" epistemology? *Jorind, 10*(3), 13–17.

Akbar, N. I. (1984). Africentric social sciences for human liberation. *Journal of Black Studies, 14*(4), 395–414.

Akom, A. A. (2003). Reexaming resistance as oppositional behavior: The Nation of Islam and the creation of a Black achievement ideology. *Sociology of Education, 76*(4), 305–325.

Amadahy, Z., & Lawrence, B. (2009). Indigenous peoples and Black people in Canada: Settlers or allies? In A. Kempf (Ed.), *Breaching the colonial contract* (pp. 105–136). Dordrecht, NL: Springer.

Asante, M. K., Miike, Y., & Yin, J. (2013). Afrocentricity: Toward a new understanding of African thought in the world. In M. K. Asante, Y. Miike, & J. Yin (Eds.), *The global intercultural communication reader* (pp. 115–124). New York, NY: Routledge.

Bagnall, J., Bailey, P., Burchall, J., Hay, B., X, C., & Nelson, L. E. (2014). *Breaking bread final report.* Retrieved from http://theblackdaddiesclub.com/wp-content/uploads/2014/01/Breaking_Bread_Final_Report_SVC_02.01.11.pdf

Bamber, J., & Murphy, H. (1999). Youth work: The possibilities for critical practice. *Journal of Youth Studies, 2*(2), 227–242.

Banks, O. C. (2014). West African dance education as spiritual capital: A perspective from the United States. *Dance, Movement & Spiritualities, 1*(1), 163–179.

Behrens, K. G. (2014). An African relational environmentalism and moral considerability. *Environmental Ethics, 36*(1), 63–82.

Benjamin, A. (2003). *The Black/Jamaican criminal: The making of ideology.* Unpublished doctoral dissertation, University of Toronto, Toronto, Ontario.

Bernard, W., & Smith, H. (2018). Injustice, justice, and Africentric practice in Canada. *Canadian Social Work Review/Revue Canadienne de service social, 35*(1), 149–157.

Biko, S. (1978). Black consciousness and the quest for a true humanity. *Ufahamu: A Journal of African Studies, 8*(3), 10–20.

Blackett, R. (2013). *Making freedom: The Underground Railroad and the politics of slavery.* Chapel Hill, NC: University of North Carolina Press.

Bonilla-Silva, E. (2013). *Racism without racists: Colorblind racism and the persistence of inequality in America* (4th Ed.). Lanham, MD: Rowman & Littlefield.

Carmichael, S., & Hamilton, C. V. (1992). *Black Power: The politics of liberation in America.* New York: Vintage.

Carroll, K. K. (2010). A genealogical analysis of the worldview framework in African-centered psychology. *The Journal of Pan African Studies, 3*(8), 109–134.

Carroll, K. K. (2014). An introduction to African-centered sociology: Worldview, epistemology, and social theory. *Critical Sociology, 40*(2), 257–270.

Collins, P. H. (2002). *Black feminist thought: Knowledge, consciousness, and the politics of empowerment.* New York, NY: Routledge.

Combahee River Collective. (1973). The Combahee River statement. *Feminism in our time: The essential writings, World War II to the present.* New York, NY: Vintage.

Datta, R. (2015). A relational theoretical framework and meanings of land, nature, and sustainability for research with Indigenous communities. *Local Environment, 20*(1), 102–113.

Dei, G. J. S. (2018). "Black like me": Reframing blackness for decolonial politics. *Educational Studies, 54*(2), 117–142.

Dei, G. J. S., & Kempf, A. (2013). *New perspectives on African-centred education in Canada.* Toronto, ON: Canadian Scholars' Press.

Dor, G.W.K. (2014). *West African drumming and dance in North American universities: An ethnomusicological perspective.* Jackson, MS: University Press of Mississippi.

Doumbia, A., & Doumbia, N. (2004). *The way of the elders: West African spirituality & tradition.* St. Paul, MN: Llewellyn Publishers.

Durden, T. R. (2007). African centered schooling: Facilitating holistic excellence for Black children. *The Negro Educational Review, 58*(1–2), 23–34.

Edwards, T. (2018, April). Redefining policies: Black Youth participation and critical civic praxis. *CYC-Online, 230,* 47–55. Retrieved from http://www.cyc-net.org/cyc-online/apr2018.pdf

Engel-Di Mauro, S., & Carroll, K. K. (2014). An African-centred approach to land education. *Environmental Education Research, 20*(1), 70–81.

Este, D. (2007). Black churches in Canada: Vehicles for fostering community development in African-Canadian communities—A historical analysis. In J. R. Graham, J. Coates, B. Swartzentruber, & B. Ouellette (Eds.), *Spirituality and social work: Selected Canadian readings* (pp. 299–322). Toronto, ON: Canadian Scholars' Press.

Fanon, F. (1963). *The wretched of the earth.* New York: Grove Press Inc.

For Youth Initiative. (2018). *The state of the youth-led sector: 10 years since the year of the gun.* Retrieved from https://d3n8a8pro7vhmx.cloudfront.net/fyi/pages/2819/attachments/original/1532351874/Laidlaw_Report_Final_%281%29.pdf?1532351874

Ford, C. L., & Airhihenbuwa, C. O. (2010). Critical race theory, race equity, and public health: Toward antiracism praxis. *American Journal of Public Health, 100*(S1), S30–S35.

Furman, E., Singh, A. K., Darko, N. A., & Wilson, C. L. (2018). Activism, intersectionality, and community psychology: The way in which Black Lives Matter Toronto helps us to examine white supremacy in Canada's LGBTQ community. *Community Psychology in Global Perspective, 4*(2), 34–54.

Garfat, T., Freeman, J., Gharabaghi, K., & Fulcher, L. C. (2018, October). Characteristics of a relational child and youth care approach revisited. *CYC-Online, 236*, 7–45. Retrieved from https://www.cyc-net.org/pdf/Characteristics%20of%20a%20 Relational%20CYC%20Approach%20Revisited.pdf

Gharabaghi, K. (2017). Why are we so white? *CYC-Online, 220*, 6–11. Retrieved from https://www.cyc-net.org/cyc-online/jun2017.pdf#page=6

Gharabaghi, K., Trocme, N., & Newman, D. (2016). *Because young people matter: Report of the Residential Services Review Panel.* Retrieved from http://www.children.gov.on.ca/htdocs/English/documents/childrensaid/residential-services-review-panel-report-feb2016.pdf

Gilbert, D. J., Harvey, A. R., & Belgrave, F. Z. (2009). Advancing the Africentric paradigm shift discourse: Building toward evidence-based Africentric interventions in social work practice with African Americans. *Social Work, 54*(3), 243–252.

Ginwright, S., & Cammarota, J. (2007). Youth activism in the urban community: Learning critical civic praxis within community organizations. *International Journal of Qualitative Studies in Education, 20*(6), 693–710.

Goggins, L. (1996). *Bringing the light into a new day: African-centered rights of passage.* Akron, OH: Saint Rest Publications.

Government of Ontario. (2017). *Anti-black racism strategy.* Retrieved from https://files.ontario.ca/ar-2002_anti-black_racism_strategy_en.pdf

Gray, E., Bailey, R., Brady, J., & Tecle, S. (2016, September). *Perspectives of Black male students in secondary school: Understanding the successes and challenges—student focus group results.* Mississauga, ON: Peel District School Board.

Harvey, A. R., & Hill, R. B. (2004). Africentric youth and family rites of passage program: Promoting resilience among at-risk African American youths. *Social Work, 49*(1), 65–74.

Hasford, J., & Boye, S. (2008). Garden culture and social diversity. *Proceedings of the Gardens as everyday culture: An international comparison International Conference,* University of Kassel, Kassel, Germany, May 22–24, 2008.

Hatcher, S. S., King, D. M., Barnett, T. M., & Burley, J. T. (2017). Mental health for youth: Applying an African-centered approach. *Journal of Human Behavior in the Social Environment, 27*(1–2), 61–72.

hooks, B. (2003). *Teaching community: A pedagogy of hope.* New York, NY: Routledge.

Ikuenobe, P. (2016). Good and beautiful: A moral-aesthetic view of personhood in African communal traditions. *Essays in Philosophy, 17*(1), 125–163.

James, C. E., & Turner, T. (2017). *Towards race equity in education: The schooling of Black students in the Greater Toronto Area.* Toronto, ON: York University. Retrieved from https://youthrex.com/report/towards-race-equity-in-education-the-schooling-of-black-students-in-the-greater-toronto-area/

Karenga, M. (1998). *Kwanzaa: A celebration of family, community, and culture*. Los Angeles, CA: University of Sankore Press.

Karenga, M. (2010). *Introduction to Black Studies*, 4th Edition. Los Angeles, CA: University of Sankore Press.

Kouri, S. (2015). The canonical self and politicized praxis: A tracing of two concepts. *International Journal of Child, Youth and Family Studies, 6*(4), 595–621.

Leonard, G., & Misumi, L. (2016). W.A.I.T. (why am I talking?): A dialogue on solidarity, allyship, and supporting the struggle for racial justice without reproducing white supremacy. *Harvard Journal of African American Public Policy, 2015–16*, 61–74.

Lewis, S. (1992). *Stephen Lewis report on race relations in Ontario*. Government of Ontario. Retrieved from https://collections.ola.org/mon/13000/134250.pdf

Mangena, F. (2016). African ethics through Ubuntu: A postmodern exposition. *Africology: The Journal of Pan African Studies, 9*(2), 66–80.

McMurtry, R., & Curling, A. (2008). *The review of the roots of violence (volume 1)*. Toronto, ON: Queen's Printer for Ontario.

Munroe, T. (2016). From college to university: What I learned navigating the child and youth care curriculum. *Relational Child and Youth Care Practice, 29*(3), 91–99.

Munroe, T. (2017). Enriching relational practices with critical anti-black racism advocacy and perspectives in schools. *Relational Child and Youth Care Practice, 30*(3), 32–45.

Nwoye, A. (2017). An Africentric theory of human personhood. *Psychology in Society, 54*, 42–66.

Ontario Association of Children's Aid Societies (OACAS). (2016). *One vision, one voice: Changing the Ontario child welfare system to better serve African Canadians*. Retrieved from http://www.oacas.org/wp-content/uploads/2016/09/One-Vision-One-Voice-Part-1_digital_english-May-2019.pdf

Ontario Child Advocate. (2018). *Hairstory: Rooted*. Toronto, ON: Ontario Child Advocate.

Saraceno, J. (2012). Mapping whiteness and coloniality in the human service field: Possibilities for a praxis of social justice in child and youth care. *International Journal of Child, Youth and Family Studies, 3*(2–3), 248–271.

Seale, B. (1991). *Seize the time: The story of the Black Panther Party and Huey P. Newton*. Baltimore, MD: Black Classic Press.

Sink, C. A., & Simpson, L. A. (2013). African-American adolescent spirituality: Implications for school counseling. *Religion & Education, 40*(2), 189–220.

Skott-Myhre, K., & Skott-Myhre, H. A. (2011). Theorizing and applying child and youth care praxis as politics of care. *Relational Child & Youth Care Practice, 24*(1/2), 42–52.

Statistics Canada. (2017). *Census profile*. 2016 Census. Catalogue no. 98-316-X2016001. Ottawa, ON: Statistics Canada. Retrieved from https://www12.statcan.gc.ca/census-recensement/2016/dp-pd/prof/index.cfm?Lang=E

Thabede, D. (2008). The African worldview as the basis of practice in the helping professions. *Social Work/Maatskaplike Werk, 44*(3), 233–245.

Thumbadoo, Z. (2011). Isibindi: Love in caring with a child and youth care approach. *Relational Child & Youth Care Practice, 24*(1/2), 193–198.

Udefi, A. (2014). The rationale for an African epistemology: A critical examination of the Igbo views on knowledge, belief, and justification. *Canadian Social Science, 10*(3), 108–117.

Walcott, R., & Abdillahi, I. (2019). *BlackLife: Post-BLM and the struggle for freedom.* Winnipeg, MB: ARP Books.

Washington, B. T. (1901). *Up from slavery.* Toronto, ON: Simon and Schuster.

Watkins, S. C. (2001). A nation of millions: Hip hop culture and the legacy of black nationalism. *The Communication Review, 4*(3), 373–398.

Watson, J., Washington, G., & Stepteau-Watson, D. (2015). Umoja: A culturally specific approach to mentoring young African American males. *Child and Adolescent Social Work Journal, 32*(1), 81–90.

Watts, R. J., Williams, N. C., & Jagers, R. J. (2003). Sociopolitical development. *American Journal of Community Psychology, 31*(1–2), 185–194.

White, J. (2007). Knowing, doing and being in context: A praxis-oriented approach to child and youth care. *Child & Youth Care Forum, 36*(5–6), 225–244.

Whitehead, R. (2013). *Black loyalists: Southern settlers of Nova Scotia's first free Black communities.* Halifax, NS: Nimbus Publishing.

Williams, Y. R. (1997). American exported black nationalism: The student nonviolent coordinating committee, the Black Panther Party, and the worldwide freedom struggle, 1967–1972. *Negro History Bulletin, 60*(3), 13–20.

CHAPTER 4

Newcomer, Immigration, and Settlement Sectors

Francis Hare

INTRODUCTION

As the new year of 2016 opened in Toronto, the newspaper headlines told of the challenges of welcoming refugee children from Syria into the school system and into Canadian society. In fact, similar challenges have become routine in the larger metropolitan areas of Canada, where issues of immigration and the settlement of newcomers often intersect with issues of services for children and youth. As such, the broad range and variety of employment opportunities for child and youth care practitioners increasingly require a familiarity with the challenges of immigration and settlement faced by the children and youth whom we serve.

This chapter will examine several ways in which the issue of immigration permeates services for children and youth in the Greater Toronto Area, while acknowledging that other population centres of varying sizes will likely recognize themselves in what is described. There will also be many ways in which the contents of this chapter will touch on issues raised in other chapters of the two volumes of *Child and Youth Care across Sectors*, including the school system, residential and foster care, health care, family dynamics, and issues of personal identity.

CURRENT STATUS OF CHILD AND YOUTH CARE PRACTITIONERS IN THIS SECTOR

This has not been a traditional area of practice in the child and youth care (CYC) field, although services for children and youth in immigrant-rich centres such as Toronto are, *de facto*, largely services for immigrant children and youth. The immigration context may not be explicitly recognized or taken into account by the practitioner, but it is likely to be an active component of the identity of the child or youth. One illustration of this was a comment made by the supervisor of a service for youth in transition from the care system. The supervisor said that since so few of the workers themselves had the experience of being immigrants, they were not especially attuned to the realities and concerns of the immigrant youth being served (Hare, 2007).

As the number of CYC practitioners who are either themselves immigrants or are the children of immigrants increases, one would hope that the awareness of and sensitivity to immigration issues in CYC practice will also increase. A myriad of employment opportunities will emerge to enhance the core of CYC practice. This chapter will attempt to illustrate the variety of ways in which CYC practitioners can respond to the needs of immigrant children and youth, drawing on CYC principles and practices and informed by an increased awareness of the significance of the immigration experience. For even greater impact, if CYC practitioners with immigration and settlement experience were to write about their own experiences as viewed through the lens of CYC theory and principles, their contribution to the CYC literature would be substantial.

CHALLENGES AND OPPORTUNITIES

Given that roughly 50 percent of the population of the Toronto Census Metropolitan Area were born outside of Canada (Ontario Ministry of Finance, 2017), it is apparent that services for children and youth in Toronto are as likely as not to be services for immigrant children and youth. Nonetheless, the focus in this chapter will be on areas of service that are explicitly linked to the immigration-related needs of children and youth as distinct from more generic services that may, by chance, be provided to immigrant children and youth. Further clarification with respect to the use of terminology is necessary. The term *immigrant* in this chapter includes those who are immigrants as well as those who meet the international criteria for being deemed refugees. The term *newcomer youth* is often used by service providers and in the literature as encompassing both immigrant youth and refugee youth, and this use will find occasional expression in this chapter.

Four areas, in particular, will be of interest to child and youth care practitioners. One was noted in the introduction to this chapter, namely, providing services for immigrant and refugee youth in school systems and other organizations and agencies. The general designation for this area would be *settlement worker*, a job designation found in school boards, municipal departments such as parks and recreation, public libraries, and organizations such as the YMCA. A second area of interest would be children and youth in the child protection system who have unresolved immigration issues. These children and youth may have arrived in Canada as unaccompanied minors or may have been taken into care from families without Canadian status. A third area involves the expectations imposed on children and youth who become linguistic and cultural brokers for their families. The fourth area involves the challenges of transnational identity, in particular for youth who came to Canada through intercountry adoption when they were very young, and find themselves in their late teens or early twenties attempting to explore their birth identity and culture.

Each of these four areas clearly resonate with child and youth care principles and practices, although none of them has been prominent in CYC literature, course work, placement opportunities, or employment options to date. The hope is that this chapter will encourage students, educators, practitioners, and service providers to explore these four new areas, which will now be considered in turn.

Child and Youth Settlement Work

As noted above, settlement work with children and youth involves providing assistance and support, often leavened with a healthy dose of advocacy, for immigrant and refugee children and youth as they navigate the systems of their new home. For many, their first encounter with such systems will be as they enter school. An article in the *Globe and Mail* (Alphonso, 2016) describes how the Toronto Catholic District School Board, the Toronto District School Board, and a local resettlement agency were collaborating on a plan to introduce approximately 100 Syrian refugee children to the school system. These school-aged children were temporarily staying in a hotel and thus did not have a permanent address, which is generally required for admission to school. However, rather than further deferring the education and socialization of these children, educators and settlement workers helped them begin their adaptation to their new home.

The job description of a school settlement worker is, in many ways, quite similar to the description that would be given for a child and youth care practitioner. A brochure published by SWIS—Canada (n.d.) describes the Settlement Workers in Schools (SWIS) program, funded by CIC (Citizenship and Immigration Canada, now Immigration, Refugees and Citizenship Canada), as a "partnership between CIC, school boards and lead community agencies" that places "approximately 200 settlement workers . . . in over 20 school boards across [Ontario]." The mandate of the settlement workers includes supporting students and parents with settlement needs, offering information sessions on what is available and how to gain access to resources, and advocating on behalf of students with school staff and relevant agencies.

Job postings in the Peel school system (immediately to the west of Toronto), in the Hamilton school system, as well as in Toronto generally call for workers to have a post-secondary education at the diploma or degree level in a social services field, a familiarity with the *Child, Youth and Family Services Act*, and demonstrated problem-solving, counselling, and interpersonal skills. Applicants should also have familiarity with immigration and settlement issues and the ability to speak at least one language in addition to English.

In addition to school-based settlement worker positions, large agencies such as the YMCA also advertise for similar qualifications, expertise, and experience. One such posting describes the responsibilities of the position, including program delivery to provide social interaction, to assist immigrant and refugee youth to integrate into the community, to assist newcomer youth to develop leadership skills, and to foster relationships and connections. That particular agency is looking for applicants with post-secondary education in psychology or counselling or child and youth development, with at least one year of experience in social work, settlement services, or youth work. Many postings indicate that the ability to speak Arabic would be an asset, as would a demonstrated ability to be sensitive to various dimensions of diversity. Second- and third-language abilities are often specified, reflecting the needs of local communities. The clear norm in these job postings is that communication skills in more than one language are essential.

Not only have school boards and major agencies begun to incorporate settlement service functions into their mandate, but public libraries have also moved in this direction. Lisa Quirke (2006) explored the self-image of Toronto libraries as settlement services as an MA student at Ryerson University. The Government of Canada (2013) launched the Library Settlement Partnerships program in 2008, funded through CIC. A recent major research paper in the Ryerson University

Child and Youth Care master's program (Orbezo, 2018) explores the ways in which child and youth care practitioners could bring their skills to library settlement programs.

Even relatively small, neighbourhood-based service agencies are hiring settlement workers to meet the needs in their communities. Take the example of a long-established agency slightly to the west of downtown Toronto. A newcomer youth settlement worker with academic qualifications in social work, child and youth work, or youth counselling was recently sought to help newcomer youth gain skills to help them integrate into the community. This particular job involves recruiting newcomer youth and volunteer mentors, coordinating their activities, and providing support to youth and volunteers. Interestingly, the settlement worker is also charged with encouraging and promoting youth and mentors in program planning and evaluation activities, a fundamental skill being taught in many child and youth care academic programs.

A final example in this group involves a pilot project organized by the municipal government of the City of Toronto (2013). While this initiative was focused on all newcomers rather than being restricted to the needs of newcomer children and youth, there were several aspects of the project that were relevant to the needs of this population. These included settlement workers assigned to work in Children's Services, in housing shelters, in Parks, Forestry and Recreation sites, and in Public Health facilities. Project highlights cited in the report include youth participation in a youth leadership certification program, youth attendance at a summer drop-in program, newcomer children engaged in a cricket summer camp, children and youth undertaking neighbourhood beautification projects, and a March Break skating program where newcomer youth were provided with skates and helmets. Parents and children sometimes arrive in Canada at different times, perhaps with a parent coming to Canada to work before sending for their children, or perhaps with a child sent ahead to live with relatives and to be joined later by the parent. In recognition of this, there were also several programs designed to facilitate the reunion of children and their parent(s) after what may have been several years of separation.

Based on this small illustrative sample of settlement worker positions, it is apparent that there is a societal need for qualified individuals to serve immigrant and refugee children and youth as they make the adjustment to their new home. It is also apparent that child and youth care practitioners have the potential to significantly contribute to this area of social service and that the salary appears to be sufficient to attract qualified individuals. Having said that, the question becomes one of whether child and youth care post-secondary programs at the diploma, BA, or MA level are in a position to provide graduates with what they will need to enter this career stream.

Most posted positions require familiarity with issues of immigration and settlement. Students themselves increasingly come from a variety of cultural and linguistic backgrounds, although it is not clear to what extent this is recognized in the curriculum. An increased availability of second- and third-language offerings that carry course credit towards graduation would be a desirable enhancement to CYC education (Gharabaghi, 2017). Adding core or elective courses with a focus on immigration and settlement would enhance employment opportunities, as would the development of a minor in the area with course contributions from child and youth care. The inclusion of settlement service placement opportunities would complement and enhance the standard placement options, perhaps even showing how these areas overlap. If the curriculum includes an independent study or research project option, students could be encouraged to view settlement services through a child and youth care lens, perhaps even drawing on their own experience as immigrants or the children of immigrants. In short, the career opportunities exist, and the various post-secondary CYC programs, with some tweaking, have the potential to rise and meet the challenge.

Youth in Care with Immigration Issues

The terms *unaccompanied minors* and *separated children* tend to be used interchangeably to refer to children up to 18 years of age who arrive in Canada without a parent or responsible guardian, or a person who was thought to be responsible but who abandons the child shortly after entering the country. If that child arrives in Ontario, they would be taken into the care of the child protection system. Through the end of 2017, the Ontario child protection system only assumed the responsibility to take someone into care up to the age of 16. The recent passage of the new *Child, Youth and Family Services Act* (Ontario Ministry of Children, Community and Social Services, 2017) raised the age of protection from 16 to 18 as of January 1, 2018, which should provide added protection to unaccompanied minors who arrive before they turn 18.

Children taken into the child protection system enter without Canadian citizenship or permanent resident status. Other children enter the child protection system after being taken into care for the usual reasons from families without Canadian status. While these children, either unaccompanied minors or others without status, are in the care of one of the children's aid societies, they have certain protections and can receive education, health care, and other social benefits. When they leave the child protection system they lose these benefits and protections, and are extremely vulnerable to exploitation and even deportation because they lack the protections inherent in having permanent resident status or Canadian citizenship. A recent example is that of Abdul Abdi, who arrived in Canada as a child refugee and grew up in the child welfare system in Nova Scotia. Coverage of his case was widespread (e.g., Lau, 2018). Abdi's lack of Canadian status made him subject to deportation after completion of his sentence in the criminal justice system. If he had obtained Canadian status while in care, completion of his sentence would have been seen, in the usual way, as having paid his debt to society.

It is only very recently that the child protection system in Ontario has recognized the importance of ensuring that children and youth in care leave care with at least initial steps taken towards obtaining Canadian status. A report by the Ontario Association of Children's Aid Societies (2014) affirmed the importance of paying attention to immigration status issues while a child is in care, and taking steps to obtain status for the child prior to leaving care. Two considerations are important here. The first is that while the child is in care, they are protected, as noted above. However, the mandate of children's aid societies does not extend beyond the time the child is in care, so the vulnerability of that child beyond the point of leaving care is quite simply not a concern of the child protection system. The second consideration is that the situations that the child protection system is mandated to monitor while the child is in care do not consider immigration status.

What are the responsibilities and opportunities for child and youth care practitioners in these situations? CYC graduates are increasingly finding employment opportunities in the child protection system, not only in Ontario but also in other provinces with significant immigrant youth populations. A CYC practitioner employed in this sector who is familiar with immigration and citizenship issues can advocate for and assist youth to ensure that, when they leave the care system, their vulnerability to exploitation and deportation is minimized. Research on the extent to which youth in care are aware of or involved in efforts to obtain Canadian status (Hare, 2007) generally indicates that the youth assumed their worker was taking care of it. However, this is not something that has been required to be monitored, and since primary workers tend to change with some frequency, youth in care with citizenship issues need the support and advocacy of those who understand the implications of different categories of Canadian status, as well as the tools, resources, and encouragement to advocate on their own behalf.

As with the opportunities presented by the settlement worker option, the unaccompanied minor child protection option presents both opportunities and challenges for CYC/CYW (child and youth worker) post-secondary education. Course work on immigration categories such as unaccompanied minors, refugees, protections offered by the child welfare system, and permanent resident status and citizenship (and the implications of each) would sensitize practitioners to these issues. As noted above, practitioners without personal experience of immigration and settlement are often unaware of how crucial such considerations can be in shaping the life trajectory of children and youth. Similarly, placements and research opportunities would contribute to a student's competence in this area.

Linguistic and Cultural Brokering

Many years ago, I was living in a predominantly immigrant section of Toronto. As I approached my house, a boy from across the street called to me. "Sir," he asked, "what language do you speak when you go inside the house?"

The reality for many immigrant children and youth is that they come to serve as the point of contact between the society of their new homeland and the language and culture that exists within the home. Children and youth will tend to pick up the local language relatively quickly through school and interactions with peers. They then find themselves expected to accompany their parents to parent-teacher meetings at school, to visits at the doctor's office or the hospital, and to a variety of municipal and social services. In other words, these children and youth become engaged in cultural and linguistic brokering, a relatively recent area of research at the intersection of immigration and settlement studies and child and family studies.

Research in this area includes the work of Dorner, Orellana, and Jiménez (2008) and Morales and Hanson (2005), as well as three major research papers by students in the Immigration and Settlement Studies master's program at Ryerson University (DelCarpio, 2007; Sarway, 2011; Mohamud, 2017). Studies such as these suggest that taking on such tasks can have a variety of implications and consequences, including stress and embarrassment on the part of the youth, mastery of key developmental skills, and an alteration of the balance of power in the family and among siblings. The title of Dorner, Orellana, and Jiménez's (2008) work is especially interesting: "It's one of those things you do to help the family," which is echoed in the title of Sarway's (2011) research project: "If we don't do it for our parents, who will?" In each case, the title emphasizes the potential for adolescent development and responsibility for others. Nonetheless, the potential for the brokering role to be a disruptive influence in family dynamics is real, as noted by Cline, Crafter, de Abreu, and O'Dell (2017).

As with the previous two areas of interest, the question becomes one of how an increased awareness of linguistic and cultural brokering could contribute to child and youth care knowledge and practice. Incorporating the challenges, responsibilities, and potential stress of the brokering task into coursework on adolescent development and family dynamics could sensitize those unfamiliar with such activities and could serve to validate the experience of those students for whom brokering was and may still be a significant task. As well, developing an ability to empathize with those who feel isolated because they are different, in this case because they lack language skills to connect with the society around them and are dependent on others to function effectively, would in and of itself contribute to effective practice.

Transnational Identity of Intercountry Adoptees

The last of these four attempts to view CYC practice through the lens of immigration considers the experience of youth who were adopted from another country at a very young age by Canadian parents. These children may or may not be able to "pass" as the parents' biological offspring, and they may or may not be raised with an awareness of their birth culture. This section will not delve into the various debates and controversies surrounding intercountry adoption (see O'Halloran, 2009; Rios-Kohn, 1998; Rotabi, 2014), nor will it describe the legal structures and international agreements that guide and regulate the practice, such as the *Hague Conference on Private International Law* (1993) and the United Nations' *Convention on the Rights of the Child* (UN General Assembly, 1989). The focus here is instead on the genealogical quest for an understanding of transnational identity on the part of intercountry adoptee youth.

Adolescent development research suggests that late adolescence and early adulthood is a prime time for exploring and solidifying personal identity, with adopted youth facing a particular set of challenges (Grotevant, 1997). Youth who were adopted as young children are faced with a gap in their ancestral line that may or may not prompt questions. If the adoption was from a different country and culture, the youth may wish to incorporate that into their identity, in which case the youth will set out on an exploration of personal transnational identity.

Transnationalism in the immigration and settlement studies literature typically refers to families who move from one country to another while maintaining personal and familial ties to their previous home (e.g., Vertovec, 2001). There is often a sense of deliberate movement, in which the family makes a decision to leave one place and go to another. The situation with intercountry adoptees is quite different. They neither initiated the process nor chose the destination.

Adoptive parents often provide details as the child grows and develops, and may even incorporate aspects of the child's birth culture or language into daily life. However, some youth will want to further explore their roots. Notwithstanding the proliferation of family tree and genealogy computer programs and software, and the growing interest in DNA testing to discover one's ancestry, there do remain a substantial number of people who either are not interested in exploring their roots or who are interested but don't really pursue it (Kramer, 2011). Recent literature on intercountry adoptees (Tieman, van der Ende, & Verhulst, 2008; Wrobel, Grotevant, Samek, & Von Korff, 2013) suggests the same pattern. Some are curious and wish to explore their roots and identity, and some are not. In fact, there is even a difference among those who are curious, in that some will actively engage in search activities and some will not. As is the case with genealogical searches in general, the extent to which a searching intercountry adoptee decides to connect with relatives is highly variable. The advent of social media with an international reach does facilitate such connections (e.g., see Smith, 2012). A scan of Facebook groups devoted to issues related to intercountry adoption shows at least a dozen such groups, some open, some restricted, but all with the goal of facilitating information sharing and support.

To once more return to the question of how this phenomenon has implications for CYC principles and practices, a starting point would be a statement that one has a right to discover and explore one's roots in the process of formulating one's identity (see Besson, 2007). CYC practitioners have the ability to help youth who are dealing with issues of identity, whether that be issues of gender identity or sexual orientation, adoptive identity, or transnational identity. Familiarity with the issues faced by intercountry adoptees as they try to explore their roots, the social media resources available, and the relevant literature would all contribute to effective CYC practice.

CONNECTIONS ACROSS SECTORS

This chapter has looked at CYC practice through the lens of immigration and settlement issues, including the importance of understanding the implications of immigration status for youth in the child protection system. Children and youth can be in care without having permanent resident status or Canadian citizenship, a situation that could arise in different ways. Protected while in care, youth who leave care without status become highly vulnerable to exploitation and deportation. Having child and youth care courses or workshops on advocacy could prepare practitioners to advocate on behalf of youth with immigration issues and to train youth to advocate on their own behalf.

Settlement service worker opportunities for CYC practitioners are found in a variety of settings spanning several sectors. These would include school systems, small community-based services, larger multi-service organizations and agencies, and municipal services including public health and recreation programming. This particular career path is an excellent match for CYC practitioners who are well versed in immigration and settlement issues, with significant potential for employment.

The family services, schools, and health care sectors have demonstrated a growing research interest in linguistic brokering. Children and youth who serve as translators for their parents in a variety of settings may find that this contributes to their developmental maturity, but it can also become a source of stress or lead to a destabilizing of family authority systems.

Finally, while adolescent identity development and genealogical interests are not sectors themselves, supporting and assisting an intercountry adoptee who is engaged in an attempt to discover their transnational identity can serve as a model for how to conduct research.

CONCLUSIONS

As the founding director of the School of Child and Youth Care at Ryerson University, I have been able to observe CYC theory, practice, curriculum, and students since the first small group was admitted in 1989. Students, curriculum, theory, and practice all tended to be white, with relatively little extension beyond institutional settings and group homes. The notion that practitioners should reflect, at least in some ways, the population being served was at best a dream at that point.

Having the potential for enrichment is not the same as realizing that potential. One of the objectives of this chapter, with its focus on immigration issues, is to goad the field in this direction, situating child and youth care in an international, global context. The more familiar CYC students and practitioners are with immigration issues, such as settlement services, youth in care with immigration concerns, the roles of children and youth serving as language and cultural brokers, and the transnational identity challenges that some youth face, the more likely CYC students and practitioners will be able to effectively counter the anti-immigrant sentiment that permeates political discussion in several countries.

Finally, as I often told my research methods classes, no self-respecting discipline would rely on other disciplines to produce its research. I hope this chapter has suggested topics that CYC students and practitioners will take up as research projects, exploring immigration-related issues from a CYC perspective.

REFERENCES

Alphonso, C. (2016, February 8). Toronto school boards taking steps to welcome all refugee children. *Globe and Mail*. Retrieved from www.theglobeandmail.com/news/toronto/toronto-school-boards-taking-steps-to-welcome-all-refugee-children/article28661753/

Besson, S. (2007). Enforcing the child's right to know her origins: Contrasting approaches under the Convention on the Rights of the Child and the European Convention on Human Rights. *International Journal of Law, Policy and the Family, 21*(2), 137–159.

City of Toronto, Social Development, Finance & Administration. (2013). *Toronto newcomer initiative program report 2012*. Retrieved from www.toronto.ca/legdocs/mmis/2013/cd/bgrd/backgroundfile-55334.pdf

Cline, T., Crafter, S., de Abreu, G., & O'Dell, L. (2017). Child language brokers' representations of parent–child relationships. In R. Antonini, L. Cirillo, L. Rossato, & I. Torresi (Eds.), *Non-professional interpreting and translating: State of the art and future of an emerging field of research* (pp. 281–294). Amsterdam, Netherlands: John Benjamins Publishing Company.

DelCarpio, L. (2007). *Bridging the gap: Immigrant children as language and cultural brokers*. Unpublished master's thesis, Ryerson University, Toronto, Ontario.

Dorner, L. M., Orellana, M. F., & Jiménez, R. (2008) "It's one of those things that you do to help the family": Language brokering and the development of immigrant adolescents. *Journal of Adolescent Research, 23*(5), 515–543.

Gharabaghi, K. (2017, August). A second language for every CYC. *CYC-Online, 222*. Retrieved from http://www.cyc-net.org/cyc-online/aug2017.pdf

Government of Canada. (2013). *Library settlement partnerships*. Retrieved from www.canada.ca/en/immigration-refugees-citizenship/corporate/partners-service-providers/immigrant-serving-organizations/best-pratices/library-settlement-partnerships.html

Grotevant, H. D. (1997). Coming to terms with adoption: The construction of identity from adolescence into adulthood. *Adoption Quarterly, 1*(1), 3–27.

Hague Conference on Private International Law. (1993). *Convention on protection of children and co-operation in respect of intercountry adoption.* Retrieved from https://www.hcch.net/en/instruments/conventions/specialised-sections/intercountry-adoption

Hare, F. G. (2007). Transition without status: The experience of youth leaving care without citizenship. *New Directions for Youth Development, 113*, 77–88.

Kramer, A.-M. (2011). Kinship, affinity and connectedness: Exploring the role of genealogy in personal lives. *Sociology, 45*(3), 379–395.

Lau, R. (2018, July 16). "He's ready to live in peace": Federal Court overturns Abdul Abdi's deportation but future still uncertain. *Global News.* Retrieved from globalnews.ca/news/4333405/abdoul-abdi-federal-court-decision

Mohamud, A. F. (2017). *The Somali diaspora experience: A focus on Somali children as cultural brokers and as ambassadors of language and culture.* Unpublished master's thesis, Ryerson University, Toronto, Ontario.

Morales, A., & Hanson, W. E. (2005). Language brokering: An integrative review of the literature. *Hispanic Journal of Behavioral Sciences, 27*(4), 471–503.

O'Halloran, K. (2009). *The politics of adoption: International perspectives on law, policy and practice* (2nd Ed.). New York, NY: Springer.

Ontario Association of Children's Aid Societies. (2014). *Immigration status matters: A guide to addressing immigration status issues for children and youth in care.* Retrieved from http://www.oacas.org/wp-content/uploads/2015/08/Immigration-Status-Matters-Guide-to-Addressing-Immigration-Status-Issues-for-Children-and-Youth-in-Care-OACAS-December-2014.pdf

Ontario Ministry of Children, Community and Social Services. (2017). *Ontario strengthens legislation for child, youth and family services.* Retrieved from http://www.children.gov.on.ca/htdocs/English/professionals/childwelfare/modern-legislation.aspx

Ontario Ministry of Finance. (2017). *2016 census highlights: Fact sheet 8.* Retrieved from www.fin.gov.on.ca/en/economy/demographics/census/cenhi/16-8.html

Orbezo, G. (2018). *Child and youth care perspective: Public libraries—A setting of support for young immigrants.* Unpublished master's thesis, Ryerson University, Toronto, Ontario.

Quirke, L. C. (2006). *Public libraries serving newcomers to Canada: A comparison of the Toronto and Windsor public libraries.* Unpublished master's thesis, Ryerson University, Toronto, Ontario.

Rios-Kohn, R. (1998). Intercountry adoption: An international perspective on the practice and standards. *Adoption Quarterly, 1*(4), 3–32.

Rotabi, K. S. (2014). Child adoption and war: "Living disappeared" children and the social worker's post-conflict role in El Salvador and Argentina. *International Social Work, 57*(2), 169–180.

Sarway, S. (2011). *If we don't do it for our parents, who will? Afghan youth as cultural/language brokers*. Unpublished master's thesis, Ryerson University, Toronto, Ontario.

Smith, C. (2012). The role of Facebook in post-adoption search and support. *Australian Journal of Adoption, 6*(1), 1–6.

SWIS—Canada. (n.d.). *SWIS—Canada brochure*. Retrieved from http://wiki.settlementatwork.org/uploads/SWIS_-_Canada_Brochure.pdf

Tieman, W., van der Ende, J., & Verhulst, F. C. (2008). Young adult international adoptees' search for birth parents. *Journal of Family Psychology, 22*(5), 678–687.

UN General Assembly. (1989, November 20). *Convention on the rights of the child*. Retrieved from https://www.unicef-irc.org/portfolios/crc.html

Vertovec, S. (2001). Transnationalism and identity. *Journal of Ethnic and Migration Studies, 27*(4), 573–582.

Wrobel, G. M., Grotevant, H. D., Samek, D. R., & Von Korff, L. (2013). Adoptees, curiosity and information-seeking about birth parents in emerging adulthood: Context, motivation and behavior. *International Journal of Behavioral Development, 37*(5), 441–450.

CHAPTER 5

Youth Homelessness and Shelter Settings

Hans Skott-Myhre

INTRODUCTION

We have all seen the pictures: the child sleeping on the sidewalk or the young person sitting on the curb with a sign asking for money. Homeless youth have become iconic, starting with a relatively small number of runaway hippie youth in the late 1960s and exploding in the 80s and 90s into the burgeoning street populations of major cities and hidden populations of rural homeless youth in the 21st century (Gaetz, 2014).

These are the young people most of our programming either fails to touch or who don't fit within the rules and regulations that would allow us to provide them with ongoing shelter (Gaetz, 2014). They are a diverse population but include certain demographic groups in higher numbers than others. Indigenous, LGBTQ, and immigrant young people, and those who have been in foster care, make up the largest populations of long-term homeless youth, while those termed runaways, castaways, or pushouts more closely match the overall demographics for Canada as a whole (Love, 2008). Over half have been in jail, a youth detention centre, or prison (Gaetz, 2014).

Estimates of the numbers of young people on the street vary considerably. One estimate was over a million (Love, 2008) and another 35,000 (Gaetz, 2014). Part of the reason for the discrepancy is the fact that the 35,000 represents youth who have been in emergency shelter programs, while the larger figure is based on estimates that include young people who are statistically invisible because they are living outside institutions and programs. These young people live at the edges of the adult world by seeking accommodations in a range of different ways, such as transitioning between unstable housing situations (couch hopping), sleeping in parks or on the streets, or illegally riding in railroad boxcars. The most common precipitating incident for young people leaving home is some form of parental abandonment or abuse, either sexual or physical (Love, 2008). However, leaving home does not and should not necessarily lead to homelessness. Gaetz argues,

> In fact we know quite well that key shifts in government policy (including the cancellation of our national housing strategy in 1993, as well as cutbacks to welfare and benefits in many jurisdictions) combined with the restructuring of the Canadian economy contributed to a rise in homelessness including among youth populations. (2014, p. 1)

While young people may experience untenable situations in their families and corresponding living situations that cause them to leave or be forced from their family or foster home, Gaetz is arguing that this cannot be separated from social and economic policies that increase the chances this relational crisis will turn into a crisis of housing and basic sustenance. This points to an important analytic distinction. Given the statistics about failed familial relations, it would be tempting to lay the blame for youth homelessness on abusive, neglectful, or rejecting parents, or rebellious and unmanageable young people. But we could go a bit further down the causal chain and hold programmatic efforts to remediate family dysfunction, programs such as foster or residential care, accountable for the increasing numbers of young people on the street.

Certainly, both families and child and youth care programs for young people have their own contested relations and horrific histories with young people (Charles, 2015). Gaetz (2014) argues that structural inadequacies in mental health, child protection, health care, and juvenile justice also contribute. The legacy of trauma levied by child and youth care initiatives, such as residential schools, asylums, and "schools" for differently abled children, cannot be ignored as factors in the tenuous constructions of social networks for marginalized and disenfranchised populations in our contemporary period (Charles, 2015). In this regard, I argue that both the family and the institutions that are designed to serve young people cannot be understood in relation to youth homelessness without an analysis of the historical moment in which they occur.

Gaetz (2014) is clearly pointing towards broader historical, political, and economic factors as intrinsic to the crisis of youth homelessness, but I would argue that we have to look beyond the contemporary situation. Youth homelessness did not only arise in the 20th century in Canada and escalate into the 21st century. This is not the first time we have seen large numbers of homeless children and youth in Canada. Indeed, in 19th-century Toronto, "it wasn't uncommon to walk the streets having to step over the sleeping bodies of abandoned children, some as young as 3 and 4" (Bell, 2008). In fact, the then-mayor of Toronto, George Allan, donated land to build a Newsboys' Home to provide health care and housing for street children in 1870. This early child and youth care initiative was followed in 1891 by the founding of the Children's Aid Society (Ontario Association of Children's Aid Societies, n.d.). If youth homelessness is not only a contemporary phenomenon in Canada, then what is its history? And what implications does that history have for us in providing care across sectors in child and youth care?

MODES OF PRODUCTION AND HOMELESSNESS

One way to read the repetitive nature of youth homelessness is to explore the possibility that the history of homeless children and youth in Canada is inextricably linked to what Marx (1978) refers to as shifts in the mode of production. Shifts in the modes of production are large-scale changes in the ways in which society produces itself, such as the shift from feudal to industrial capitalism or industrial capitalism to global cyber-capitalism. Such shifts have an immense impact on civil society and the ability of society to care for its constituents. In the period of upheaval between different modes of economy, entire sectors of people who had previously had a role in an earlier form of production are displaced and relegated to the margins of the emerging system. Such groups become what Marx (1978) has called the lumpen proletariat; Luhmann (1995), the radically excluded; or Hardt and Negri (2005), The Poors.

These are groups of people with little or no access to the economic system of a given historical period. There are specific reasons for this exclusion, which can encompass such variables as an oversaturated labour market or a shift in types of production that eliminate certain categories of work and attendant skill sets. However, there are more complex factors that tend to correlate with the status of exclusion itself, its emotional and psychological influence on poverty and marginalization, and the direct and indirect interactions with social apparatuses of society designed to manage and control those no longer of useful to the emerging mode of production.

For our concerns here, the shifts in the mode of production in the middle of the 19th century and the 20th century hold both similarities and differences. Both periods produced large numbers of what were termed *abandoned children* in the 19th century and *homeless and runaway children* today. The two historical periods have one significant similarity in common and a number of echoes that resonate from the 19th century to the 20th. The fundamental similarity is that in both historical periods, capitalism as an economic system extended its range and influence as a global economic system. As it did so, it eliminated whole sectors of value, modes of labour, and ways of life.

In the 19th century, capitalism extended its reach through imperialism and colonialism. European capitalism colonized much of the globe, transforming the peoples it touched by appropriating their labour into either the production of raw materials to be sent from the colonies to factories and mills in Europe and North America or turning farmers and peasants into workers in those mills. Industrial capitalism severely disrupted the lives and cultures of peoples across the world, initiating immense flows of people in motion across the globe in service to its colonial desires (Hardt & Negri, 2009).

In Europe, emerging forms of industrialization disrupted feudal economies by forcing large numbers of people off of the land they had farmed for subsistence and on behalf of aristocratic landlords. These peasant farmers were forced into the cities as potential labour for the new factories and mills being built to process raw materials flowing from the colonies. By design, there were not enough jobs in these factories, leaving many of these immigrants from the countryside without a way to survive. Many were left to live in the streets, including large numbers of children. This excess labour force was then forced into prostitution and petty crime, or sent off to the colonies as labour for the appropriation of land as settlers, of resources as labour, or of Indigenous populations as soldiers (DuPlessis, 1997).

Children had an integral role in all of these activities, with poverty, social dissolution, and the mental or emotional collapse of adult family members resulting in high rates of child abandonment. Miller (2012) tells us that child abandonment "occurs in societies with inadequate social welfare arrangements or in which adoption procedures are difficult or orphanages are rare or overcrowded" (pp. 235–236). Miller also notes that child abandonment was very rare in the early 19th century, but escalated in the middle half of that century.[1] These abandoned children were sent into mines and factories, when work was available, as young as four or five years old. Immigrants to Canada from Europe during this period also included families who abandoned children because of abject poverty.

These abandoned children are the ones we find living on the streets of Toronto in the 1850s.

Early child and youth care efforts to be of assistance in England included the founding of the Children's Aid Society by minister Charles Loring Brace, who "was determined to do something about the problem of 'street arabs'" (Miller, 2012, p. 236). The solution was initially to apprentice such children to British farmers and manor houses. However, when the number of children exceeded the capacity of apprenticeship programs, numerous child saving organizations sent well over 100,000 children from the United Kingdom to Canada between the 1820s and 1939 (Charles, 2015). Although called orphans, many were not and had been taken away from their parents due to poverty. The boys were distributed to farms to serve as labourers while the girls were "employed" as domestic servants. All were held in indenture until coming to the age of majority.

The social and cultural brutality of capitalism as a system that would view children's bodies as labour to produce capital is echoed in an even more pronounced form in the related residential schools for Indigenous young people, as well as slavery for both Indigenous and African children and youth.

The enslavement of Africans in Canada began in 1628, with the introduction of a young slave boy into New France, and ended in 1834 when the British outlawed slavery (Winks, 1997). Although it never reached the scale of slavery as an institution as in the United States, there were still over 4,000 Africans enslaved in colonial Canada over nearly 200 years of legal slavery. Indeed, New France adopted as customary law the French legal code established to protect slave owners in the Caribbean and Louisiana, the Code Noir, to regulate and control the practice and management of slaves in 1685 (Winks, 1997). A significant number of these slaves (over 2,000) were brought into Canada as white Loyalists fled the US revolution in 1783 and brought their slaves with them (Winks, 1997). While there were no child and youth care initiatives for the children of slaves in Canada during the 19th century, the legacy of slavery has echoes in the 21st century, as we will see later.

Charles (2015) traces the legacy of child and youth care (CYC) complicity in what he calls "the establishment of 'serving' organizations that were rooted in the oppression of marginalized populations" (p. 52). Charles notes that the practices of 19th-century CYC were rooted in a belief that certain ways of living were morally superior to all others. Any child or family who represented an alternative set of values was considered morally inferior and in need of remediation. The critical distinguishing characteristic of a child or family who was morally unfit was an inability or unwillingness to become what Foucault (1977) terms a *docile body*, that is, a body shaped to the needs of the dominant mode of production. Docile bodies were *productive* in the sense that they were available as labour to be appropriated and exploited to the ends of the colonial project and emerging industrial capitalism. This was particularly true of colonized populations globally.

Foucault (1977) details the social mechanisms designed to produce docile bodies. The capacity to discipline and shape bodies to the ends of the dominant mode of production in the 19th century was through spaces of enclosure where dangerous bodies could be removed from general society, placed under observation, and subjected to social and moral re-education. Charles (2015) argues that the roots of many of current practices and programs in child and youth care are to be found in these residential and community-based moral movements (p. 53). Particularly egregious in Canada was the development of residential schools for Indigenous young people.

The residential school movement in North America was designed to "kill the Indian, save the man." This quote, by the American founder of the first off-reservation residential school, Richard Pratt, succinctly encompasses a movement that impacted Indigenous peoples across the United States and Canada.[2] As Ward Churchill (2004) points out in his book named for Pratt's edict, residential schools were designed to eradicate any trace of Indigenous language, culture, or spiritual practices and belief in the children subjected to its regimes of discipline and control. Churchill refers to this as cultural genocide through forced assimilation. These schools had very high rates physical and sexual abuse, poor nutrition, tuberculosis, and forced labour. The death rate for Indigenous children in these schools vastly exceeded that of other populations of youth in Canada. These schools are one of the few institutions that persist, largely intact, across the 19th and 20th centuries, with the last residential school closing in the 1990s (Truth and Reconciliation Commission of Canada, 2015). While the residential schools actually kept young people off the streets and provided shelter, their effects can be felt in the contemporary crisis of homeless Indigenous young people in Canada today. As Churchill puts it,

> Of all the malignancies embodied in twentieth-century U.S./Canadian Indian policy, the schools were arguably the worst. The profundity of their destructive effects upon native people, both individually and collectively, not only in the immediacy of their operational existence but in the aftermath as well, was and remains by any reasonable estimation incalculable. (2004, p. xlv)

The response to the crisis in social structure brought about by the shift in the mode of production in the 19th century was tied directly to producing labouring bodies in the factories and colonial projects of emerging capitalism. The release of flows of bodies, including those of children and youth, produced new apparatuses of capture and assimilation designed to assimilate young bodies into the machinery of production. Arguably, early child and youth care initiatives comprised important elements in this effort at social and cultural re-engineering of how bodies of all kinds were valued and how young people's bodies in particular were to be produced, shaped, and integrated in the broader social dynamic.

A NEW MODE OF PRODUCTION AND ITS IMPLICATIONS

As we enter the middle of 20th century, this begins to change. Some scholars (Negri, 1999) consider the year 1968 as the point at which there is a full turn to the new mode of production, which Hardt and Negri (2009) term Empire; Baudrillard (1981), "the advent of homo-cyberneticus"; and other scholars, "global" or "postmodern" capitalism (Jameson, 1991). It is also the moment that we begin to see a resurgence in homeless young people, as we have noted above. The fundamental structural crisis is not dissimilar, in its broad outlines, from what occurred in the 19th century. The crisis is one in which the skill sets of workers trained under industrial capitalism were no longer in demand in the new regime of production that Negri (1996) has termed "immaterial labour." This new form of labour is premised in the escalating and proliferating capacities of digital and virtual production. The rapid emergence of new technologies that allow for the virtual transfer and production of money on an unprecedented scale produced a new ruling elite with unimaginable monetary wealth. The wealth of this class is increasingly concentrated and insulated from the material world of commodities and (at least in the short term) the effects of rapacious production on the planet.

This shift in production has immense implications for those not in the ruling class. Some of the most notable developments effecting young people are:

1. the robotization of ever-increasing sectors of the economy, reducing the possibilities of previous sectors of gainful employment;
2. the emergence of outsourcing and contingent modes of production that allow large corporations to add or eliminate aspects of production, leading to increasingly precarious employment, where the job one has been trained for may simply disappear or be modified in ways that disqualify further employment;

3. the dismantling and/or radical restructuring of education so that schools no longer serve the community but the interests of corporations;
4. the elimination or modification of housing stock so that it becomes increasingly unaffordable to those being displaced by the new economy;
5. the efforts by neoliberal governments to eliminate social safety nets that have provided services to poor and marginalized populations;
6. shifts in the methods and modes of colonization, with the elimination of direct colonial rule in many parts of the world while sustaining colonial control in settler states like Canada;
7. the escalation of wars and conflicts globally;
8. the increasing privatization or elimination of those institutions founded in the 19th century designed to manage unmanageable bodies; and
9. the proliferation of corporate efforts to appropriate and exploit our emotions, social capacities, and unconscious desiring production.

These shifts in the organization of society and the field of labour have once again set millions of bodies into motion across the planet as refugees, asylum seekers, and economic migrants. These flows of living human force include those in motion on a more local scale, such as homeless and runaway children and youth in Canada.

MOVING FORWARD UNDER GLOBAL CAPITALISM

If the historical solution for abandoned young people in the 19th century was to create spaces of enclosure, observation, and moral/psychological training, then what are the contemporary solutions under global postmodern capitalism? I would argue that contemporary CYC, like the rest of global society, operates in a transitional space in which the spaces of enclosure—such as residential programs, foster care, juvenile justice facilities, mental hospitals, and treatment programs—still exist but are turned to a different purpose. Since there are a number of other chapters dealing with these practices and institutions in both volume 1 and volume 2 of this series (see Gharabaghi & Charles, volume 1; Modlin & Legett, volume 1; Charles & Quinn, volume 2), I won't belabour the details of this shift here, except to say that the project of reshaping young people continues to be a central feature, often to the detriment of the relational aspects of CYC praxis. Reshaping, however, has moved from creating docile bodies to practices of obfuscation and infinite deferral. There is a tendency to focus programming on the reshaping of internal attributes of young people, such as their neurology, attachment deficits, or trauma. In this there is often little attention to the material realities young people will face upon exiting the program, much less any mobilization to assist them in challenging or changing those realities.

For homeless young people in Canada, the future is now. They have already experienced the maximal effects of 21st century neoliberal capitalism. There are, of course, differences for youth compared to the situation in the 19th century. Put succinctly, unlike abandoned youth in the past, there are increasingly limited options to remediate the escalating crisis of homelessness for these young people. Although Canada has a network of shelter programs in major cities such as Montreal, Toronto, Calgary, and Vancouver, most of these are at capacity the majority of the time, and in my experience have been for decades. CYC programs also provide street outreach to those youth who are on the street. However, these programs struggle for resources on an ongoing basis and have to fight against political and social campaigns that demonize street-engaged youth and/or wish to eliminate or curtail harm reduction strategies (Gaetz, 2014).

In rural areas, programming is spotty at best, and young people are harder to locate because they are not as visible. There are generally no areas where homeless youth congregate in rural areas. They tend to move from couch to couch, live in cars parked out of sight of police, or camp in out-of-the-way places. This makes it quite hard to make a case for funding for programs if the population is not visible to policy-makers and citizens (Skott-Myhre, Raby, & Nikolaou, 2008).

The legacy of colonialism, slavery, and efforts at forced assimilation can be seen in the disproportionate numbers of immigrant, Indigenous, and African-Canadian young people who are street-engaged. The legacy of racism and colonial superiority remains active in the dominant discourses of "assimilate or leave," as well as anti-Indigenous sentiment that denies or obscures the legitimacy of claims to sovereignty and land. The colonial period, as Foucault (1979) points out, also included the production of sexual minorities as a marginalized group, and this legacy is also to be found in the disproportionate numbers of LGBTQ young people in runaway or homeless situations. The legacy of the importing of "orphans" and their subsequent development in the system of foster care can also be found in the high number of foster children who have fled care or who aged out of care with no follow-up support.

The direct services provided to these runaway and homeless youth were largely developed in the late 1960s in response to large numbers of young people leaving home to join hippie communities in large urban centres. The lack of housing, medical services, clothing, and food led to the creation of free medical clinics, stores, and food pantries, as well as to what were termed *crash pads* where young people could find shelter. Over the intervening 50 years, these grassroots initiatives have become funded programs, such as street outreach that includes medical triage, condom and needle distribution, harm reduction education, the distribution of clothing and sleeping bags, case management of street-based trauma, emotional and psychological crisis management, and efforts to work with young people engaged in sex work. In addition, crash pads, which were initially youth-driven free spaces where hippie youth could find freedom from the dictates of the dominant society, have become emergency shelters and transitional living programs with adult-driven agendas and corresponding sets of rules and program expectations.

BEST PRACTICE RECOMMENDATIONS

The best practice recommendations (Sloane, Radday, & Stanzler, 2012) for working with street-engaged young people fit well with my experience in the field, as well as with basic principles of good child and youth care practice. They include using an approach that is flexible and works with the individual circumstances of the young person. Generally, there are two routes for attempting to assist young people in exiting the street. In the instance of short-term street engagement or runaway, the recommendation is intensive efforts to achieve family reconciliation. In my work in emergency shelters, the deployment of brief family therapy approaches had considerable positive effects in remediating the family conflict causing the young person to flee the home. The other route for those young people unable to reintegrate into their family (either biological or foster) or who have been unable to fit into various forms of "therapeutic" care, such as residential treatment or group homes, is transitional housing.

Ideally, the structure of care would include a continuum of services, including emergency phone lines that would allow a young person or family to access assistance immediately 24 hours a day, 7 days a week. This phone service would then be able to provide an array of possible services, including in-home family counselling that would remediate crisis situations when they arise, street-based services that could meet young people on the street and triage the situation whatever time day or night, emergency shelters that young people and their families could access for short-term stays, intermediate-term transitional housing that would prepare young people who are unable to return home with transitional living skills, and, finally, an array of long-term housing options in apartments and group living situations. All of these options would be fully staffed with child and youth care workers to provide a full array of support services. Having worked in programs that provide this array of services, this approach is quite successful for the majority of young people able to access it. Regrettably, it is rare if not impossible to find such a program that has sufficient staff or beds to meet the numbers of young people who could benefit from such a service.

The recommended approach for the worker to engage young people in such programs is pretty consistent with CYC best practices. This should include positive youth development that focuses on young people's strengths and capacities, being tolerant of errors and flexible in the approach taken, using an unconditional care approach that resists expelling young people from care, working with young people long term, allowing for variability in behaviour over the duration of the relationship, making relationship-building a fundamental aspect of the approach, and taking into account culture and trauma.

FINAL THOUGHTS

In his call for an end to young people's homelessness in Canada, Gaetz (2014) recommends a very similar approach of integrated systems of care that result in permanent housing for young people. He remarks that we have a tendency to see youth homelessness as a crisis and respond with triage measures. He argues that we have not put sufficient resources or attention into a comprehensive approach. While I agree with Gaetz, I believe that he has not taken into account the shifts in the mode of production I have noted above. In his work, Gaetz points to the British system as being one of the most integrated and successful he has investigated. I would note that under the neoliberal regimes of governance in Britain the very system he describes is being taking apart piece by piece. In the US and Australia, which are two other examples he points to as possible models for a Canadian response, the systems of care for homeless young people are also being defunded. In this sense, it could be argued that street-engaged young people are the canaries in the coal mine. What is happening to them may indicate future trends in what is coming for the rest of us as wealth disparity grows, employment becomes increasingly precarious, and governments are less responsive to the bulk of the citizenry and more driven by the interests of the capitalist class.

What, then, is the future of CYC work with street-engaged youth under such circumstances? I would propose that there are two things that probably won't work, at least in the foreseeable future. It seems unlikely that we will see increases in governmental support for CYC-driven initiatives for the development of a comprehensive system of care. The likelihood of seeing significant increases in affordable housing for the homeless seems to be overshadowed by gentrification and our inner cities turning into urban theme parks for well-to-do tourists. Homeless young people don't fit well into this scenario.

I would suggest, then, that the remedy is to be found in relationship and care. Relationship in the sense of truly founding our work with homeless young people on an understanding that we share more in common than we may have previously thought. Care, I would propose, is founded in an acknowledgement that we must insist on reconfiguring society so that all of us can reasonably care for each other. This requires thinking outside the professional box and re-engaging our relations with young people as profoundly personal.

Some years back I gave a talk at a CYC conference in Scotland. This was at the very beginning of the dismantling of the youth care sector in Britain. There was some considerable anxiety among those gathered about job security and the continued ability to serve young people in effective ways. I asked them the following question, which I will close with here.

> When they close your group home, will you simply leave and seek other employment or will you squat the program with the young people and claim it as your own? Will you have enough relationship with the young people that they will join you in insisting that the home is yours together?

For me, this is the only real question left under the current regime of rule: Are our relationships powerful enough to join together to reclaim the world?

NOTES

1. Miller (2012) notes an earlier instance of child abandonment in 13th-century Europe due to social instability and poverty. This was also a period of a shift in production, in this case the move into a feudal economy through the appropriation of land farmed in common.
2. There were similar initiatives across the colonial project, with Australia initiating residential schools similar to North America's and India establishing a mix of residential and non-residential education systems with very similar goals (Seth, 2007; Corntassel & Holder 2008). The case of the development of kindergarten in Indonesia is also an egregious one (Stoler, 1995).

REFERENCES

Baudrillard, J. (1981). *A critique of the political economy of the sign*. New York, NY: Telos Press.

Bell, B. (2008, September 17). Old Town patriarch endured horrid misfortunes. *The Bulletin—Downtown Toronto, IX*(VIII).

Charles, G. (2015). Doomed to repeat it: The selective and collective ignorance of the shadowy historical foundations of child and youth care. *International Child and Youth Care, 200*, 52–58.

Churchill, W. (2004). *Kill the Indian, save the man: The genocidal impact of American Indian residential schools*. San Francisco, CA: City Lights Books.

Corntassel, J., & Holder, C. (2008). Who's sorry now? Government apologies, truth commissions, and Indigenous self-determination in Australia, Canada, Guatemala, and Peru. *Human Rights Review, 9*(4), 465–489.

DuPlessis, R. S. (1997). *Transitions to capitalism in early modern Europe* (Vol. 10). Cambridge, UK: Cambridge University Press.

Foucault, M. (1977). *Discipline and punish: The birth of the prison*. New York, NY: Vintage.

Foucault, M. (1979). *The history of sexuality*. New York, NY: Penguin.

Gaetz, S.A. (2014) *Coming of age: Reimagining the response to youth homelessness in Canada*. Toronto, ON: The Canadian Observatory on Homelessness Press. Retrieved from http://www.homelesshub.ca/sites/default/files/ComingOfAgeHH_0.pdf

Hardt, M., & Negri, A. (2005). *Multitude: War and democracy in the age of empire*. New York, NY: Penguin.

Hardt, M., & Negri, A. (2009). *Empire*. Cambridge, MA: Harvard University Press.

Jameson, F. (1991). *Postmodernism, or, the cultural logic of late capitalism*. Durham, NC: Duke University Press.

Love, J. R. (2008). Runaway and street kids: Risks and interventions for homeless youth. *Graduate Journal of Counselling Psychology, 1*(1), Article 7.

Luhmann, N. (1995). *Social systems*. Palo Alto, CA: Stanford University Press.

Marx, K. (1978). The German ideology. In R. C. Tucker (Ed.), *The Marx-Engels reader* (pp. 146–202). New York, NY: W. W. Norton & Company.

Miller, W. R. (2012). *The social history of crime and punishment in America: An encyclopedia*. New York, NY: Sage Press.

Negri, A. (1996). Twenty theses on Marx: Interpretation of the class situation today. In S. Makdisi, C. Casarino, & R. E. Karl (Eds.), *Marxism beyond Marxism* (pp. 149–180). New York, NY: Routledge.

Negri, A. (1999). *Insurgencies: Constituent power and the modern state*. Minneapolis, MN: University of Minnesota Press.

Ontario Association of Children's Aid Societies. (n.d.). *History of child welfare*. Retrieved from http://www.oacas.org/childwelfare/history.htm

Seth, S. (2007). *Subject lessons: The western education of colonial India*. Durham, NC: Duke University Press.

Skott-Myhre, H. A., Raby, R., & Nikolaou, J. (2008). Towards a delivery system of services for rural homeless youth: A literature review and case study. *Child & Youth Care Forum, 37*(2), 87–102.

Sloane, P., Radday, A., & Stanzler, C. (2012). *Improving outcomes for homeless youth*. Retrieved from https://rootcause.org/wp-content/uploads/2019/05/Improving-Outcomes-for-Homeless-Youth-Social-Issue-Report.pdf

Stoler, A. L. (1995). *Race and the education of desire: Foucault's history of sexuality and the colonial order of things*. Durham, NC: Duke University Press.

Truth and Reconciliation Commission of Canada. (2015). *Honouring the truth, reconciling for the future: Summary of the final report of the Truth and Reconciliation Commission of Canada*. Retrieved from http://www.trc.ca/websites/trcinstitution/File/2015/Honouring_the_Truth_Reconciling_for_the_Future_July_23_2015.pdf

Winks, R. W. (1997). *Blacks in Canada: A history*. Montreal, QC: McGill-Queen's University Press.

CHAPTER 6

Child and Youth Care in the North

Heather Modlin, Kelly Shaw, Sheldon Lane, and Jennifer Oliver

INTRODUCTION

The majority of Inuit in Canada (60 percent) reside in Inuit traditional territories, known as Inuit Nunangat, which consists of Nunatsiavut (in Labrador), Nunavut Territory, Nunavik (in Northern Quebec), and Inuvialuit (in the Northwest Territories) (Tungasuvvingat Inuit, 2018). As Qallunaaq or Kallunât, those of us who are non-Indigenous recognize our position working in Inuit Nunangat, an Inuktitut word that means *homeland*. We know that we are viewed as interlopers by some, and by others, as experts. We know that we have knowledge of child and youth care (CYC) practice, in the context that we know it—specifically in eastern Canada, both urban and rural, residential and community, family-based and substitute care.

We have spent the past several years developing relationships in community with Inuit who are natural carers. We are learning about Inuit culture and politics, and the regions and territories where we have been invited to work. We wear the skin of our ancestors and speak only the language of colonization, and we recognize there are significant complexities that our European heritage brings to our work in child welfare, and into our CYC practice in Nunangat. We acknowledge the role of our ancestors in the colonizing of this country and harms done to Indigenous people. We believe that we have a responsibility in truth and reconciliation. Together with our Inuit colleagues, we are committed to child and youth care practice that is decolonizing and grounded in Inuit values and culture.

BACKGROUND

To appreciate the complexity of child and youth care practice in the North, it is important to have some awareness of the history of Inuit communities in Canada. Colonization has been widely accepted as a determinant of the health and social problems currently experienced by Indigenous communities (Maxwell, 2014). Further, historical trauma has become a recognized framework for describing the impact of colonization, oppression, and cultural suppression of Indigenous peoples in Canada (Kirmayer, Gone, & Moses, 2014). "Colonization is clearly understood as both historical and *ongoing* incursions by Canadian institutions and professionals into Indigenous family life, and the imposition of dominant Euro-Canadian values via these and other systemic channels" (Maxwell, 2014, p. 423).

There has been a misperception, historically, that all Indigenous cultures and communities are the same. It has been presumed, therefore, that research findings, clinical assessment tools and instruments, and associated prevention strategies are applicable to all communities. There are considerable differences, however, within Inuit, First Nations, and Métis groups and communities (Zamparo & Spraggon, 2005).

Similar to that of numerous Indigenous communities across Canada, the history of the Northern Inuit includes the forced transition from being self-reliant, self-governing, and semi-nomadic to coerced settlement by government. The Inuit experience is unique compared to that of other Indigenous groups, however, in that the process of assimilation and relocation for the Northern Inuit is more recent, resulting in rapid, sweeping change to their culture and traditional way of life over the last 60–70 years. Essentially, "they transitioned from igloos to iPhones in one generation" (C. Lund, personal correspondence, October 25, 2018). Compounding this were the pressures on the Inuit to adapt to mainstream societal expectations, underpinned by policies and actions that have since been determined to be a violation of human rights, autonomy, and dignity (Crawford, 2014).

In one example, in the 1950s, the Government of Canada relocated Inuit families from Northern Quebec to the Arctic with the promise of abundant hunting opportunities. Once there, the Inuit encountered a harsh environment that was unlike the more temperate region with which they were familiar. They were not permitted to return to Quebec, as they had been promised, which resulted in family separation and associated losses of their traditional belief system, language, and relationship with the land (Crawford, 2014).

The Labrador Inuit are distinct among Canadian Inuit groups, who typically did not have regular contact with Europeans until the 20th century. Having settled further south than other Inuit communities, the Labrador Inuit had ongoing contact with Europeans, and specifically with Moravian missionaries, starting in the 1760s. The Moravians moved into the Inuit communities to promote Christianity. They also participated in trading furs. The Moravian influence is still evident in the Nunatsiavut communities of Nain, Hopedale, and Makkovik (Virtual Museum of Labrador, 2018).

When Newfoundland and Labrador joined Canada in 1949, there were approximately 700 Inuit in Labrador. In spite of the widespread conversion to Christianity, other aspects of Inuit culture, such as language, relationship to the land, and traditional hunting and fishing activities, remained intact. After confederation, much of this changed. The provincial and federal governments began delivering programs in health, education, and other areas without any consideration of preserving Inuit language or culture. This contributed to a decline in the use of Inuktitut and increased alienation from a school curriculum that was already irrelevant. As the Inuit became further marginalized by mainstream society, poverty, alcoholism, and other forms of substance abuse became pervasive issues in many communities (Heritage Newfoundland and Labrador, 2018).

Currently, the Labrador Inuit are self-governing under the Nunatsiavut Government, which represents approximately 5,000 people. Although there are still many struggles to overcome, they have made significant strides towards preserving the Inuit language and culture (Heritage Newfoundland and Labrador, 2018).

INTERGENERATIONAL TRAUMA

The concept of historical, or intergenerational, trauma has been widely accepted as a framework for understanding some of the current challenges experienced in Indigenous communities (Menzies, 2010; Truth and Reconciliation Commission of Canada, 2015). This framework extends beyond the individual and emphasizes the complex effects of pervasive traumatic events on the family and community, and cross-generational impacts (Crawford, 2014). The traumatic events that lead to historical trauma "are theorized to be collective, inflicted upon a group that has a shared identity or affiliation by outsiders with destructive intent; widespread, affecting many members of the group; result in contemporary collective distress or mourning; and this distress is both psychological and social, affecting multiple levels of the individual, family, and community" (Crawford, 2014, pp. 342–343).

The intergenerational impact of colonization has contributed to the violation and erosion of traditional livelihoods, forced relocation, systematic marginalization of Indigenous peoples, imposition of the welfare system, and residential schools (Maxwell, 2014). The manifestations of colonialism and the associated inequities continue to this day, with "profound implications for parenting and family relations: substandard and overcrowded reserve housing, huge inequalities in funding for reserve education, entire cohorts of young people forced to choose between living with their family or pursuing education and employment, everyday experiences of racist violence, a woeful shortage of affordable child care services, and the disproportionate removal of Indigenous children from their families and communities in the name of child 'protection'" (Maxwell, 2014, p. 426).

These systemic issues impact the overall well-being of individuals and communities and contribute to a disproportionate need for mental health services in Indigenous communities (Menzies, 2010). One of the challenges in providing mental health services in Indigenous communities is the need to blend the traditional with the modern. This is particularly salient for young people, who have been described as having "lost their identity" by living between two worlds (Inungni Sapujjijiit Task Force, 2003, p. 17). Youth must be provided with the opportunity to resolve the confusion of living very different lifestyles between these two cultural worlds (Inungni Sapujjijiit Task Force, 2003).

Young people who have left their community to receive child welfare care or mental health treatment are in a particularly vulnerable position upon their return. They have, quite literally, had to straddle two worlds without fully belonging to either. It is often difficult for them to reintegrate into the community and difficult for the community to accept them. This leads to many young people experiencing regression, losing all treatment gains, and/or leaving their community permanently. "Re-entry into the community after being away for a period of time always requires adjustment for everyone. Youth need to be carefully monitored as they learn to share their new knowledge and live their lives differently. Without the community's support and appreciation of the transition youth are going through, they are at risk" (Zamparo & Spraggon, 2005, p. 16).

Zamparo and Spraggon (2005) have identified that best practices in mental health promotion for Inuit youth include teaching youth their traditions; adding traditional food to their diet; facilitating youth involvement and leadership; and providing a community gathering place and activity centre. Other key themes include involving family and community members in programs and activities; offering classes that teach coping and problem-solving skills; engaging and training natural helpers and establishing mentoring programs; setting high standards for cultural awareness and usage; and providing school-based interventions promoting resilience (Zamparo and Spraggon, 2005).

COMMUNITY ISSUES

For child and youth care programs to be successful in the provision of out-of-home care in Northern communities, it is essential that they be fully integrated into the community. In her report on mental wellness and healing for Labrador Inuit, Mayo (2009) recommended a service delivery model that is holistic, strengths-based, grounded in traditional Inuit values and beliefs, and community-based. Mental health services must be integrated into each community in a way that supports rather than takes away from existing services and resources (Raphael, 2000) and should focus on the broader determinants of health that address the whole person.

Consistent with this, in a review of the treatment literature for First Nations, Métis and Inuit youth, the Newfoundland and Labrador Centre for Applied Health Research (2009, p. 37) identified the following common themes as being important for effective intervention:

1. culturally sensitive programming and service delivery;
2. service delivery that encompasses a holistic perspective of the person (individual, social, cultural, spiritual);
3. community involvement and control over programs; and
4. outreach as the preferred model of service delivery.

VALUES AND PRACTICES OF CHILD AND YOUTH CARE AND INUIT CULTURE

Child and youth care practice is experiential—focused on engaging young people and families in experiences that are different from their previous experiences—and occurs in the life-space, wherever that life-space may be (Garfat & Fulcher, 2011; Gharabaghi & Stuart, 2013). In our assessment, there is congruence between the values and practices of child and youth care and Inuit culture. This is illustrated in Table 6.1.

Table 6.1: Labrador Inuit and Child and Youth Care Values

Labrador Inuit	Child and Youth Care
Holistic approach to wellness	Holistic and ecological approach to practice
Focus on promoting strengths and resilience	Focus on promoting strengths and resilience
Emphasis on the importance of physical, mental, social, and spiritual well-being within the context of a strong Inuit cultural system	Emphasis on the importance of the physical, mental, social, and spiritual well-being within the context of culture and community
Practising and promoting Labrador Inuit culture and language	Focus on promoting culture, and maintaining cultural sensitivity and "rituals of encounter"
Promoting the balance between rights and responsibilities	Promoting the balance between rights and responsibilities
Client-centred approaches (where clients refer to the people served)	Child and family-centred approaches and needs-based intervention; meeting people "where they're at" and adapting a "non-expert" stance
Respecting yourself and others	Respect for self and other
Empowerment: fostering independence, self-reliance, and self-worth	Focus on empowerment: fostering safety, trust, attachment, self-reliance, self-worth, and independence
Collaboration: working together	Collaborative practice: working "with" not "to" or "for" and participating with people as they live their lives
Accountability: being answerable to clients and stakeholders in a clear manner	Responsibility and accountability
Consultation: sharing knowledge and exchanging information	Focus on connection and engagement and "being in relationship" with other
Leadership: demonstrating and fostering positive role modelling	Positive role modelling, "walking the talk"
Communication: open sharing of information	Open sharing of information "where they're at" and adapting a "non-expert" stance

Source: Table created with information from Nunatsiavut Government (2013) and Garfat & Fulcher (2011).

CHALLENGES

One of the biggest challenges associated with working in the North is that there are so many Inuit children not living with their families. It is difficult to cite an exact percentage, since statistics pertaining to Indigenous children in care tend to lump all "Aboriginal" children together rather than break them down into First Nations, Inuit, and Métis. It is also a challenge to find these numbers analyzed across provincial and territorial jurisdictions. Regardless of how the numbers are broken down, however, the percentage of Indigenous children in care is much higher than for non-Indigenous children. This is the result of many complex factors associated with the impact of colonization, one of the most prominent being the intergenerational trauma experienced in these communities. Due to the complexity of social issues in the communities within which we work, placement options for children in care are limited. Family members are sometimes able to assist with care through traditional adoption (custom adoption) or kinship care, and there are a number of foster homes; however, these options are not enough to meet the need identified by the community. A significant percentage of the children involved with the child welfare system have been impacted by complex developmental trauma, and their specific needs influenced by their histories of trauma include behavioural issues, diagnoses of fetal alcohol spectrum disorders (FASD), poor emotional regulation, and delays in meeting developmental milestones. Due to the lack of suitable placement options, many children in care have multiple placements, siblings are often separated, and too many children are placed outside of their communities, sometimes in other provinces, regions, or territories (Roberts, 2017).

There are also challenges associated with hiring child and youth care workers from Inuit communities. The communities in which we operate are small (as few as 190 people), and often isolated (only accessible by boat or plane). There is a limited pool of people to draw from; therefore, we simply cannot (and should not) have the same hiring criteria as for larger centres. Most child and youth care workers are hired for aptitude and in spite of a lack of prior education or experience. In such small communities, it is not difficult to run out of adults with the "aptitude" for the job. In such situations we have had to become creative to ensure the availability of sufficient staffing. Examples of creative hiring practices are provided in the case study.

An unanticipated challenge is that there are so many jobs available in some of the communities. It is not unusual to lose staff to other programs, such as the daycare. The hours associated with working in residential care are somewhat incongruent with the lifestyle preferred by some. Cultural differences can also impact the employee-employer relationship. For example, employees may unexpectedly take time off (in some cases up to a few months) to "go on the land." While this is of considerable importance to the individuals partaking in this experience, it can take some time, as an employer, to come to grips with employees going on unpaid leave for extended periods of time with no prior notice. Employers must straddle being culturally sensitive while also remaining focused on the needs of the children in the program and the impact on them of staff absenteeism and turnover. This is the type of situation in which there can be tension between cultural traditions and practices and professional child and youth care practice.

In some communities, the entire community shuts down for lunch. All children must leave school and go home for lunch, and all parents/guardians must be available to provide lunch to their children. This leads to an interesting dynamic for staff who are working during the day but who are also parents.

STRENGTHS

While acknowledging the impact of colonization on Indigenous peoples is important, it is equally important to recognize the individual and collective strengths and resilience that exist within Indigenous communities. Our experience in Northern and Labrador Inuit communities has been that community members are welcoming and appreciative. Child and youth care supervisors from outside of the community hold a role as one of the few "outsiders," but also often as someone trusted by the community.

Working in isolated communities provides opportunities to engage collaboratively with other service providers. There is generally more room for creativity and a willingness to "think outside the box" when there are limited resources available within a community.

A significant strength, in the context of out-of-home care, is that families are in close proximity. To the extent possible, family members need to be engaged and involved. Ideally, family involvement includes utilizing the strengths of the parents, or other family members, to support the program. For example, a mom who loves to cook could help prepare a meal once a week. A dad who carves can lead a carving session. A grandparent could spend time storytelling with all of the young people or passing along Inuit traditions or customs.

CHILD AND YOUTH CARE PRACTICE EXAMPLES

With such a high percentage of children from Inuit communities in care, it is critical that service provision is offered in the community and is specifically geared towards meeting the community's needs as well as the needs of each individual child or youth. While there are no quick fixes, some promising practices have emerged. One of these is the shift in focus from pathology to strengths-based practice. Specifically, the promotion of resilience in Indigenous youth in care has been demonstrated to be effective in achieving positive outcomes (Filbert & Flynn, 2010). This generally involves focusing on building developmental and cultural assets. Increased cultural resilience occurs through the promotion of Indigenous culture and has been found to contribute to positive outcomes at the individual and community levels (Lalonde, 2006).

Working with Inuit children in their home community, and using Inuit child and youth care workers from the community, provides a multitude of opportunities for meaningful, culturally based activity programming. Young people are engaged in traditional activities like hunting (for seal, partridge, geese, duck, porpoise, and black bear), trapping and snaring (for fur and meat such as fox, rabbits, arctic hare, and lynx), and fishing (for trout, char, salmon, cod, rock cod, and capelin). Young people are taught how to skin the animals they have caught and butcher the meat into chunks for proper storage and cooking. They are also taught to gut and fillet their fish to fry, dry, smoke, and freeze while also helping to cook the meals.

Young people are engaged in "wooding," which involves travelling by snowmobile to cut and gather wood for a source of heat. They are taught what to look for on the land such as animal tracks, landmarks, weather tendencies, and navigating to cabins or hunting and trapping grounds. Child and youth care workers introduce and teach arts and crafts in traditional ways, such as sewing and making seal skin mitts with the addition of furs around the cuffs. They also learn to make necklaces, bracelets, slippers, and earrings.

Young people are enlisted to help with repairing and maintaining snowmobiles, ATVs, and boat motors, and to assist in making flats or any other woodworking projects they can participate in, such as hunting tools and toys. Music is also used regularly as an intervention, with much success. Frequently, Elders can be seen singing to youth in Inuktitut—it is a way of soothing and can be helpful in de-escalation.

To assist young people to learn and/or maintain their traditional language, Inuktitut, child and youth care workers put Inuktitut words and numbers around the house. They also have Inuit colouring books, words, songs, and books to review and read, and they encourage the young people to read back what they understand.

When working with Inuit young people, it is important to be aware of the many different ways of communicating with the Inuit. With body language, for example, lifting your eyebrows means yes, and pointing with your head and squinting your cheeks and eyes means no, or it could also mean the person is upset. It takes time and effort to learn each other's ways of communicating, especially as some young people speak multiple languages. They may speak Innu, Inuktitut, and English. A lot of patience may be required.

Speaking in an Inuit language may help at times in de-escalation by distraction or re-direction. This may bring back good memories but also bad memories, so the staff need to be aware of how it is communicated and received.

Understanding Inuit culture ensures that our child and youth care workers are able to accurately interpret behaviour and respond accordingly. For example, non-Inuit practitioners might see children being "aggressive" and think they are fighting or being rough with one another. Most times, this is just the Inuit culture. They sometimes hit (softly), push, or nudge as a sign of affection. It is important to be aware of these things in order not to make a wrong decision and enforce a consequence when, in fact, they are just showing they care for each other.

One of the authors (Oliver), a graduate from the first CYC diploma program offered in Nunatsiavut, and an Inuk, shared the following:

> Through my experience growing up and moving back to Nain, Nunatsiavut, I can see the child welfare system is guided by objectivity; step-by-step rules for parents to abide by in order for their children to come back home. Inuit are subjective. We learn through storytelling from Elders and aunts and uncles and community members and "going off" on the land instead of more formally like with mental health counsellors and non-Indigenous treatment centres. Inuit heal through lived relational experiences with other Inuit.
>
> As a child and youth care diploma graduate, child and youth care practice relates to Inuit values, beliefs and engagement. If child welfare adopted a child and youth care approach in our communities, prevention work can happen to avoid "crisis driven apprehension." Helping, being with and supporting, growing and healing through engagement in our communities would allow an approach similar to Inuit pre-colonization.

> Traditional Inuit practice was informal and lead by Elders in our communities. Elders were the most knowledgeable people, the ones everyone turned to for support. We need to include our leaders and community members in circles of support to allow our people to heal and grow for our children in order for them to thrive.

What we may describe as child and youth care practice is often not recognized as such, or at least not named in this way throughout most of Nunangat. As in other parts of the country, in Northern Canada child and youth care jobs may be hidden in the roles of educational behavioural support, community youth engagement, community support, youth group facilitation, youth centre, and child and adolescent mental health. Individuals in these roles who are able to engage the edgy young people from the community typically have the attitudes and attributes that are commonly associated with an individual who is a child and youth care worker.

An understanding of what a CYC-educated person might be able to do, however, is still limited. In Nunavik, the hiring of CYC-educated individuals from southern Canada has introduced the language of child and youth care practice into the vernacular, yet it has been expressed that many still don't understand what the role is unless it is juxtaposed with the more common term in Quebec, psychoeducator.

CASE STUDY: NUNATSIAVUT

In this section we present an example of a child and youth care program established in a particular Inuit community.

One of the authors is involved with an organization that provides residential care to young people in a small, coastal community in Labrador. They were invited to establish services by the Nunatsiavut Government, responsible for the Labrador Inuit communities of Hopedale, Nain, Rigolet, Makkovik, and Postville. Prior to establishing programs in the Nunatsiavut region, it was necessary for the organization to become integrated into and accepted by the community. Since there were not yet any individuals living in the community qualified to manage residential care, one of the managers from St. John's agreed to move there for three to six months to develop relationships with community members, learn about Inuit culture and practices, and establish an organizational presence. Becoming integrated into the community required involvement in community activities (with bingo being the most popular) and working to navigate an understanding of respectful engagement with all community members.

It also required an examination of the pre-conceived notion of boundaries and professionalism. While still important, personal and professional boundaries are very different in a small, isolated Indigenous community. Everyone knows everyone else and most people are related. All community members know where the staff live. Separating personal life from work life can therefore be a struggle and it is difficult for staff to ever be fully "off." While this can be problematic, it can also be an asset. The staff are able to incorporate their whole selves directly into their work with the young people and engage the young people in a way that keeps them fully connected to their community. For example, in some cases the staff can go to work, go out in the boat all day, and take their own children along with the children with whom they are working (as long as there are no safety issues). Perhaps the biggest strength is the opportunity to have an impact on an entire community—which will happen whether intentional or not.

When the organization first set up in Nunatsiavut, community inclusion was part of the goal. It is typical on a cold winter's day that children from around the community come to our houses to warm up, get a glass of water, use the bathroom, and then head back out to play. At lunchtime, when our manager is in the community, all of the school children, upon spotting her, run up to her for a hug on their way home for lunch. Our organization sponsored the community volleyball team (volleyball is a popular sport in Labrador and the North).

When establishing our organization in Labrador, our initial goal was to hire all front-line staff from the community. Congruent with the recommendation by Zamparo and Spraggon (2005), child and youth care workers were hired for aptitude rather than educational qualifications. We started with nine employees and provided extensive training, over a five-month period, in crisis intervention, child development, attachment, trauma, activity programming, suicide intervention, FASD, the purposeful use of daily life events, and related areas. Much of the training was experiential and took place out on the land rather than in a classroom setting. The manager also had the staff practise implementing a daily routine in the home, from morning to night, prior to the arrival of the first children.

As presented in Table 6.1 and reinforced through the experience of the Inuk authors of this chapter, there is congruence between Inuit traditional values and child and youth care. It is perhaps because of this that the local staff were so accepting of the material covered in training. In some ways, becoming a child and youth care professional in this context means embracing traditional Inuit values and ways of being and doing.

Concurrent to the training, we worked in partnership with the Nunatsiavut Government to research child and youth care education programs available for Indigenous students in Canada and selected the Nova Scotia Community College to offer a two-year diploma in child and youth care for Labrador Inuit. The delivery of this program is unique in that it is delivered in Nunatsiavut face-to-face in community and via distance delivery (which is primarily telephone because of the challenges of Internet access in remote Canada). The assessment and delivery have been designed so that they meet the needs of the individuals in the program who are currently employed by or associated with the Nunatsiavut Government in some capacity, delivering services to children and youth.

Initially, we anticipated that all of our employees would participate in this program. Several registered upfront, but by the end of the program, we only had one employee enrolled, along with four other students from various Inuit communities. The reasons for this are varied and complex, not the least of which is the reality that all of the participants were employed full-time, balancing family, community, and work commitments. Add onto this the demands of a child and youth care education program. Some individuals changed jobs and decided it was no longer relevant for them to participate. Some individuals were not prepared for the intensity of the program, and others were simply unable to negotiate the demands to meet the structured deadlines required by the funder. It should be noted that the attrition for this program is similar to the attrition for the delivery of the same program in full-time classroom attendance, and the reasons for attrition may also be the same. Those five students who graduated with a child and youth care diploma were the first in Nunatsiavut. They are intent on using their new credentials to help improve services for children, youth, and families in their communities and to push for professional credentials for all those in helping roles. Many are exploring the next step in their post-secondary career.

Although the initial intent of our organization had been to utilize only community members in child and youth care worker roles, after three years of operating, we were running out of local people to hire. We initiated a fly in/fly out model in which child and youth care workers spend six weeks in the community and six weeks out. At first, we were hesitant to develop this type of staffing model, as we were committed to ensuring that all of our front-line staff were from the community. It was members of the community and Nunatsiavut Government who convinced us to try this approach. They were eager for us to expand our services so that we could keep more children in their home communities. During a conversation in which we were discussing our difficulty hiring staff from the community, we were asked, "Why aren't you using your staff from other regions?" The community and Nunatsiavut Government were more concerned about us expanding than they were about flying in staff—this was our own issue that we had projected onto them. Interestingly, when we advertised within our organization for the fly in/fly out positions, they were mostly filled by Inuit employees who had moved out of their communities and viewed these positions as a way to get home more often while not having to return full-time. The fly in/fly out model, while temporarily meeting a need, has some drawbacks. Most notable, it is not sustainable as a long-term employment option for most people. Many non-Indigenous practitioners struggle with the isolation, and none of them have remained in the role for longer than a few months.

After three years in community, our organization has provided care to several children and youth so that they could remain in their home community. Our founding manager is still connected to the service delivery, although no longer living in the community full-time. She is the only non-Indigenous team member, yet she has been fully adopted by the community as one of theirs. She has stood in weddings as a maid of honour and is godmother to more than one Inuit child. When she is in the community, the children (not just those in our care) and adults are drawn to her. She knows every community member by name. Because of the work she has done, and that by our local Inuit staff team, we have established trust as an organization. This is critical, in any setting, to providing quality care. After they had gained at least a year of experience and demonstrated their effectiveness as child and youth care workers, two of our Inuit child and youth care practitioners were promoted into program supervisor roles, and they continue to oversee operations in their community.

Child and youth care in Labrador includes Happy Valley-Goose Bay. Although this is not part of the Nunatsiavut territory, it does encompass the area where Southern Labrador Inuit live, known as NunatuKavut, and therefore we have many Inuit children in our care in this community. It is even more important, in this context, that we focus on keeping them connected to their culture. We utilize the Labrador Friendship Centre and engage in traditional activities, such as land-based programming. We also bring children to their home coastal communities for holidays and other special occasions. There have been circumstances where our Inuit employees have acknowledged that our programs have introduced traditional Inuit activities to them. They had not been exposed to such activities because they grew up out of region, outside of territory, or because the impact of colonization on their own family had resulted in loss of culture.

SUMMARY

The Ottawa Inuit Children's Centre (2015) conducted a literature review on promising practices in service provision to Inuit children and youth. They identified that services need to be Inuit driven and Inuit specific. They highlighted the importance of recognizing that the Inuit have a culture and history that is different from that of First Nations and Métis, and that Inuit community is distinct from the other Indigenous communities. Programs operating in Inuit communities must:

1. be based on Inuit culture and values—as illustrated in Table 6.1, these are congruent with child and youth care philosophy and practice;
2. involve Elders, who are recognized as having a key role as the carriers of Inuit culture and teachers of Inuit values;
3. integrate traditional knowledge, practices, land-based activities, and celebrations into the daily routines;
4. focus on family and community involvement;
5. ensure that child and youth care staff are trained to understand and deal with some of the complex challenges faced by Inuit children and families, including trauma, speech and language difficulties, FASD, autism, learning disabilities, and other special needs;
6. ensure that child and youth care workers have an understanding of the impact of cultural disruption and intergenerational trauma;
7. promote a holistic approach to care and intervention;
8. promote strength- and resilience-based approaches; and
9. have qualified Inuit staff, an important component of high-quality, effective services for children and youth.

As discussed by the Ottawa Inuit Children's Centre (2015), Inuit culture and practices are unique and distinct from those of other Indigenous peoples. "A pan-Aboriginal approach, in which First Nations, Métis and Inuit are dealt with through the same service, is really predominantly focused on First Nations. The experience of Inuit is that services are provided to them as if they were First Nations" (Patrick & Tomiak, as cited in Ottawa Inuit Children's Centre, 2015). It is important to ensure that any program offered to the Inuit is tailored to their specific needs.

As we continue our work in Inuit Nunangat, we continue learning. Even as the drafts of this chapter evolved, we made significant changes in order to most accurately reflect our current engagement and understanding. At some point, in order to meet publishing deadlines, we have to identify a place to stop. To stop writing, however—definitely not to stop learning. As previously mentioned, two of the authors descend from settler colonizers, and we both recognize our responsibility in truth and reconciliation, yet we continue to learn about that too.

Working in Indigenous regions and territories in the colonial systems of education and child welfare pose ethical dilemmas at every turn, and these dilemmas are not easily resolved. We are confident that this submission will be criticized, and we welcome that because we believe it is only through honest, respectful, and open dialogue that we can ensure we are doing our best work, ensure we are not repeating mistakes of the past, and ensure we are able to continue to support the growth and change in our profession. It is our hope that through the decolonization of child and youth care education, and child welfare in general, there will be increased opportunities for engagement in pre-service CYC education and subsequently for the child and youth care profession to continue to contribute, perhaps even more meaningfully, towards community capacity building and the healing that is occurring across Nunangat.

REFERENCES

Crawford, A. (2014). "The trauma experienced by generations past having an effect in their descendants": Narrative and historical trauma among Inuit in Nunavut, Canada. *Transcultural Psychiatry, 51*(3), 339–369.

Filbert, K., & Flynn, R. (2010). Developmental and cultural assets and resilient outcomes in First Nations young people in care: An initial test of an explanatory model. *Children and Youth Services Review, 32*, 560–564.

Garfat, T., & Fulcher, L. (2011). Characteristics of a child and youth care approach. *Relational Child and Youth Care Practice, 24*(1/2), 7–19.

Gharabaghi, K., & Stuart, C. (2013). *Right here, right now: Exploring life space interventions for children and youth.* Toronto, ON: Pearson Education Canada.

Heritage Newfoundland and Labrador. (2018). *Impact of non-Aboriginal activities on the Inuit.* Retrieved from https://www.heritage.nf.ca/articles/aboriginal/inuit-impacts.php

Inungni Sapujjijiit Task Force. (2003). *Our words must come back to us.* Iqaluit, NU: Government of Nunavut. Retrieved from http://www.gov.nu.ca/hsssite/sreport.html

Kirmayer, L. J., Gone, J. P., & Moses, J. (2014). Rethinking historical trauma. *Transcultural Psychiatry, 51*(3), 299–319.

Lalonde, C. (2006). Identity formation and cultural resilience in Aboriginal communities. In R. J. Flynn, P. M. Dudding, & J. G. Barber (Eds.), *Promoting resilience in child welfare* (pp. 52–71). Ottawa, ON: University of Ottawa Press.

Maxwell, K. (2014). Historicizing historical trauma theory: Troubling the transgenerational transmission paradigm. *Transcultural Psychiatry, 51*(3), 407–435.

Mayo, M. (2009). *Service delivery model for mental wellness & healing, program area, Nunatsiavut Government: The strength of our Inuit.* Report prepared for the Department of Health and Social Development, Nunatsiavut Government, Happy Valley-Goose Bay.

Menzies, P. (2010). Intergenerational trauma from a mental health perspective. *Native Social Work Journal, 7,* 63–85.

Newfoundland and Labrador Centre for Applied Health Research. (2009). *Youth residential treatment: Contextualized research synthesis program.* Draft report prepared for the Government of Newfoundland and Labrador.

Nunatsiavut Government. (2013). *Department of Health and Social Development: Regional health plan 2013–2018.* Retrieved from http://www.nunatsiavut.com/wp-content/uploads/2014/03/2013-2018.pdf

Ottawa Inuit Children's Centre. (2015). *Research report: Background for an Inuit children and youth strategy for Ontario.* Retrieved from http://www.ottawainuitchildrens.com/wp-content/uploads/2015/01/OICC_Final-Report_WEB.pdf

Raphael, B. (2000). *Promoting the mental health and wellbeing of children and young people. Discussion paper: Key principles and directions.* National Mental Health Strategy, Commonwealth of Australia. Retrieved from http://www.health.gov.au

Roberts, T. (2017). *Uprooted: Why so many of Labrador's children are in foster care so far away from home.* Retrieved from https://www.cbc.ca/news2/interactives/uprooted

Truth and Reconciliation Commission of Canada. (2015). The survivors speak: A report of the Truth and Reconciliation Commission of Canada. Retrieved from http://www.trc.ca/assets/pdf/Survivors_Speak_English_Web.pdf

Tungasuvvingat Inuit. (2018). Making space for Inuit specific approaches beyond the North: A pathway to inclusion, non-Nunangat policy framework. Presentation at National Child Welfare Conference, Calgary, Alberta, October 25, 2018.

Virtual Museum of Labrador. (2018). *History of the Labrador Inuit.* Retrieved at http://www.labradorvirtualmuseum.ca/home/inuit_history.htm

Zamparo, J., & Spraggon, D. (2005). *Echoes and Reflections: A discussion of best practices in Inuit mental health: A comparative cross-jurisdictional analysis of the literature on services, program models, and best practices in mental health, with a focus on interdisciplinary, intersectoral approaches emphasizing Inuit youth.* Iqaluit, NU: Centre of Excellence for Children and Adolescents with Special Needs.

CHAPTER 7

Child and Youth Care Practice in Hospital Settings

Agnes Quittard and Grant Charles

INTRODUCTION

Child and youth care (CYC) practice within the health care system, and particularly within hospital settings, has been rapidly growing in recent years. The health care sector has increasingly acknowledged the need to address the psychosocial aspects of health even within acute care settings. While other professions also provide services in this area, the focus of child and youth care on relational practice has provided a unique opportunity for the profession to create innovative ways of providing support and care to children and youth struggling with health and mental health challenges. Child and youth care practitioners (CYCPs) provide interventions through mental health and child life services. This chapter will discuss these two broad service roles and specific functions crossing the roles, and explore the challenges of working with a hierarchical, multi-disciplinary system. It should be noted that while child and youth care practitioners work in these roles, they are performed by members of other professions as well. They are not exclusive to child and youth care.

MENTAL HEALTH

Originally employed in psychiatric hospitals, child and youth care practitioners are now employed in a wide range of health care settings. One of the core contributions of CYCPs in hospital settings is the focus on relational practices that build capacity for young people to become meaningfully engaged in their treatment plans. This is an important contribution given that treatment outcomes are often far more achievable and sustainable when young people feel engaged during treatment and have a sense of ownership and agency within the context of their discharge plans and follow-up care (Dobbs, 2010; Hilton & Jepson, 2012; Hilton, Watson, Walmsley, & Jepson, 2004; Watson, 2004; Yates, Payne, & Dyson, 2009). A CYCP's ability connect through relationship so as to hone in on young peoples' anxieties, fears, and struggles provides an opening to rebuild an ability to find more healthy ways of coping with stressful life events.

Within the hospital milieu, CYCPs have a variety of roles and responsibilities related to the day-to-day workings of the unit. Appreciating CYC's foundation is in relational practice, CYCPs have an opportunity to interact with the young person in a manner that permits "a stream of immediacies" (Garfat, 2008, as cited in Swanzen, 2011, p. 73). Our ability to be in the moment and use life-space interactions provides the ideal backdrop where "hospital youth work can be effective in creating bridges between institutions and young people's perspectives, enabling . . . their role in consenting to and owning their own treatment and . . . in relation to medical decisions and wider life choices" (Yates, Payne, & Dyson, 2009, p. 83).

The foundation of CYC practice is relational work with young people. Swanzen (2011) suggests that "relational practice is a dynamic, rich, flexible, and continually evolving process of co-constructed inquiry" (p. 73). Adolescents in hospital tend to face many challenges and have very different needs than adults. There can be related issues of stigmatization, anxiety, and low self-esteem (Hilton & Jepson, 2012; Yates, Payne, & Dyson, 2009). Furthermore, young people in hospitals, depending on their circumstances, can also experience social isolation and disconnection from their sources of support (Hilton & Jepson, 2012; Watson 2004; Yates, Payne, & Dyson, 2009). As CYCPs, we work in "the natural place, not a neutral space" (Phelan, 2005; as cited in Phelan, 2008, p. 3). Using "life space interactions to create connections and change, CYCPs are experiential and physically present in a way that most other professionals avoid" (Phelan, 2008, p. 3).

Further, Coyne (2006) suggests that young people "want to be involved in their care and decisions so that they can exercise some control over what is happening to them in hospital" (pp. 62–63). The goal of CYCPs is to engage young people to be active and involved in their care as a way of raising their awareness and understanding of what is taking place (Yates, Payne, & Dyson, 2009).

Attempting to promote strength and facilitate self-agency is an active component of CYC practice. Through building relationships and being in relation with the young people we work with, CYCPs help others "achieve order within themselves and in their daily lives" (Phelan, 2008, p. 2).

PRACTICE CHALLENGES

Role Ambiguity

Notwithstanding the roles of CYCPs articulated above, there is often some confusion amongst members of the hospital clinical team, as both CYCPs and their colleagues from other disciplines can find it challenging to understand their respective roles. Sometimes the roles and responsibilities of CYCPs appear as very similar to those of their colleagues. This can cause territorial conflict that can be quite destructive to the well-functioning of a team (Charles, Alexander, & Oliver, 2015; Charles, Bainbridge, & Gilbert, 2010).

Child and youth care practice is "characterized by its flexibility of approach with young people" (Yates, Payne, & Dyson, 2009, p. 85), and as a result it tends to be difficult to access a standard description of what CYCPs do within any sector—not just hospitals. Generally, child and youth care practice can entail one-to-one work, group work, advocacy, crisis intervention, working within a multi-disciplinary team, and mediation on various levels (Yates, Payne, & Dyson, 2009). It could also include various other roles and responsibilities depending on the organization one works for and where in the organization one works. Ultimately, the role of the CYCP tends to be ambiguous, regardless of the job description, contingent on where one works, who one works for, what team one works with, who that team is composed of, and what types of individuals one works with.

One of the professional issues for CYCPs is the notion of role ambiguity. Literature suggests that the role of the CYCP is reliant on the bureaucratic system (Rose, 2001). Given that the hospital-based CYCP typically falls into the legislative and regulatory context of a provincial or territorial ministry of health (as opposed to a ministry of social services, such as in child welfare or other sectors), they are required to function within health care systems while figuring out how to maintain their own scope of practice. While Hilton and Jepson (2012) argue that the introduction of child and youth care practice into multi-disciplinary teams has been beneficial, others find CYCPs at times continue to get lost within their multi-disciplinary team. Many CYCPs, regardless of the sector they work in, at some point struggle with recognition from professional colleagues.

Interprofessional Issues

Interprofessional work has evolved over time within health care setting as the number of health professions have grown. Child and youth care has been well placed to prosper in this context, as team-based approaches to working with young people have long been at the forefront in the delivery of care and treatment by CYCPs beyond the health care sector (Buljac-Samardzic, van Wijngaarden, van Wijk, & van Excel, 2001; Gharabaghi, 2010; Krueger, 1986). For CYCPs, being a member of a team is both important and professionally satisfying as it cultivates the capacity to work together to augment the type of care that can be provided (Krueger, 1986). Given that one of the main challenges is the inability to define exactly who we are and what we do, other professionals can sometimes have a hard time seeing our interventions as relevant and important (Salhani & Charles, 2007), resulting in challenges with collaboration.

One of the more significant challenges in working within a hospital setting is the constant tension of having to function within a medical model while maintaining the core fundamental values of our profession. As CYCPs move into this sector, adjustments to practice are required. No longer is there the opportunity to primarily function as a CYCP, focusing on activities of daily living, milieu, recreation, and relationships. Instead, a new challenge has emerged with respect to learning about the health care system (Solinski, 2010).

As our practice has expanded within a setting that incorporates and supports medication as the primary choice of treatment, CYCPs have had to adjust our scope of practice to incorporate an alternative way of thinking. This shift requires that we understand that relationships are often not considered to be at the forefront of treatment methods, but rather medications manage behaviours and diagnoses guide care plans and interventions. This may hinder and impede on young people's capacity to connect with practitioners and develop a therapeutic relationship. For example, a young person with a severe mental health concern who is heavily medicated, and cannot engage in activities due to psychotropic sedation, cannot be present for in-the-moment experiences and will not likely be concerned with engaging and connecting with others (Solinski, 2010). As a result, CYCPs must find alternative ways of connecting and being in the life-space of young people.

Contrary to the medical model of care, CYCPs have traditionally focused on growth and development and not on labels or pathology (Durrant, 1993; Ferguson, Pence & Denholm, 1993; Maier, 1991), but in doing so we place ourselves in a complex dance as CYCPs work as part of a multi-disciplinary team within the hospital sector. This team approach often promotes a deficit-focused model of care, which, in conjunction with the medical model hierarchy, places the CYCP at a disadvantage when providing treatment and care to young people.

When evaluating deficit-focused discourses, we must understand that these have a long history within our culture, and have guided much of the work that has taken place within the health care system. We are constantly challenged to straddle two ways of thinking and being as the young people we work alongside often continue to be classified by this deficit-focused model, reinforcing the oppressive discourses that can take place with clinical settings.

Hospital-based child and youth care practice calls for a modification in our philosophical framework. CYCPs are encouraged to direct their attention to more clinically driven therapeutic interventions that then shape the type of care one provides to individuals in treatment. In this context, CYCPs are confronted with the dilemma of finding their place within this sector while also demonstrating the capacity to maintain a balance between the assortment of principles embedded in medical models and ecological approaches, problem-focused and strength-based interventions, relational work and boundaries. This needs to occur while at the same time communicating to our colleagues our uniqueness and the expertise and understanding we bring to the clinical table.

Our work in health care settings has brought CYC in contact with a wide range of professions. Within this system are numerous professions, including physicians, nurses, social workers, teachers, physiotherapists, occupational therapists, pharmacists, dieticians, and many others. This has created new opportunities for collaboration but also comes with challenges. Working in interprofessional teams requires a great deal of ongoing negotiation, education, flexibility, and patience. There can be a great deal of misunderstanding when multiple professionals work together. Many stories emerge from CYCPs about challenging and sometimes negative experiences with nurses and social workers, who may feel threatened by the appearance of CYCPs in their traditional domains, and are uncertain of what this could mean for their own positions within the milieu (Salhani & Charles, 2007). Issues of mistrust and lack of understanding arise given the absence of literature or professional culture associated with hospital-based child and youth care practice, resulting in CYCPs having to advocate for the creation of roles and criteria for practice.

In spite of these negative experiences in the context of employment-related matters and negotiating roles across disciplines, there is enormous support for the value of child and youth care practice in hospital settings. Relational approaches that engage young people and are meaningful with respect to their healing journeys are highly relevant to the goals of hospital-based psychiatric units.

It is also important to highlight that, currently, working within a hospital setting is a highly sought-after position within our field. The employment context of hospitals often offers some of the highest compensation packages for direct care work in child and youth care, and the social status associated with working in clinical settings such as hospitals provides for constant reinforcement of professional satisfaction. Competition for hospital-based jobs in child and youth care is often fierce. The high demand for such clinical positions has challenged post-secondary education institutions to respond through increasingly sophisticated curriculum that accounts for current discussions of evidence-based clinical intervention strategies.

Child and youth care is a profession that finds itself continuously adapting to any role that is required in a wide range of settings and contexts. It is possible that the capacity to demonstrate such flexibility and adaptability contributes to the themes of lack of respect and understanding of the work CYCPs do with children and youth. Although some earlier literature reviews the notion of defining standards of practice for CYCPs (Beker, 2001a, 2001b, 2001c; Lochead, 2001; Phelan, 2005), the articulation of such standards is clearly underdeveloped in the context of hospital-based settings.

No Regulatory Body

CYCPs working within the hospital milieu constantly face the challenge of proving their value within the clinical team. On the political stage this has been a continuing debate, as matters of vagueness regarding roles remain at the forefront of many discussions within the CYC field. Concerns with clinical multi-disciplinary teams not recognizing the role or understanding the skill sets of CYCPs puts the field at a disadvantage. CYC does not have a professionally regulated body, whereas most of the other disciplines at the clinical table do. The absence of this regulatory body can be seen as a factor in the debates that occur, as some may associate professional competency with such a body. It has been recognized by others that a professional association with a regulatory body has the ability to contribute to the status of that particular discipline within the health care sector (Lingard, Reznick, Debita, & Epsin, 2002). Additionally, it affects how the profession is positioned within this system and how others view the discipline in question.

Hierarchies

CYCPs within the hospital sector have a tendency to feel undervalued and not respected within the clinical team in terms of institutional hierarchy, even though it can be argued that CYCPs often tend to know the young person best, given the amount of time they engage with them and the relationship typically established with the individual (Gharabaghi, 2010; Salhani & Charles, 2007; Demers & Gudgeon, 2004). Despite this, CYCPs within clinical settings tend to rank lowest amongst other disciplines in a multi-disciplinary capacity (Salhani & Charles, 2007). Our position could be improved if we conducted more research on our place within the team (Yates, Payne, & Dyson, 2009).

RECOMMENDATIONS FOR MOVING FORWARD

Literature on hospital-based child and youth care practice is limited. Yates, Payne, and Dyson (2009) explain that while "very short discussions of youth work in hospitals have been produced, there remains the need for more detailed analysis on the ways youth work can operate in hospitals and its potential benefits" (p. 78). The various roles and different perceptions about what it is CYCPs do or should be doing in various settings need further research. "Much work needs to be done to further develop and consolidate child and youth work as a profession" (Hoffman, 2002, p. 3).

Research Opportunities

Providing more opportunities for research to examine current trends and practices within this sector could substantiate and bring credibility to the work we do within the hospital sector. Using the momentum currently taking place within the field to further advance standardization and professionalization will additionally solidify our acceptance at the table with other professions.

A core challenge to child and youth care practice in the hospital sector is that there is little literature to support current practices within this field. Although some literature has been produced (Dobbs, 2010; Hilton & Jepson, 2012; Hilton, Watson, Walmsley, & Jepson, 2004; Watson, 2004), we need to develop a better understanding of our roles and responsibilities and our ways of practice in order to fully understand how CYCPs function within this sector. Questions about why roles and responsibilities in this sector vary so significantly would be a critical theme for future research to explore, as it directly impacts scope of practice within the hospital sector. This would be an invaluable aspect of future studies, as the role of the CYCPs within hospitals is like that of no other profession, given that its unique relational approach is all-encompassing and imperative to the treatment and care of the young people they work alongside.

Opportunities for Education within the Organization

As CYCPs, we must continue to create opportunities for education about who we are and what we do within health care organizations. Promoting who we are while articulating what we do in a manner that transcends various systems will be essential to the advancement of CYC. Many CYCPs acknowledge the importance of the organization they work for gaining a stronger understanding of the field of child and youth care, and of CYCPs knowing how to navigate the various systems within the hospital sector. In order to be viewed by others as a distinct entity within a clinical team, we must be able to defend why and how this is so (Davie, 2011). Understanding the system one works in and appreciating the culture and language of the organization is vital to the education of others with respect to our scope of practice. Developing a stronger capacity to articulate precisely how CYCPs impact the treatment process in hospital settings would go a long way to mitigating some of the professional issues practitioners encounter in this setting (Gharabaghi, 2010).

CONCLUSION

CYCPs within the hospital sector are an invaluable part of the clinical team. Our capacity to engage young people at various levels has the ability to impact the young person's experience, recovery, and healing while in hospital. CYCP's relational work provides opportunities for in-the-moment work to take place and demonstrates the ability to connect with a young person during a critical time in their lives. The unique ability to work with young people in this manner should be seen as an asset on any clinical team and embraced to ensure the most holistic and collaborative type of care is provided to young people and their families. Young people in hospital with chronic conditions experience a variety of psychosocial challenges, such as stigmatization, family discord, stress, and anxiety (Hilton & Jepson, 2012; Hilton, Watson, Walmsley, & Jepson, 2004; Watson, 2004; Yates, Payne, & Dyson, 2009). The skill CYCPs have to relate to young people and "meet them where they are at" (Garfat, Freeman, Gharabaghi, & Fulcher, 2018) can have a positive impact on how the young person understands their current situation, and can help facilitate the rapport and relationship the young person has with medical staff. Far too often the language that is used by other professions is focused on diagnosis and geared to a specific understanding of the medical model. This can, at times, result in young people feeling pathologized and have a ripple effect on the young person's attitude towards staff, which could be misunderstood as "problem behaviour" instead of frustration and lack of understanding (Yates, Paine, & Dyson, 2009).

As CYCPs, we must not be frightened by change. We must be open to evolving and growing independently and professionally. CYCPs tend to be flexible in nature and have the ability to adapt to various working conditions within various teams. Although this can be seen as a strength within our field, it can be a challenge as well. As the systems around us change, we must be willing to step up and advocate for ourselves, our profession, and, most importantly, for the young people we work alongside. Our advancement within the hospital sector has a direct impact on the young people we engage with on a daily basis. Our ability to have a voice at the clinical table has a ripple effect on the quality of care they receive and amount of involvement they have in their treatment. Appreciating how teams work, which teams are most effective, and how to find our place within these teams will create opportunities for dialogue, education, and a sense of belonging. It is important as we move forward to develop balance between our strengths and areas of growth, while at the same time working towards change, recognition, and acceptance within the teams to which we belong (Hoffman, 2002).

REFERENCES

Beker, J. (2001a). Development of a professional identity for the child and youth worker. *Child and Youth Care Forum, 30*(6), 345–354.

Beker, J. (2001b). The emergence of clinical youth work as a profession: Implications for the youthwork field. *Child and Youth Care Forum, 30*(6), 363–376.

Beker, J. (2001c). Toward the unification of the child care field as a profession. *Child and Youth Care Forum, 30*(6), 355–362.

Buljac-Samardzic, M., van Wijngaarden, J., van Wijk, K., & van Excel, N. (2001). Perceptions of team workers in youth care of what makes teamwork effective. *Health and Science Care in the Community, 19*(3), 307–316.

Charles, G., Alexander, C., & Oliver, C. (2015). Overcoming isolation: Making the case for the development of blended service learning and social work interprofessional field education experiences to improve university-community engagement. *Currents: Scholarship in the Human Services, 13*(1), 1–17.

Charles, G., Bainbridge, L., & Gilbert, J. (2010). The University of British Columbia model of interprofessional education. *Journal of Interprofessional Care, 24*(1), 8–18.

Coyne, I. (2006). Consultation with children in hospital: Children, parents' and nurses' perspectives. *Journal of Clinical Nursing, 15*(1), 61–71.

Davie, A. (2011). A code of ethics for youth work? Notes for a national discussion. *Youth Studies Australia, 30*(2), 57–59.

Demers, M., & Gudgeon, C. (2004). Abbott and Costello meet the multi-disciplinary team. *International Child and Youth Care Network, 60*, 1–9.

Dobbs, H. (2010). Meeting the needs of young people in the hospital. *Paediatric Nursing, 22*(9), 14–18.

Durrant, M. (1993). *Residential treatment: A cooperative, competency-based approach to therapy and program design*. New York, NY: W. W. Norton & Company.

Ferguson, R., Pence, A., & Denholm, C. (Eds.). (1993). *Professional child and youth care* (2nd Ed.). Vancouver, BC: UBC Press.

Garfat, T., Freeman, J., Gharabaghi, K., & Fulcher, L. (2018, October). Characteristics of a relational child and youth care approach revisited. *CYC-Online, 236*. Retrieved from https://www.cyc-net.org/cyc-online/oct2018.pdf

Gharabaghi, K. (2010). *Professional issues in child and youth care*. New York, NY: Routledge.

Hilton, D., & Jepson, S. (2012). Evolution of youth work service in hospital. *Nursing Children and Young People, 24*(6), 14–28.

Hilton, D., Watson, A. R., Walmsley, P., & Jepson, S. (2004). Youth work in hospital: The impact of a youth worker on the lives of adolescents with chronic conditions is evaluated. *Paediatric Nursing, 16*(1), 36–39.

Hoffman, W. (2002). Challenges facing the child and youth care profession. *The International Child and Youth Care Network, 8*, 1–3.

Krueger, M. A. (1986). *Job satisfaction for child and youth care workers*. Washington, DC: Child Welfare League of America.

Lingard, L., Reznick, P., Debita, I., & Espin, P. (2002). Forming professional identities of the health care team: Discursive construction of the "other" in the operating room. *Medical Education, 36*, 728–734.

Lochead, A. (2001). Reflecting on professionalization in child and youth care. *Child & Youth Care Forum, 30*(2), 73–82.

Maier, H. (1991). Developmental foundations of child and youth care work. In J. Beker & Z. Eisikovits (Eds.), *Knowledge utilization in child and youth care practice* (pp. 25–48). Washington, DC: Child Welfare League of America.

Phelan, J. (2005). Child and youth care education: The creation of articulate practitioners. *Child and Youth Care Forum, 34*(5), 347–355.

Phelan, J. (2008, March). The profession called child and youth care work. *CYC-Online, 109*. Retrieved from https://www.cyc-net.org/cyc-online/cycol-0308-phelanguest.html

Rose, L. (2001, April). On being a child and youth care worker. *CYC-Online, 27*. Retrieved from https://www.cyc-net.org/cyc-online/cycol-0401-rose.html

Salhani, D., & Charles, G. (2007). The dynamics of an interprofessional team: The interplay of child and youth care with other professions within a residential treatment milieu. *Relational Child and Youth Care Practice, 20*(4), 12–20.

Solinski, R. J. (2010). *An inquiry into child and youth care narratives of experiences in children's mental health treatment.* Unpublished dissertation, University of Victoria, Victoria, British Columbia.

Swanzen, R. (2011). Relational child and youth care involves emotional intelligence. *Relational Child and Youth Care Practice, 24*(1–2), 73–81.

Watson, A. R. (2004). Hospital youth work and adolescent support. *Archives of Disease in Childhood, 89*, 440–442.

Yates, S., Payne, M., & Dyson, S. (2009). Children and young people in hospitals: Doing youth work in medical settings. *Journal of Youth Studies, 12*(1), 77–92.

CHAPTER 8

School-Based Child and Youth Care Practice: A Case Study of Ontario

Saira Batasar-Johnie and Kiaras Gharabaghi

INTRODUCTION

In Ontario, schools are the largest employer of child and youth care (CYC) practitioners, although child and youth care practitioners hold jobs in schools that often are not actually child and youth care positions. In fact, the largest proportion of child and youth care practitioners working in schools across Ontario are employed in educational assistant positions or other, not clearly defined, support positions typically focused on identified students but sometimes extended to cover classroom-based work. Nevertheless, a not insubstantial number (perhaps 1,000)[1] across Ontario work in both elementary and secondary schools as CYC practitioners with a range of assigned roles and job descriptions. In some cases, CYC practitioners also work in specialized programs outside of mainstream schools, such as suspension and expulsion programs, although not all school boards across Ontario offer such programs.

The history and current status of child and youth care practice in Ontario's schools is complex. On the one hand, schools are spaces of learning and formal education that serve nearly all of Ontario's children and youth. For this reason, schools represent meaningful spaces to be with young people and support young people's growth, not only with respect to academic performance but also with respect to civic engagement, personal growth, and cultural development. On the other hand, schools are spaces of enormous diversity, not only with respect to culture, race, gender, sexual orientation, faith, and socio-economic status, but also with respect to academic ability, learning abilities and disabilities, behaviour, mental health, and substance use. Teachers are the primary professional resource in schools. This creates limitations with respect to meaningfully serving young people with unique learning needs, particular identity profiles, and personal circumstances. To this end, schools have been reliant on other professional resources to ensure that they can fulfill their mandate as educational institutions. Currently, common professional profiles involved in schools include social workers; psychologists; psychiatrists; occupational therapists; speech and language therapists; medical, addictions, and mental health nurses; child and youth care practitioners; and educational assistants.

In Ontario, and across most jurisdictions in Canada, the results of the efforts of schools to respond to diversity have ranged from positive to disastrous. This is especially obvious in relation to embedded racism and the consequences for Black Youth and Indigenous young people in particular, as evidenced by the very high rates of drop out and suspensions/expulsions of these students (James & Turner, 2017). Efforts to deal with gender and sexual diversity have had mixed results, but in many cases have failed to provide adequate learning environments to students outside of gender binaries or heteronormative cultures (Little, 2001). The integration of newcomer youth has often been fraught with challenges. Young people with mental health challenges, or those with disabilities, in particular autism spectrum disorders (ASD) and fetal alcohol spectrum disorders (FASD), often find themselves excluded from mainstream schools or segregated from mainstream school curriculum, culture, and social activity (Ontario Autism Coalition, 2019).

Schools do not exist in isolation from other social dynamics and institutions. Policy contexts that have driven school culture have evolved significantly over the decades, with perhaps the single most influential policy initiative being the introduction of the Safe Schools Act (2000). This piece of legislation, which was framed as a way of ensuring that learning spaces provided at schools reflect safety and peace of mind for students and parents alike, has resulted in arguably one of the gravest attacks on equity considerations, accentuated by enforcement measures that have explicitly disadvantaged racialized communities first and foremost, and also young people impacted by mental health or developmental challenges that often include externalizing behaviours (Daniel & Bondy, 2008; James & Turner, 2017). One outcome of this policy initiative and related enforcement measures is that the already deeply embedded institutional racism of education systems has been strengthened through the pathologizing of individual behaviours and actions as deviant and unsuitable for the school environment (Milne & Aurini, 2017). Multi-disciplinary support teams have, as a result, become interprofessional expert teams presiding over matters of inclusion and exclusion based on the location of power and influence in education—a colonial, largely white-driven system of authority, values, and appropriate identity markers.

It is in this complex landscape of interprofessional practices, institutional cultures, and policy contexts that we wish to consider the roles and practices of child and youth care practitioners in schools. Both of the authors are associated with the School of Child and Youth Care at Ryerson University in Toronto, which is noteworthy specifically because it was founded in 1989 in response to requests from what at the time was the Toronto Board of Education (TBE), which was seeking to enhance the qualifications of its child and youth care practitioners in an effort to create opportunities for upward mobility in compensation and professional roles. Ryerson University became the first degree-granting institution for the field of child and youth care in Ontario. In this chapter, we will consider the range of roles and responsibilities of a school-based CYC practitioner, as narrated by a practitioner with long-time professional roles in schools—Saira Batasar-Johnie. Then we will outline some of the challenges associated with school-based CYC practice, focusing in particular on issues of racism and exclusion, the limited scope of the job description, and challenges associated with supervision and professional growth. Finally, we will provide a synthesis of where the field of child and youth care fits with respect to practising in schools today and some thoughts on what the possibilities for the future might be.

CHILD AND YOUTH CARE ROLES AND RESPONSIBILITIES IN ONTARIO SCHOOLS TODAY

Child and youth care practitioners working in the education system face many challenges. For instance, every school board has a different job description and deploys CYC practitioners differently. This may vary from working one-on-one with a child, to working in a specific classroom, to working across a whole school with all students, to being an itinerate practitioner, deployed where and when needed. In any position, CYC practitioners may work with children with disabilities, be members of behaviour support teams, and more. The challenges of different roles and job descriptions that CYC practitioners can have is further complicated by the myriad job titles they are assigned. They are not often called CYC practitioners. The Ministry of Colleges, Unviersities and Trades recently changed the colleges' program name to Child and Youth Care, whereas before it was Child and Youth Worker. Many school boards still hire Child and Youth Workers, but most often practitioners are hired as Educational Assistants (EA). Once labelled in this way, it is difficult for CYC practitioners to maintain their professional identity because of the title of EA. This causes role confusion and an imbalance of power and respect for CYC practitioners. Another result of this misnaming is issues with pay equity. CYC practitioners and EAs are paid significantly lower than other disciplines in most school boards, excluding Dufferin-Peel Catholic School Board and Toronto District School Board, as they both recognize the role of CYC practitioners as distinct from EAs. At the Toronto District School Board, a further divide exists between Child and Youth Workers (CYWs) and CYC practitioners. CYWs are unable to practise as CYC practitioners. There is also a pay difference between these titles, which can lead to frustration for those who have trained to complete the same role but find themselves paid significantly less.

Whole School Child and Youth Care Practitioners

A whole school child and youth care practitioner (CYCP) is assigned to an elementary or secondary school in order to provide support to all students of all grades within the school. The CYCP is supervised by the principal or an external person. The CYCP will be given a caseload based on the needs of the children. They will work with the special education department to determine which students are identified with specific social, emotional, and behavioural needs. The CYCP can also provide short-term one-on-one counselling support, social skills programming within classrooms, and specific programming throughout the school, such as girls or boys groups, anger management support groups, and friendship clubs. The CYC practitioner is expected to execute a variety of different tasks within the job, work during non-work hours, and have their own space within the school (office/small classroom). They also work closely with teachers and facilitate parenting workshops on themes arising within the school (Denholm & Watkins, 1993; De Salvo, 2017).

Classroom-Based Child and Youth Care Practitioners

A classroom-based CYCP is attached to a specific classroom and works with the entire classroom on social, emotional, and behavioural development to support all students to be successful academically. They are supervised by the principal or an external person and work in partnership with a teacher (Denholm & Watkins, 1993; De Salvo, 2017).

One-on-One Child and Youth Care Practitioners

This role works in either an elementary or secondary school with an exclusive focus on one young person for the day. The CYC practitioner will be supervised directly by the principal or an external person. They may be expected to complete specific tasks, such as supporting students with transportation, teaching social and life skills, communicating with parents/guardians, and meeting the needs of the student's Individual Education Plan (IEP). The CYC practitioner works solely to support the child with their daily school routine.

Itinerate Workers/Intervention Support Workers

These roles look different across all school boards. Typically, in this role the CYC practitioner will be assigned several schools. They are supervised by the principal of the itinerate team or an external person. They work with a variety of different professionals and provide additional strategies and support on different caseloads at the school. They also support students struggling with attendance.

Specialized Classrooms: Student Success

This position may exist in both elementary or secondary schools. The CYCP would be supervised by the principal or an external person. This involves a small classroom environment ranging from four to ten students experiencing a variety of challenges. The CYC practitioner focuses on the social, emotional, and behavioural aspects of the students' school experience. They work alongside the classroom teacher to facilitate programming.

Outside Agency Child and Youth Care Practitioners

Sometimes schools lack the specific human resource needed to support a student. In such cases, the school may call in a CYC practitioner from an outside agency in order to provide support in a specialized classroom working with students with developmental delays. This person typically reports to the principal of the school and abides by the policies and protocols of the community agency where they are permanently employed.

CHALLENGES FOR SCHOOL-BASED CYC PRACTICE

Child and youth care practice in schools is a rewarding career path. Aside from the terms of employment, which generally compare favourably with many other settings where child and youth care practitioners are employed, school-based child and youth care practice offers opportunities for the application of a wide range of child and youth care competencies, and it typically allows for professional growth and development, at least horizontally; upward mobility in the education sector is, however, often a challenge for child and youth care practitioners.

In spite of many positive aspects related to child and youth care practice in this sector, there are challenges as well. In Ontario, such challenges include everything from increasingly precarious work contexts through contracts and casual positions, to issues related to professional hierarchies and interprofessional practices and a lack of clarity on job roles and responsibilities. For the purpose of this chapter, we want to highlight two types of challenges in particular: (1) issues related to anti-Black racism in schools and how these intersect with child and youth care practice, and (2) issues related to supervision for child and youth care practitioners.

Anti-Black Racism in School Settings

Although child and youth care practitioners working in Ontario schools are themselves a very diverse group, with strong representation of African Canadian CYC practitioners as well as other racialized groups, the decisions impacting Black and racialized students rest primarily with teachers and school administrators who are considerably less diverse and reflect the ongoing dominance of white professionals in school settings (Carr & Klassen, 1997; Maynard, 2017). In this context, there are clear patterns embedded in systemic approaches to meeting the educational aspirations of racialized students. These include the following:

1. The academic expectations of Black and racialized youth are often lower than those for white youth. Black students in particular are very often streamed into more vocational and/or sports-related courses and educational trajectories (James & Turner, 2017; Maynard, 2017; Sefa Dei, 2008; Smith, Schneider, & Ruck, 2005).
2. The behavioural expectations of Black and racialized youth are often higher than they are for white youth. Many behaviours on the part

of white youth are seen as disruptive but not aggressive and result in minimal consequences; behaviours of Black Youth are often framed as aggressive and therefore disruptive, and often result in major consequences, including lengthy suspensions and even expulsions (almost always in the name of safety) (James & Turner, 2017; Maynard, 2017).
3. Black bodies are considered in relation to school safety; white bodies are considered in relation to individual learning needs (Cooper Diallo, 2016; James & Turner, 2017).
4. Racialized parents are often less welcome to advocate on behalf of their children than white parents, and to the extent that they do advocate on behalf of their children, their style of advocacy is often reduced to stereotypes of the "angry Black woman." When they do not advocate for their children or when they simply do not respond to school concerns, they are assumed to be negligent and the young person is assumed to be living in dysfunctional or uncaring family environments. School administrators do not typically take systemic barriers of racialized families into account when responding to behaviour incidents or academic weakness (Lechuga-Pena & Brisson, 2018; Schniedewind & Tanis, 2018).

From the perspective of CYC practitioners, these embedded patterns create major challenges. While their training allows them to quickly identify broader systemic and policy issues as the root of specific circumstances or crises, there are few opportunities to engage school professionals in discussions about these. A common scenario for CYC practitioners in schools, therefore, is a frustrating and sometimes harmful process of deflecting youth claims of racism and injustice in order to move forward with job responsibilities related to supporting healthy and safe school climates. Also challenging are the limitations placed on practitioners in engaging with parents or caregivers. This work falls primarily on teachers, even in circumstances where the importance of matching racial and cultural contexts of family and professional is readily apparent.

These challenges with respect to issues of anti-Black racism, as well as anti-Indigenous racism, are especially pronounced for practitioners working in school suspension and school expulsion programs. They are constantly frustrated with the narratives of Black and Indigenous young people about the reasons for their suspensions and expulsions (James & Turner, 2017), and unlike those working in regular schools, these practitioners have access to information pursuant to all of their students. This means that they are particularly well placed to identify patterns of unreasonable, and often explicitly racist, experiences on the part of the young people placed in their programs. The voices of these practitioners are rarely invited, which results in a deafening silence about this problematic aspect of schools across Ontario.

Supervision in the Education System

As of June 2019, of the 76 school boards in Ontario, only two have managerial roles for CYC practitioners: Manager of Child and Youth Services at the Toronto District School Board, and Chief Support Officer at the Dufferin Peel District School Board. The other school boards position the CYC role under special education services or mental health services, and these positions are overseen by a chief of social work, head of special education, or chief of social services. Even at the two boards where there are CYC practitioners in managerial roles, it is clearly not possible for one person in an institution to provide supervision to over 100 employees in a 10-month span. This is where the system is flawed, because a model of supervision has not yet been created to provide supervision to school-based CYC practitioners, and there has not been any literature written about their supervision in the education system. In other disciplines, such as social work and psychology, supervision has been mandated by their professional colleges. Similar to the child and youth care field, social workers and psychologists have had to advocate for the practice of supervision in the education system. The practice of supervision is typically seen in a "support group" format (Clemans, 2010; Bogo & McKnight, 2006; Vito, 2015; Clark et al., 2008). Psychologists are supposed to receive clinical one-on-one supervision in the education system (Fischetti & Crespi, 1999; Chafouleas, Clonan, & Vanauken, 2002). These professions have governing bodies that provide handbooks of the importance of supervision and its impact (National Association of Social Workers, 2013; Canadian Psychological Association, 2000). In the education system in Ontario, CYC practitioners often work in environments where they may feel professionally isolated due to being the only CYCP in the school. Every school is structured differently, and every supervisor is different for the practitioner; it could be a teacher or a principal depending on the job description and the administrative culture of the school. There is an insufficient amount of literature about school-based CYC practitioners. The literature that has been written is currently over 30 years old, and began in the mid-1980s and early 1990s with authors such as Carry Delhom and Jim Anglin from British Columbia. Often, supervision in the education setting is practised more as a performance appraisal or evaluation.

The lack of attention to the issue of supervision for CYC practitioners in the education setting may relate to the high turnover and burnout rate (Batasar-Johnie, 2019).

MOVING FORWARD

Opportunities for CYC Practice in Schools

The field of child and youth care in the education system has a great deal of opportunity to continue to grow and evolve into an established profession. Regulation has been spoken about for many years as the Ontario Association of Child and Youth Care continues to advocate for regulation and legislation to be created for the field. There are currently two school boards that have child and youth care–trained managers that are overseeing CYC practitioners. This role ideally would exist in all school boards in order to optimize the value of CYC practitioners in schools through supervision, advocacy, and support. Most boards of education recognize the need for CYC practitioners in schools, which is why they continue to hire child and youth workers and child and youth care practitioners, even if they don't refer to them as such.

A core priority for the further development of a child and youth care workforce in schools is the establishment of a consistent job description across all school boards and a commitment to an equitable pay scale. Currently, the compensation for CYC practitioners in schools can vary from $39,000 to $80,000, with the high end of this scale reserved for CYC practitioners with a university degree. There is a huge discrepancy of pay and employment benefits across school boards, which creates tensions within the field itself. CYC practitioners need to have more opportunities for both horizontal and upward mobility within school boards, including access to management positions in the education system. In order for CYC practitioners to get there, they must come together and advocate for themselves with their unions and schools boards.

The benefit of having CYC practitioners in schools is that they solely focus on children and youth. This is what CYC practitioners are taught in their pre-service education: to support children, youth, and families. CYC practitioners are able to provide programming, one-on-one support, short-term counselling, support in the classroom, de-escalation of crises, problem solving in and out of the classroom, parent support programming, and much more. There have been many studies documenting that students feel more empowered and supported when they have a caring adult in their lives, and they are more likely to be successful academically (Dods, 2013; Woolley & Bowen, 2007). While teachers can be this person, CYC practitioners have a role just as important because they are in the daily life-space working with young people and focusing on their needs and success.

Participatory Structures Aimed at ASD and FASD

Autistic young people and those impacted by FASD respectively make up significant sub-populations of students in Ontario (Ontario Ministry of Education, 2007; Government of Ontario, 2007). School responses to these students have been entirely inadequate, even in circumstances where staffing and learning supports are provided. Missing almost entirely are any kind of participatory structures and processes either for parents or for students so that they have a stake in their own education pathways (Harwood & Murray, 2019). Moving forward, child and youth care practitioners are particularly well positioned to begin to shift this object-focused approach to serving the education needs of these young people. Relational approaches enriched with specialized techniques to centre autistic young people and those impacted by FASD can facilitate much more person-centred and subject-focused experiences for students (Marshall & Thorn, 2017).

In order to facilitate such a shift, post-secondary training for child and youth care practitioners ought to develop courses and thematic concentrations on working with this sub-population of students. Child and youth care practitioners are themselves often hesitant to challenge the focus on Applied Behaviour Analysis (ABA) in schools, which, although not without benefits, marginalizes young people for much of the school day when ABA resources are not offered. It is furthermore self-evident that autistic young people and those impacted by FASD have social and emotional needs and desires that cannot be met through ABA strategies. A child and youth care approach can meaningfully enrich and add a social justice dimension to the way in which we offer both academic and social elements of school to these young people (Marshall, Wilton, & Weinroth, 2018).

Advocacy and Activism with Respect to Anti-Racism and Anti-Colonialism

Issues of anti-Black racism and colonial practices with respect to Indigenous students have been identified in Ontario schools for many decades (James & Turner, 2017; Maynard, 2017). There is no reason to believe that the professional hegemony of teachers and school administrators will shift in their complacency towards these issues. This means that there is an opportunity for child and youth care practitioners to intervene and demand change. This, however, cannot happen until child and youth care practitioners significantly improve their own understanding of these issues and become fully committed to expanding their roles in schools to include high levels of activism and advocacy. Once again, post-secondary training in these areas is essential. Child and youth care practitioners require specialized skills to engage in activism and advocacy in education systems that are highly protected from larger social narratives by the hegemony of a singular professional group that is itself strongly protected by its union—teachers (Munroe, 2017).

The need to find opportunities to challenge injustice in schools requires a capacity on the part of CYC practitioners to develop strong arguments that are backed up by research and evidence. In this context, a praxis approach in which practice and research are inherently complementary and mutually reinforcing may well be a path forward to make real and lasting change.

CONCLUSION

Child and youth care practice in schools is alive and well as the largest employment sector for the field, but it is a much under-studied service setting. However, this service sector offers enormous opportunities both for individual practitioners and for the field of child and youth care as a whole. Schools are where virtually all issues and themes relevant to youth can be found. From the role of cyber-technologies to the integration or marginalization of young people with disabilities, from racism and oppression to learning and academic achievement, from the complex manifestations and intersections of identities to the experiences of newcomers and the development of communities, child and youth care practitioners can apply their strong focus on relational practices and their increasing commitments to social justice in virtually every context of school dynamics. The field itself can prove its worth in this setting by fundamentally and substantively improving the outcomes not only for privileged young people but for all young people who have a right to an education that speaks to their fullest potential.

At the same time, working in schools requires much more than a focus on educational outcomes. As is congruent with the characteristics of a CYC approach, it is this field that can ensure that schools are settings that are trauma-informed, participatory, and engaged with young people; socially just and anti-oppressive; and, ultimately, responsive to the full range of issues facing young people in the 21st century. Child and youth care practitioners individually and the field as a whole are our hope for innovation in this setting. We are not limited by standardized curriculum, nor by the latest trends in pedagogic methods. Our work is life-space work, and schools are one critical element of every young person's life-space.

NOTE

1. There are no available statistics on how many CYC practitioners actually are employed across school boards in Ontario. The estimate of 1,000 is based on the authors' experience with engaging many different school boards in the context of field placements.

REFERENCES

Batasar-Johnie, S. (2019). Exploring the role of supervision for child and youth care practitioners in the education system in Ontario. *Relational Child and Youth Care Practice, 32*(1), 56–71.

Bogo, M., & McKnight, K. (2006). Clinical supervision in social work: A review of the research literature. *The Clinical Supervisor, 24*(1–2), 49–67.

Canadian Psychological Association. (2000). *Canadian code of ethics for psychologists* (3rd Ed.). Ottawa, ON: Canadian Psychological Association.

Carr, P., & Klassen, T. (1997). Different perception of race in education: Minority and white teachers. *Canadian Journal of Education, 22*(1), 67–81.

Chafouleas, S. M., Clonan, S. M., & Vanauken, T. L. (2002). A national survey of current supervision and evaluation practices of school psychologists. *Psychology in the Schools, 39*(3), 317–325.

Clark, S., Gilman, E., Jacquet, S., Johnson, B., Mathias, C., Paris, R., & Zeitler, L. (2008). Line worker, supervisor and manager perceptions of supervisory practices and tasks in child welfare. *Journal of Public Child Welfare, 2*(1), 3–32.

Clemans, S. E. (2010). The transformation of the purpose of a school-based supervision group during tough economic times: Challenges and considerations for the worker. *Social Work with Groups, 33*(1), 41–52.

Cooper Diallo, H. (2016). High school and the Black body in Canada: A recollection of a female high school student. In A. Ibrahim & A. Abdi (Eds.), *The education of African-Canadian children: Critical perspectives* (pp. 90–95). Montreal, QC: McGill-Queen's University Press.

Daniel, Y., & Bondy, K. (2008). Safe schools and zero tolerance: Policy, programs and practice in Ontario. *Canadian Journal of Education Administration and Policy, 70*, 1–20.

Denholm, C., & Watkins, D. (1993). Canadian school-based child and youth care. In R. Ferguson, A. Pence, & C. Denholm (Eds.), *Professional child and youth care* (2nd ed., pp. 79–104). Vancouver, BC: UBC Press.

De Salvo, A. (2017). School connectedness in the field of child and youth care. *Relational Child and Youth Care Practice, 30*, 6–12.

Dods, J. (2013). Enhancing understanding of the nature of supportive school-based relationships for youth who have experienced trauma. *Canadian Journal of Education / Revue Canadienne De L'éducation, 36*(1), 71–95.

Fischetti, B. A., & Crespi, T. D. (1999). Clinical supervision for school psychologists: National practices, trends and future implications. *School Psychology International, 20*(3), 278–288.

Government of Ontario. (2007). *Making a difference for students with Autism Spectrum Disorders in Ontario schools*. Retrieved from http://www.edugains.ca/resourcesSpecEd/SystemLeader/ASD/autismFeb07.pdf

Harwood, V., & Murray, N. (2019). Strategic discourse production and parent involvement: Including parent knowledge and practices in the Lead My Learning campaign. *International Journal of Inclusive Education, 23*(4), 353–368.

James, C. E., & Turner, T. (2017). Towards race equity in education: The schooling of Black students in the Greater Toronto Area. Toronto, ON: York University. Retrieved from https://youthrex.com/report/towards-race-equity-in-education-the-schooling-of-black-students-in-the-greater-toronto-area

Lechuga-Pena, S., & Brisson, D. (2018). Barriers to school-based parent involvement while living in public housing: A mother's perspective. *The Qualitative Report, 23*(5), 1176–1187.

Little, J. N. (2001). Embracing gay, lesbian, bisexual and transgendered youth in school based settings. *Child & Youth Care Forum, 30*(2), 99–110.

Marshall, N., & Thorn, C. (2017, December). Establishing relational care to support young people living with disabilities. *CYC-Online, 226*. Retrieved from https://www.cyc-net.org/cyc-online/dec2017.pdf

Marshall, N., Wilton, F., & Weinroth, S. (2018). It's our turn! Autistic young people inform praxis and policy. *Relational Child & Youth Care Practice, 31*(2), 36–50.

Maynard, R. (2017). *Policing Black lives: State violence in Canada from slavery to the present*. Halifax, NS: Fernwood Publishing.

Milne, E., & Aurini, J. (2017). A tale of two policies: The case of school discipline in an Ontario school board. *Canadian Journal of Educational Administration and Policy, 183*, 30–43.

Munroe, T. (2017). Enriching relational practices with critical anti-Black racism advocacy and perspectives in schools. *Relational Child & Youth Care Practice, 30*(3), 32–45.

National Association of Social Workers. (2013). *Best practice standards in social work supervision*. Retrieved from https://www.socialworkers.org/LinkClick.aspx?fileticket=GBrLbl4BuwI%3D&portalid=0

Ontario Autism Coalition. (2019). *Briefing note: Recommendations for special education in Ontario's public schools: Exclusions, suspensions and expulsions*. Retrieved from https://ontarioautismcoalition.com/wp-content/uploads/2019/01/BRIEFINGNOTE_-Recommendations-for-Special-Education-in-Ontario%E2%80%99s-PublicSchools.pdf

Ontario Ministry of Education. (2007). *Effective educational practices for students with Autism Spectrum Disorders*. Retrieved from http://www.edu.gov.on.ca/eng/general/elemsec/speced/autismspecdis.pdf

Schniedewind, N., & Tanis, B. (2018). Learning from parents of colour in the effort to preserve multicultural and public education. *Multicultural Education, 25*(1), 29–33.

Sefa Dei, G. (2008). Schooling as community: Race, schooling and the education of African youth. *Journal of Black Studies, 38*(3), 346–366.

Smith, A., Schneider, B., & Ruck, M. (2005). "Thinking about makin' it": Black Canadian students' belief regarding education and academic achievement. *Journal of Youth and Adolescence, 34*(4), 347–367.

Vito, R. (2015). Leadership support of supervision in social work practice: Challenges and enablers to achieve success. *Canadian Social Work Review, 32*(2), 151–165.

Woolley, M., & Bowen, G. (2007). In the context of risk: Supportive adults and the school engagement of middle school students. *Family Relations, 56*(1), 92–104.

CHAPTER 9

Child and Youth Care Practice in Day Treatment Settings

Jessica Carriere and Kiaras Gharabaghi

INTRODUCTION

Not every young person engaged in education pathways finds themselves attending school as we traditionally think of it. By *traditional* we mean school that follows specific patterns and routines, reflecting mainstream expectations of young people, their behaviour, their academic capacity, their social skills, and their ability to spend dedicated time focused on learning. For some young people, *learning* is not a simple matter; instead, the intersections of mental health, social engagement, emotional complexity, and even family constellations and circumstances may render the traditional school a challenging concept (Fahlman, Hall, & Lock, 2006). Often, broader social challenges such as racism, binary gender constructions, and stigmatization of disability also significantly impact the experiences of young people in traditional schools (Jay, 2009). For these young people, whose everyday lives may feature complex intersections of ways of being, school needs to be reimagined and restructured to respond to their individual needs. One response to their needs has been the development of day treatment programs, which, in Ontario at least, are programs featuring a wide range of design, operating dynamics, and collaborations with other systems, including school boards and child and youth mental health organizations (Government of Ontario, 2017).

In this chapter, we will explore the nature of day treatment programs in Ontario, their structure, operating dynamics, and role within the broader education and mental health systems in the province. In particular, we will highlight the roles of child and youth care practice in day treatment programs, including elements of treatment activities, academic support, mental health support, and advocacy. In addition, we will explore the process of transitioning into and out of day treatment and the collaborative processes between day treatment programs and school boards. Finally, we will highlight some of the areas of day treatment programs, child and youth care practice within such programs, and the broader systems and contexts of these programs that one might engage for future development or augmentation.

Although often not a very visible part of education and mental health systems, day treatment serves to ensure opportunities for growth and development for young people who often are chronically excluded or disadvantaged in traditional schools. Such programs have been around for a very long time, and were found to be meaningful enhancements of both education and mental health service systems as early as the 1960s (La Vietes, Cohen, Reens, & Ronall, 1965; Grimes, Gardiner, & Weiss, 1983). Day treatment represents an opportunity for child and youth care practitioners and other professionals to enrich, strengthen, and broaden young people's pathways in education and in their well-being within social and family contexts. Perhaps most importantly, child and youth care practitioners can utilize the day treatment context to guide young people's perception of their own strengths and capacities, and to reduce their anxieties about mental health challenges and feeling "other," or feeling like they are not "normal." Day treatment provides contexts where academic and mental health challenges and strengths can be incorporated into adult–youth relationships without judgment so that more functional tasks related to academic performance can be engaged without pressure and in a context of mitigated barriers to success.

Below, we will first provide a description of the systemic and operational landscape of day treatment in Ontario, including its legislative context, service system context, and broader connection to education and mental health systems and processes. We will also provide a description of operational dynamics such as the human resources, program structures, and routines typically in place, as well as referral systems, client profiles, and operational and clinical oversight of such programs. The roles of child and youth care practitioners will also be delineated.

The following section will provide a more in depth exploration of the everyday practice and relational contexts of working in day treatment as a child and youth care practitioner. It will include discussions about the way in which this work might be approached, the patterns of collaboration with other professionals, and the ambiguities inherently embedded in this context of practice. We will additionally focus on issues of child and youth participation and more broadly the centring of young people within the everyday practice that unfolds.

Given the importance of transition work in day treatment, the third section will describe and critically explore the processes of transitioning into and out of day treatment, and the ways in which child and youth care practitioners utilize aspects of relational practice, interprofessional collaboration across sectors, and client-based and systemic advocacy in their work. The section will highlight the ways in which transition work in day treatment has evolved over time.

Finally, the chapter will end with a discussion of current challenges and opportunities embedded in day treatment programs themselves, as well as in the broader context of the way in which day treatment connects to larger education and mental health systems. At the systems level, we will focus in particular on the limitations of education pathways available for young people that are inclusive and relevant to the whole diversity of young people. At the operational level, we will focus on the opportunities to strengthen the roles and impacts of young people and their families who participate in decisions affecting their education and well-being, while at the same time developing more effective, collaborative, and inclusive mechanisms for intersectorial and interprofessional collaborations in the context of case planning and coordination, as well as professional development that is inclusive of education and mental health professionals.

STRUCTURE AND PROCESSES IN DAY TREATMENT

Day treatment programs exist in a variety of contexts; some programs are physically housed in a mainstream school, usually in one or more classrooms that are somewhat distant from the centre of the school. Other programs are housed in residential treatment programs, often in the basement. Again others are in separate buildings, either on a campus of residential services or sometimes stand-alone buildings in the community. In some cases, day treatment is attached to specific kinds of services, such as custody programs for youth who still have to attend school (Government of Ontario, 2017). In Ontario, the specific parameters of day treatment are laid out in the *Ontario Education Act*. For a long time, these provisions were under section 23 of this act, which is why the terms *day treatment* and *section 23 classrooms* are often used interchangeably. Currently, the provisions appear under section 171(1). In fact, while all day treatment programs are section 23 classrooms, one could argue that not all section 23 classrooms are day treatment programs. The specific characteristic of a day treatment program is the dual focus, ideally fully integrated, on academic work and treatment processes that unfold through a range of modalities, including family systems practices, narrative practices, and cognitive-behavioural approaches to practice.

Day treatment is only one type of alternative education program in Ontario. There are many others, including behaviour classrooms in mainstream schools, alternative schools, suspension and expulsion programs, arts-based schools, African-centred schools, and others (Government of Ontario, 2017). What sets day treatment apart from other forms of alternative education is that students enrolled in day treatment are de-registered from their local board of education; they are clients of the agency operating the day treatment program, albeit in partnership with the board of education. This is different than the aforementioned alternative education programs, which typically are operated by the board of education or at least on behalf of the board, and students in these programs remain students within the local board. The explicit purpose of day treatment programs, as per section 171 of the *Ontario Education Act*, is to serve as a temporary intervention for students with mental health issues, and the mandate is to aim for reintegration into mainstream schools as soon as possible. Day treatment, in other words, is not designed as an alternative to mainstream school on a long-term basis; it is designed to build capacity in students, their families, and schools to provide education to young people after acute mental health issues have been addressed through treatment interventions.

Students referred to day treatment typically have encountered major challenges in mainstream schools. While such challenges might manifest behaviourally, there is broad agreement on the part of educators, psychologists, and others who may be involved that the student's challenges are directly connected to mental health issues, or to family issues that require mental health services as part of the intervention. It is in this context that one can quickly identify some troubling aspects of the education system and its construction of behaviour. Although there are no firm data available to corroborate this, a common observation has been that day treatment programs serve a relatively small number of racialized young people, while suspension and expulsion programs often serve disproportionately large numbers of racialized, and especially Black and Indigenous, young people. This may well be yet another feature of what has been referred to as the school-to-prison pipeline in the education system (Faulconbridge, 2018).

The defining characteristics of day treatment programs are the size of the programs and the human resources associated with these. Most day treatment programs have a maximum capacity of 10 students, and they are staffed at minimum by a teacher (supplied by the local board) and a child and youth care practitioner. Sometimes there is also an educational assistant (EA) available, either designated to a particular young person or as a general support person for academic matters. In rare cases, day treatment programs that are operated by child and youth mental health agencies provide additional clinical support, which may take the form of a child and youth care practitioner providing family and community supports or a clinical therapist attached to each student. Most programs have at least a psychologist on a consulting basis available, and some programs even have a consulting psychiatrist.

It is important to note that day treatment programs are not operated directly by school boards. They are operated instead through a partnership between boards and mental health agencies, private agencies providing residential care, or custody facilities. The students referred to day treatment cease to be students in the school board and instead become clients of the agency operating the program. The program itself is cost-shared between the school board, which typically provides the teacher, sometimes an EA, and often some small amount of operational funding, and the child and youth serving agency, which provides the child and youth care practitioner and additional operational funding, as well as often the space for the program.

Day treatment programs, or section 23 programs, are quite common in Ontario, although the exact number of such programs is not in fact available, because each board develops partnerships to operate section 23 classrooms quite separately from any other board. As a result, there is no central information portal that could provide information on all day treatment programs in the province. Furthermore, there is almost no research on day treatment settings specifically. Instead, to the extent that any day treatment provides research-informed programming, such research is usually drawn from a wide range of alternative education programs, some of which are based in United States (Milin, Coupland, Walker, & Fisher-Bloom, 2000; Rittner, Nochajski, Crofford, & Chen, 2015; Svedin & Wadsby, 2000).

Given the limited number of students involved in any given day treatment classroom, the focus is on providing individualized educational plans (IEPs) for each student. Students are able to sign up for any number of credit courses and then work on these through modules that are provided by the teacher. Day treatment programs do not follow the semester schedules of mainstream schools, which allows students to work on credits within timeframes that are workable for them. Some students experience success by completing fewer credits than what would have been required in mainstream schools; others actually accelerate their work and complete more credits, each credit in a shorter time than the pre-scheduled semester in mainstream schools. The pace of learning is negotiated between the student and the teacher with the support of the child and youth care practitioners, with a focus on enabling academic success at whatever pace or rate.

THE EVERYDAY DYNAMICS OF DAY TREATMENT: A CASE EXAMPLE

There is significant variation in how different day treatment programs operate on a day-to-day basis. Some programs are very structured, focused on behaviour, and provide limited input into academic aspirations or success. Others take a different approach and provide students with strength-based and success-oriented pathways through education (Powell, Calkins, Quealy-Berge, & Bardos, 1999). Below, I (Carriere) will describe day treatment routines and processes as I experience them where I work, but the reader is encouraged to remember that, much like in the context of residential care and treatment, the variations in the quality of practice in day treatment is such that my experience may not be representative of everyone's experience.

At New Path, where I work, our primary concern is to re-engage young people in their learning. For this reason, we take a highly participatory approach to planning academic pathways, and students are strongly encouraged to articulate their own goals and ambitions with respect to education as well as future career aspirations. We always meet students where they are at; there is no pressure to perform academically right from the outset. As one student commented:

> I feel like the teachers were able to communicate to me "more than a teacher would," such as joking around and having a good time. I feel like being able to discuss and communicate with the teachers helped me a lot. I feel like the teachers also understood my emotions and tried to talk to me and make me feel better when I wasn't happy. That stuff made the classroom much better for me.

We measure their performance, and provide feedback to students, based on their progress in meeting their own goals. In addition, as part of the child and youth care role in day treatment, we engage the students in their lives more generally, including their family dynamics, social issues and strengths, recreational likes and dislikes, and emotional well-being. In order to take this approach, we have learned that pre-set daily structures and routines do not work very well; we structure each day as it comes, always with the input and direct participation of the students present. As a result, unlike residential care and treatment, our experience of day treatment is much less routinized; while we encourage some rituals and regular routines, we also deviate from these almost every day in order to use the day to optimal effect based on what young people tell us they need and want. Some days this means that we provide more recreational and social activity than academic activity; other days, students are eager to complete modules or credits and we shift gears to support them in that.

One element of our approach is that we centre discussions about future goals and career aspirations. We have learned that students who are able to connect their academic progress to some goal or aspiration that they have articulated themselves are more eager to make progress in their work. We have also learned that teachers and child and youth care practitioners find common ground in promoting young people working towards their future goals, which is helpful in the context of interprofessional practices and multi-disciplinary team dynamics.

Finally, it is worth mentioning that we place considerable emphasis on ensuring that young people in our program remain connected with broader issues and themes affecting youth in our communities. To this end, we ensure that we acknowledge and engage special events such as Orange Shirt Day, which acknowledges the legacy of residential schools in Canada, as well as wearing pink on anti-bullying day, amongst other initiatives.

CHILD AND YOUTH CARE PRACTICE IN DAY TREATMENT SETTINGS

Perhaps the most important attribute of effective child and youth care (CYC) in day treatment settings is the capacity to respond with flexibility to whatever might unfold in the setting. This includes circumstances directly related to the young people in the setting, but it also includes the organizational context of day treatment and the need to be responsive to teachers, school board personnel, mental health professionals, and clinical professionals with goals and objectives that extend beyond the educational context of a young person. In addition, while young people often thrive in the smaller and much more intimate environment provided by day treatment, the reality is that academic work continues to be challenging, both substantively and also logistically, as it often requires young people to confront their deficits, such as concentrating for longer periods of time, paying attention, interacting with others calmly and constructively, listening to instructions, and so on (Hughes & Adera, 2006). For this reason, child and youth care practitioners in day treatment settings need to be flexible enough to know when to deviate from program expectations or routines. Sometimes, a young person needs a break when this is not part of the schedule. Sometimes, behavioural outbursts are needed in order to transition from one task to another. Regardless, the CYC practitioner's role is to maintain a supportive stance, to facilitate sufficient opportunities for young people to meet their needs in the moments (such as breaks, walks, music, and distraction), and to refocus young people on academic work when those young people have the capacity to do so.

A significant part of the work is to continuously assess the strengths of the young person in their approach to learning. Very often, young people frustrated with a particular academic activity are quite capable of completing the academic aspects of the activity, but may need a different medium to do so. This then requires the CYC practitioner (CYCP) to work with the teacher to develop creative and individually tailored academic assignments and work modules that the young person can become engaged with.

Transitioning into and out of the Program

Young people enter day treatment through referrals, which are typically made by the special education consultants at the school board. A referral package provides comprehensive information about the student's academic, behavioural, and social history. The referral package is initially vetted by a program manager from within the mental health agency that operates the day treatment program. If the package seems reasonable, a series of meetings are arranged with the student, their parent(s) or guardian(s), and staff from both the board of education and the mental health agency. Often, other professionals are involved as well, depending on the context of the student (e.g., probation workers, counsellors). Great care is taken to ensure that the student has a central voice in discussing possible ways forward. The child and youth care practitioner is chiefly responsible for responding to the student's anxiety in this context. To this end, an experienced child and youth care practitioner would typically seek out opportunities for relational practice even at this early stage, which often involves taking the student on a tour of the setting and explaining the program while at the same time engaging the student on their aspirations, preferences, anxieties, and dislikes.

At this stage, it has not yet been decided whether or not to admit the student into the day treatment program. Other alternatives are also discussed, which often include special education programs and alternative schools, typically operated by the school board. If the decision is made to admit the student to the day treatment program, attention shifts to the logistics of planning the student's integration into the program. This can look quite different depending on where the student is at. In many cases, considerations include sleep patterns (does the student need time to get used to getting up early to come to the program in the mornings?), academic needs (how many credits should the student be working on and which ones?), behavioural supports (can we plan for breaks, activities, and connections that may assist the student mitigate behavioural patterns?), and other factors. The child and youth care practitioner has a central role in determining plans with respect to these considerations, largely because any such plans require that the student feels their voice has been heard and remains central to decision-making. While the end goal is normally for the student to participate fully and on a full-time basis in the program, for many it takes some time to get to this stage, and part of the benefits of a day treatment program is that there are always provisions to respect the pace of the student and their capacity to engage.

Much as the student is at the centre of transitioning into the program, they are also at the centre of transitioning out of the program. This process can range from straightforward to complicated, depending on the specific circumstances of the student, their placement scenarios, the responsiveness of the school board, and, where applicable, the home school of the student. Typically, students experience enormous anxiety as the transition out of the program approaches. For this reason, planning for this transition must happen very early, with the full team of support people from both the mental health agency and the school board involved. A great deal of attention is paid to gradual integration into mainstream schools or into alternative schools, depending on the circumstances. Some day treatment programs offer integration support workers who connect with the student while they are still in the day treatment program but then accompany the student to the elementary or high school to which they are transitioning (Buchanan, Nese, & Clark, 2016). The day treatment child and youth care practitioner plays a significant part in the transitioning out of the program process, ensuring that they are available to respond to the student's anxieties, worries, and fears, and also their hopes, aspirations, and preferences.

A core challenge in transition process is the anxiety experienced by the receiving school. In many cases, the receiving school already knows the student from previous years, and may have had negative experiences with the student. Often, teachers and school administrators are unable to see the growth and progress a student has made while in day treatment, and receive the student back into their school environment with trepidation. This is reflected in the emphasis placed on safety plans, which school administrators typically demand from the day treatment program as the transition approaches. Day treatment programs often don't articulate safety plans per se, as these are seen to have a strong deficit focus. In this context, child and youth care practitioners must engage in considerable advocacy and education efforts to ensure that students are not *a priori* tagged as risks or problems as they re-enter their mainstream school.

Collaborating with School Boards

Collaboration with school board staff and school administrators is critically important in the day treatment context, particularly with respect to planning smooth transitions back to mainstream schools. Unfortunately, there often are different cultures at play, and as a day treatment CYC practitioner it is sometimes frustrating to deal with the de-centring of student voice by school board staff and school administrators (Duncan, Forness, & Hartsough, 1995). Not infrequently, their focus is on policies and procedures, and their primary source of information is not student voice but the student file. In this context, strong advocacy skills are necessary that allow the child and youth care practitioner to uphold and amplify the voice of the student while at the same time maintaining respect for the procedural cultures in each institution.

In recent years, there has been a marked improvement in the collaboration with school boards and school administrators. This can be attributed to the development of more trusting relationships and the emergence of respect for the knowledge and experience of the day treatment child and youth care practitioner. Conversations about students can now take place with students, although the encounters are rarely without challenges.

One strategy to strengthen the day treatment perspective in the context of meetings with school boards is to ensure that different day treatment programs and agencies collaborate with one another in order to present a united position to the school board. This facilitates greater understanding and more streamlined processes in which everyone at the table is familiar with each other's priorities.

Working with the Teacher

The cornerstone of day treatment is the collaboration between the teacher assigned to the classroom and the CYC practitioner. This can often be problematic, as the assignment of the teacher to a day treatment classroom is at the discretion of the board of education. Not infrequently, teachers assigned to day treatment are not particularly pleased about this assignment (Conley & You,

2017), which means that struggles can ensue in the team. On the other hand, many teachers assigned to work in day treatment discover the enormously rewarding nature of this work, and in those cases, the collaboration between teacher and CYC generally works well. Nevertheless, in all circumstances it is important to maintain a sense of respect for the particular role of each position. Teachers need to provide curriculum and assess performance based on curriculum guidelines, while CYC practitioners need to take into account the specific treatment context of individual young people and develop plans congruent with such contexts. Good collaboration is usually a function of good communication. In my work context (Carriere), all aspects of the work and of the program are discussed jointly between teacher and CYCP, and we make decisions as a team. Given that we are focused on ensuring young people are participating in those decisions, it is often the young person who helps the teacher and I collaborate effectively, because their voice and their needs are centred in our discussions and in our program planning processes.

A further helpful step, when possible, is to involve the teacher in processes of the mental health service provider beyond the classroom. It is possible, for example, to have a teacher participate in clinical meetings at the residential program where the students might live. In fact, the more the teacher is invited to become part of the overall treatment team, the better the collaboration in the classroom works. At the same time, it is important for the CYC practitioner to be flexible in their role. Often, CYC practitioners reject tasks that are specific to academic activities, arguing that they are not a teacher or tutor. This is not a helpful position to take. Collaboration in the intimate context of day treatment means that roles sometimes must overlap, and that teacher and CYCP are available to support each other in part by strengthening each other's work and actively participating in the goals and practices of the other. Tutoring math, assisting with English assignments, or other academic activities are very much within the role of the CYC practitioner in this context when this is needed.

Working as Part of the Mental Health Team

Day treatment is as much of an education intervention as it is a mental health intervention. This means that the work that unfolds in day treatment is directly tied to work that unfolds either in residential treatment settings or in community-based treatment programs, and all of this work is facilitated by multi-disciplinary teams that may include psychologists and psychiatrists, clinical social workers, and other child and youth care practitioners. One common aspect of this interprofessional process is that different members of the team often see young people very differently (see also Quittard and Charles, this volume). In residential care contexts, young people often display much more behaviour and less cooperation than what they present in the day treatment context. As a result, the day treatment CYCP may have a much more strength-based orientation towards the young person than their residential colleagues. At the same time, the educational accomplishments of young people in day treatment settings often are not a fully integrated component of the clinical assessment, which can be frustrating, particularly as behavioural considerations often take precedence over academic achievement.

For these reasons, it is critical for the day treatment CYCP to maintain very close connections and communication with the mental health treatment team. In many cases, this involves tireless repetition of the strengths of the young person in clinical meetings in order to ensure that the wholeness of the young person is considered as treatment goals and objectives are articulated. Similarly, the day treatment CYCP must maintain an active interest in the assessment work of clinical team members, who can enrich the day treatment process by helping to understand the learning needs of the young person in the broader context of family and community. Maintaining respect for how interactions with young people in different settings and contexts might impact larger treatment planning is an important skill required for the day treatment CYCP, but a preparedness to advocate on behalf of the young person with respect to educational aspirations and learning success is the flip side of this skill and is equally necessary.

STIGMATIZATION AND ADVOCACY ACTIVITIES

In spite of the supportive and enriching nature of day treatment by design, the reality is that there is considerable stigma associated with being placed in a day treatment setting instead of mainstream school (Shifrer, 2013). Young people themselves often express disappointment that they are unable to attend a mainstream school, and suggest that alternative school formats such as day treatment are an embarrassment and not a meaningful way of shaping their educational journeys. Schools also perpetuate stigma in this context. This is often readily apparent as young people seek to transition back to mainstream schools from a day treatment program. Principals and teachers in mainstream schools often have little knowledge about day treatment and assume these settings to be representative of school failure, behavioural problems, and deviance more generally.

It is unhelpful when day treatment settings are quite obviously makeshift alternatives to mainstream schools. Where such settings are really rooms in the basement of a residential program, for example, it becomes enormously difficult to convince anyone, and especially young people, that they are attending school, even if it looks and feels a little different. For this reason, some day treatment settings work hard to present themselves as real schools but in alternative format. At New Path, for example, our day treatment program is located in its own building, on the campus of some residential programs, but separate and aesthetically quite different from these programs. We refer to the day treatment program as the New Path Academy in order to give the program an aura of legitimate educational institution. We also work with mainstream schools to include young people in our Academy in some regular school rituals, such as annual picture taking and obtaining a student ID card. While we cannot replicate all mainstream school rituals and opportunities, we have managed to ensure that our students feel like students rather than patients or clients. While they cannot join school-based sports teams or field trips, they can nevertheless experience every day at school as fundamentally different than their days at the residence or in the community. Somewhat counterintuitively, then, we work hard to infuse some level of institutionalism in our day treatment program in order for students to feel part of something, while at the same time maintaining a more intimate environment in order to facilitate individualized and very personal education journeys based on strengths and regular experiences of success.

In spite of all of our efforts, advocacy remains a major part of the work. The students in our academy are "othered" by the education system, having been dropped as official students of their local board of education and admitted instead to a mental health agency. Advocacy in the context of day treatment really takes at least three forms (see also Maletsky & Evans, 2017):

1. We advocate for additional resources, as school boards are not always prepared to resource day treatment programs in the same way they resource mainstream schools. This applies to mundane things like sports and recreational equipment, and also to more substantive items such as learning technologies and white boards.
2. We advocate for recognition of young people's learning efforts and academic successes in our interprofessional networks. This is particularly important with respect to mental health services that often remain concerned about deficits and behavioural issues while neglecting to see and celebrate the accomplishments of the young people.

3. Perhaps most challenging, we advocate with respect to transitioning young people to mainstream schools. Unfortunately, education systems are designed to place barriers to seamless transitions from one setting to another. Stigma and fear often drive negative responses to our students from principals and school board personnel.

VOICE AND THE PARTICIPATION OF YOUNG PEOPLE

As a result of the smaller setting provided by day treatment compared to mainstream schools, young people have ample opportunity to speak to their concerns as well as their aspirations. The reality, however, is that for many young people, using their voice is difficult; they are anxious, they wonder about the usefulness of sharing what is on their minds, and they are not sure how to operationalize their voice and their agency (Weiss, 2016). One strategy we use on a regular basis is that we tailor academic assignments in such a way that young people can complete them by drawing on their own lived experiences, and by sharing their perspectives on things that affect them right now. This may include issues related to our program, various peer relationships, and also issues unfolding within family or the broader community. Our experience has been that young people will use their voice more often and more effectively when they have multiple pathways for doing so, and perhaps surprisingly, academic work is one particularly useful pathway.

As mentioned previously, all the young people in day treatment settings are on an Individualized Education Plan, which is a living document prepared for (or, in our case, with) young people with special educational needs. In mainstream settings, IEPs are often prepared by teachers and principals, with young people themselves and also their families playing at best a minor role. In day treatment settings, in part because of the dual focus on treatment and education, young people can play a much more instrumental role in the drafting (and re-drafting) of this document, and their families can also be involved and have a voice.

As is always the case in child and youth care practice, the most important way to facilitate the voices of young people is through the medium of relationship (Serido, Borden, & Perkins, 2011). Child and youth care practitioners in day treatment settings have many opportunities to become engaged with young people relationally, and it is usually in the context of such relational practice that young people find their voice. This really sets day treatment apart from mainstream schools; it is a setting where the education and healing journeys of young people are taken up as a joint activity between young people and child and youth care practitioners, and in good scenarios, the teachers too.

THE EMPLOYMENT CONTEXT FOR CHILD AND YOUTH CARE PRACTITIONERS

At least in Ontario, the employment context for child and youth care practitioners in day treatment settings is positive. Day treatment settings usually follow the work hours of schools, which means CYCPs can rely on a regular schedule of daytime work, with weekend commitments relatively rare. Day treatment positions are compensated similarly to residential care positions; if the day treatment program is operated by a child and youth mental health centre or a children's aid society (which are publicly funded institutions), the compensation is relatively good. It might range from a low of $45,000 a year to a high of $70,000. If, on the other hand, the setting is operated by a private agency, the compensation may not be as positive, similar to positions in the private residential care sector (see Gharabaghi & Charles, volume 1).

Unlike child and youth care positions in mainstream schools (see Batasar-Johnni & Gharabaghi, this volume), day treatment settings provide ample opportunities for relational practice and for operationalizing the competencies of child and youth care practitioners. The setting is flexible and the work itself requires drawing on a wide range of CYC skills. As a result of the much less regulated nature of the day treatment setting compared to schools, as well as the less entrenched hierarchy of professional roles in day treatment settings compared to schools, the collaborative relationship between CYCPs and teachers also tends to be stronger and more constructive. CYCPs and teachers, along with mental health professionals involved in the treatment process, often work in well-functioning teams that benefit from the richness of perspectives and the opportunities presented by multiple types of skill sets and roles.

Perhaps most significantly, the employment context of CYCPs in day treatment provides opportunities for them to be connected to young people's families and their communities. Again unlike mainstream schools, where family work and community practice are well outside of the role, day treatment CYCPs can adjust their focus based on the needs and circumstances, presenting themselves with each individual young person.

Finally, day treatment programs operated by child and youth mental health centres provide CYCPs with supervision that is meaningful and regular, and usually (but not always) based on an understanding of their practice and principles. This again is quite different than what CYC practitioners experience in mainstream school settings, where supervision is very often non-existent, or alternatively provided by principals or teachers with a very limited understanding of child and youth care practice (Batasar-Johnni & Gharabaghi, this volume).

MOVING FORWARD: THEMES AND ISSUES

Day treatment settings offer hope to young people whose experiences in mainstream school settings have been deflating and sometimes invalidating. From the perspective of the child and youth care practitioner, these settings provide an excellent context in which to utilize one's relational practice skills and other competencies. Nevertheless, there are huge variations in the ways in which day treatment settings operate across Ontario, and likely across Canada, which means that there continue to be themes and issues that need to be improved and constantly re-evaluated.

Perhaps the most important theme is the inclusion of the child and youth worker in broader team decision-making. Many professionals involved in the lives of the young people enrolled in day treatment do not get to know the young people in the context of their education journey. Sometimes, decisions made about or for young people in one context serve to dismantle strength and progress in another context, such as education. While there are agencies that have done exceptionally well in ensuring fully integrated team work and interprofessional practices, there are still moments of decision-making and professional activity that exclude the child and youth care practitioner from the day treatment setting. Moving forward, a much closer and reliable collaboration is needed between both the child and youth care practitioner and the teacher working in the day treatment setting, and the diverse professionals involved with the young person and their family as part of a broader mental health intervention strategy. To some degree, the need to tighten collaboration also applies across child and youth care practitioners in different settings. Since it is not uncommon for young people enrolled in day treatment programs to also be living in residential treatment programs, the mutual inclusion of CYCPs in team meetings is essential.

Finally, there continue to be many challenges associated with the education journey of young people at the systemic level, and day treatment settings are not above these issues. Racial inequities and exclusions, gender biases, ableism, and heteronormative practices abound. So does the stigma associated with mental health settings for young people, and the sometimes poor responses on the part of education professionals in mainstream school systems. These issues will require further engagement and constant advocacy efforts with and on behalf of young people.

REFERENCES

Buchanan, R., Nese, R. N. T., & Clark, M. (2016). Stakeholders' voices: Defining needs of students with emotional and behavioral disorders transitioning between school settings. *Behavioral Disorders, 41*(3), 135–147. doi:10.17988/BD-15-73.1

Conley, S., & You, S. (2017). Key influences on special education teachers' intentions to leave: The effects of administrative support and teacher team efficacy in a mediational model. *Educational Management Administration & Leadership, 45*(3), 521–540. doi:10.1177/1741143215608859

Duncan, B. B., Forness, S. R., & Hartsough, C. (1995). Students identified as seriously emotionally disturbed in school-based day treatment: Cognitive, psychiatric, and special education characteristics. *Behavioral Disorders, 20*(4), 238–252. doi:10.1177/019874299502000403

Fahlman, M. M., Hall, H. L., & Lock, R. (2006). Ethnic and socioeconomic comparisons of fitness, activity levels, and barriers to exercise in high school females. *Journal of School Health, 76*(1), 12–17. doi:10.1111/j.1746-1561.2006.00061.x

Faulconbridge, O. (2018). *Suspensions and expulsions: A look at the racial injustice of school punishment.* Retrieved from https://rsekn.ca/suspensions-and-expulsions/

Government of Ontario (2017). *Special education in Ontario: Kindergarten to grade 12.* Retrieved from http://www.edu.gov.on.ca/eng/document/policy/os/onschools_2017e.pdf

Grimes, C., Gardner, L., & Weiss, D. (1983). A day treatment programme for children of school age. *Canadian Psychology, 24*(2), 131.

Hughes, A. F., & Adera, B. (2006). Education and day treatment opportunities in schools: Strategies that work. *Preventing School Failure: Alternative Education for Children and Youth, 51*(1), 26–30. doi:10.3200/PSFL.51.1.26–30

Jay, M. (2009). Race-ing through the school day: African American educators' experiences with race and racism in schools. *International Journal of Qualitative Studies in Education, 22*(6), 671–685. doi:10.1080/09518390903333855

La Vietes, R., Cohen, R., Reens, R., & Ronall, R. (1965). Day treatment center and school: Seven years experience. *The American Journal of Orthopsychiatry, 35*(1), 160–169. doi:10.1111/j.1939-0025.1965.tb02280.x

Maletsky, L. D., & Evans, W. P. (2017). Organizational factors that contribute to youth workers' promotion of youth voice. *Child & Youth Services, 38*(1), 53–68. doi:10.1080/0145935X.2016.1204538

Milin, R., Coupland, K., Walker, S., & Fisher-Bloom, E. (2000). Outcome and follow-up study of an adolescent psychiatric day treatment school program. *Journal of the American Academy of Child & Adolescent Psychiatry, 39*(3), 320–328. doi:10.1097/00004583-200003000-00014

Powell, S., Calkins, C., Quealy-Berge, D., & Bardos, A. N. (1999). Adolescent day treatment: A school and community based alternative to residential care. *Journal of Developmental and Physical Disabilities, 11*(3), 275–286. doi:10.1023/A:1021804817301

Rittner, B., Nochajski, T., Crofford, R., & Chen, Y. (2015). Demographic and environmental factors associated with successful day school treatment program outcomes. *Journal of Evidence-Informed Social Work, 12*(6), 601–613. doi:10.1080/15433714.2014.976695

Serido, J., Borden, L. M., & Perkins, D. F. (2011). Moving beyond youth voice. *Youth & Society, 43*(1), 44–63. doi:10.1177/0044118X09351280

Shifrer, D. (2013). Stigma of a label: Educational expectations for high school students labeled with learning disabilities. *Journal of Health and Social Behavior, 54*(4), 462–480. doi:10.1177/0022146513503346

Svedin, C. G., & Wadsby, M., (2000). Day school treatment in Sweden: A 4-year follow-up study of maladjusted pupils. *Children and Youth Services Review, 22*(6), 465–486. doi:10.1016/S0190-7409(00)00097-9

Weiss, J. (2016). Amplifying youth voice and acting on it. *Connect,* (220), 19–20.

CHAPTER 10

Child and Youth Care and the Youth Criminal Justice System

Grant Charles and Ashley Quinn

INTRODUCTION

While not widely recognized, the roots of child and youth care can be traced in part to the youth criminal justice system (Charles & Gabor, 2006; Charles & Garfat, 2013). Along with residential care, youth justice was one of the first state-run systems to employ staff who had a particular focus on working with young people. Although child and youth care has only been considered a profession for approximately 50 years, its foundation was laid at least 100 years ago from these untrained staff groups who worked in the original youth-serving institutions. While the profession has significantly expanded beyond these beginnings, many practitioners are still employed in or come in regular contact with the youth justice system. As such, it is important to have an understanding of the philosophical and historical foundation of the work in this sector as well as the current roles of members of the profession.

The current youth criminal justice system is deeply rooted in early French and English colonial ways of viewing children and criminals (Bennett, 1988; Demerson, 2004; Houston, 1972; Myers, 2006). The youth criminal justice system has significantly changed in the past 50 years with what can be seen as more progressive practices, but much of the system remains rooted in these colonial beginnings. This chapter will discuss the origins of the youth justice system, changes in how the system works, and the role of child and youth practitioners. It is only recently that Indigenous justice values have begun to influence how the justice system is operationalized. This will be discussed later in the chapter.

Prior to the establishment of the child saving movement in the early to mid-1800s, children were seen in what became Canada as miniature adults (Carrigan, 1998; Pinchbeck & Hewitt, 1973). Children breaking the law were seen as miniature criminals and were judged by adult standards. This meant that they were held responsible for their actions in the same way as adults. While there could be some leniency for younger children based upon their age, most received the same types and levels of punishments as adults (Carrigan, 1998). Public whippings were a common form of punishment. Children could be and were hanged. If sentenced to jail or prison, they would be housed with adults in harsh living conditions with poor food and little medical attention. Beatings were common. A 10-year-old sentenced to time in the Kingston Prison was lashed 57 times in a less than nine-month period. An eight-year-old was lashed within days of being sent to the prison. Boys and girls received similar sentences and punishments.

The driving force behind this type of treatment was the belief that people who committed crimes, regardless of their age, had deep character and moral flaws (Wheatley, 2013). It was widely accepted in mainstream society that the only way to stop people with these "flaws" from committing another crime was to harshly punish them. It was thought leniency only led to the commission of further crime. While not nearly as widespread as in the past, this belief is still held by a significant proportion of the Canadian population. It still influences our current youth justice system.

However, the Canadian youth justice system is, as are many of our care systems, also a legacy of the child saving movement (Houston, 1972; Pinchbeck & Hewitt, 1973; Rooke & Schnell, 1983). There are two ways to interpret the establishment of the child saving movement. The first is that it can be considered a progressive movement started by child advocates that was founded to promote the growth and well-being of young people. There can be no doubt that many young people in Canada in the 1800s were living in adverse conditions and were being exploited by adults in any number of ways (Carrigan, 1998). Child labour was common in Canada during the 1800s, especially on the marginal farms where many Canadian families lived during that time period. Families relied upon cheap labour provided by their own children or by young people who were forced to work for survival (Carrigan, 1998; Kohli, 2003). As urbanization and industrialization took place during that century, young people often worked under adverse conditions in factories and mines.

There were few legal or workplace safety protections for children, and the rates of injury and death were high. Poverty was also widespread, and the mortality rate for children, especially from lower-class families, was high. Severe physical punishment was commonplace. There were also high levels of child sexual exploitation. While all children were vulnerable during this era, the young people most at risk were those who were poor and marginalized. The two conditions were often interchangeable. It was these conditions that led to the call for improvements in the lives of children and youth. The people calling for these changes saw themselves as being progressive and part of a larger movement to improve the lives of people in general.

However, much of this progressive thought was based upon a widespread self-righteous sense of moral, class, racial, gender, and ability superiority held particularly by members of the middle class towards the lower classes (Charles, 2015). The middle class during that era was small, relatively new, and insecure. Perhaps in an attempt to differentiate themselves from the lower classes by making themselves feel morally superior or, more likely, in an attempt to protect themselves from their fear of being overwhelmed by the masses of people they deemed inferior, many middle-class people supported the child saving movement.

While many of the child saving schemes did contribute to such advances as the establishment of universal public education and decreases in child mortality rates, these initiatives were often more beneficial to middle-class children rather than those of the lower class. Many of the child saving initiatives directed towards lower-class young people, families, and communities were focused on social control rather than social improvement. As such, we saw the establishment of large-scale institutions such as the "institutions for idiots," "institutions for the feeble-minded," and "schools for the deaf and dumb" (Charles, 2015). Rather than benefiting young people, these institutions were simply ways of ensuring that young people who did not fit the tight definition of "normal" were kept out of sight and out of mind, in order to ensure that these children and youth did not "contaminate" the general public.

It was this philosophy and societal attitude that was behind the establishment of a youth justice system in Canada. Children and youth who were deemed dangerous or potentially harmful to public well-being and morality needed to be controlled. As in the rest of the child saving era, there were some positive benefits for children and youth. For example, prior to the 1800s young people were subject to the same justice system as adults. This changed during the middle part of the century with the establishment of separate facilities for young people in Quebec and Ontario (Smandych, 2012). Conditions did improve for youth but only in a relative manner. Conditions were still harsh and often brutal. The child and youth justice system remained largely an adult system for younger people despite the early efforts at reform.

LEGISLATION

Juvenile Delinquents Act

The youth justice system began to change more significantly with the introduction of specific federal legislation that delineated the differences between the adult and youth justice systems. The first federal legislation was passed in 1894 as a direct result of lobbying by social reformers associated with the child saving movement. The *Act Respecting Arrest, Trial and Imprisonment of Youthful Offenders* was the first overarching piece of legislation directed at young people, although there had been an earlier amendment to the *Criminal Code* in 1892 that prohibited the intermingling of child and adult populations in prison, prohibited the conviction of children under age 7, and restricted the laying of charges against young people under the age of 14 if they were deemed unable to appreciate the difference between right and wrong. This legislation also allowed for the placement of young people in foster homes under the supervision of child protection agencies. The legislation recognized that young offenders were in need of understanding and support rather than just being morally weak perpetrators of criminal activities. This was a significant step towards an acknowledgement that factors other than character flaws influenced criminal behaviour.

The *Juvenile Delinquents Act* (JDA) took the reforms a step further. The legislation was enacted in 1908 and stayed in force, although with amendments, until 1984. The legislation applied to any young person who violated any municipal, provincial, or federal law, and later included behaviour deemed to be sexually immoral (Smandych, 2012). The age at which the law applied was determined by the individual provinces and, while it generally applied to 7- to 15-year-olds, it could be extended to people until they reached the age of 21. There were also different ages for males and females. The provinces tended to apply the legislation to girls at an older age than boys.

The *Juvenile Delinquents Act* mandated the establishment of separate courts for young people, although those over the age of 14 could be transferred to adult court if the crime was deemed severe enough by a juvenile court judge to warrant serious consideration. The Act also enshrined the right of young people to be held in facilities separate from those of adults, to have their trials held in private, and to not have their names published. Judges were also granted wider discretionary powers over sentencing, placement, and confinement.

Perhaps the most significant part of the Act was the underlying assumption that young offenders should be treated as misguided children rather than as criminals. The legislation was still punitive by current standards, as it allowed for the sentencing of a young person to industrial schools or reformatories for unmanageable or incorrigible behaviour until they were either considered no longer a threat to society or until they aged out at 21, whichever came first. The legislation gave sweeping authority to police and courts to determine the definition of unmanageable and incorrigible. For example, it was common for girls to be deemed incorrigible if they were sexually active or seen as being outspoken. How the legislation was applied reflected local norms, but overall tended to reflect a rigid middle-class, Anglo-Saxon, and Protestant interpretation of what was considered acceptable moral behaviour (Charles & Gabor, 2006; Smandych, 2012). While it was progressive in that it differentiated between the needs of young people and adults, and despite the reformist language in the Act, it was still very much a mechanism for social control meant to ensure the supremacy of the upper and middle classes over the lower class.

The Young Offenders Act

The *Juvenile Delinquent Act* was replaced in 1984 by the *Young Offender Act* (YOA) after a great deal of debate based upon previous punitive-versus-progressive arguments. The new legislation tried to find a balance between the two positions by providing support to young offenders while at the same time holding them accountable for their actions. The Act was highly influenced by the passing of the Canadian Charter of Rights and Freedoms in 1982. The previous Act had tended to ignore or at least minimize the rights of young offenders. The YOA provided young people with the same legal rights as adults. This included the right to a lawyer, the right to appeal a conviction, and the right to due process.

While still allowing the transfer of young offenders to adult court for serious offences, the legislation also set maximum custodial sentences to two years for most offences. Sentencing for more serious crimes such as murder, if not transferred to the adult system, allowed for sentences of up to five years. It also abolished the discretionary powers of the provinces to set the age limits applicable to young offenders, replacing this with a uniform provision across the country. The minimum age for being charged was set at 12 years while the maximum age was 17. The legislation also allowed for a wider range of judicial outcomes, including fines and mandated community service. While these provisions for alternative measures decreased the incarceration rates when compared to the JDA, the number of young offenders being sentenced to custody remained high. Despite the improvements from the JDA, the YOA did not quiet the dissent of either those who continued to call for a more punitive approach or those who thought less intrusive measures would better address the rehabilitation needs of young offenders.

The Youth Criminal Justice Act

In a further attempt to resolve these conflicting viewpoints and to address the needs of young offenders, their victims, and their communities, the federal government enacted the *Youth Criminal Justice Act* (YCJA) in 2003. This current legislation defers significantly from the YOA in that it uses the formal court system less while focusing on decreasing detention and incarceration using alternative methods of responsibility. It is a far more prescriptive piece of legislation in that it clearly outlines possible courses of action when dealing with young people who have committed crimes. It is based upon six underlying principles: restraint, accountability, proportionality, structured discretion, protection of the public, and rehabilitation and the addressing of needs (Green, 2012). Restraint and accountability refer to minimizing, whenever possible, the use of the courts and maximizing the use of meaningful consequences that promote rehabilitation. Proportionality, structured discretion, and protection of the public refer to ensuring the intervention matches the seriousness of the crime while also ensuring that public safety is maintained. All actions should be taken with the goal of meeting the needs of the young person in terms of rehabilitation. This Act makes a distinction between young people who commit serious violent offenses and those who commit less serious crimes.

The YCJA builds upon the earlier alternative measures of the YOA through the use of extrajudicial measures. Meant to primarily be used for people who have committed non-violent offences, the purpose of these measures is to allow for the provision of interventions outside of the judicial system, encouraging the young person to acknowledge and repair the harm they have done to the victim and encouraging the involvement of the young person's family, the victim, and the community in the process while respecting the rights of the young offender and being proportional to the crime. When addressing youth in conflict with the law, the YCJA provides police with the option of doing nothing, giving the young person a warning, or, with their permission, referring them to a community agency for involvement in alternative processes. This is a mechanism for keeping less serious charges out of the courts so that the resources can be directed towards dealing more effectively with serious offences (Green, 2012).

The YCJA also formalizes the use of community conferencing to assist in making decisions related to the Act. The purpose of the conferencing is to allow interested parties who would have been denied input under previous legislation to contribute to the decision-making process. Conferencing is most often used during the bail stage of the court process to help set conditions and community support, and during sentencing to determine what would be appropriate (Green, 2012). It may involve the young person, parents, other family members, the victim and people associated with them, members of the local community, and members of the professional community. This mechanism, along with the use of local youth justice committees, not only ensures wider community ownership of the outcome, but also permits a greater degree of service coordination between the youth justice system and other services such as child protection, mental health, and education. The underlying belief is that the wider the circle of support, the more likely positive outcomes for the young person.

The application of the legislation varies significantly amongst the provinces and territories, especially in regard to incarceration rates (Malakieh, 2018). For example, British Columbia has the lowest rate with 2 per 10,000 of their youth population being incarcerated, while Manitoba is the highest with 22 per 10,000. The average rate in Canada is 5 per 10,000. Overall, there has been a significant drop in incarceration rates since the introduction of the YCJA, although in 2016 and 2017, there were 897 youth in locked facilities across the country out of a total of 7,616 young people in formal contact with the youth justice system.

DISPROPORTIONALITY

There are different contact and incarceration rates amongst young people (Malakieh, 2018). Males are overrepresented in the system, and make up over three-quarters (76 percent) of the youth in contact with the system. Older males are more likely to be placed in locked facilities, although females are incarcerated at an earlier age than males.

There is a significant imbalance in the youth justice system in Canada, with a disproportional representation of certain peoples. The overrepresentation of youth in care who are involved in the youth justice system is noteworthy (Kendall & Turpel Lafond, 2009). Young people who have experienced trauma, mental health, or substance misuse issues, and/or have fetal alcohol spectrum disorder, are disproportionately in contact with the system (Dowden, 2003; Oudshoorn, 2015; Verbrugge, 2003). Black Youth are also overrepresented in custodial and residential care (Gharabaghi, 2019).

However, this imbalance is most evident with Indigenous youth who, from 2016 to 2017, accounted for 8 percent of the overall youth population in Canada and yet made up 46 percent of admissions to correctional services (Statistics Canada, 2018). Compared to their peers, youth who identify as Indigenous and are involved in the child welfare system are at an even higher risk of being involved with the youth justice system (Kendall & Turpel Lafond, 2009). Involvement of the child welfare and youth justice systems in the lives of Indigenous youth creates increased risk of social dislocation, detachment from family and community, and missed opportunities (Cesaroni, Grol, & Federicks, 2018). The impact of colonialism on Indigenous persons is reflected in historical, structural, socio-economical, and systemic factors (Corrado, Freedman, & Blatier, 2011).

A number of initiatives have been developed to address issues related to disproportionality within the youth justice system. While we will discuss them in connection with Indigenous youth, many of the values, principles, and practices associated with them can be used with other disproportionately represented groups. One of the ways in which this disproportionality is being addressed is through the use of extrajudicial measures that build upon traditional Indigenous systems of justice. While built upon traditional Indigenous values and beliefs, the processes being implemented can in many cases be applied to non-Indigenous peoples.

Restorative justice has been practised among various Indigenous communities for thousands of years and is now being recognized as a tool for addressing conflict resolution within the youth justice system in Canada. Although there is no universal definition of restorative justice (Chartrand & Horn, 2016), Tony Marshall (1996) provides the following commonly used definition: "Restorative justice is a process whereby all the parties with a stake in a particular offence come together to resolve collectively how to deal with the aftermath of the offence and its implications for the future" (p. 37). Participation in the restorative justice process for resolving conflict focuses on relationship building, reconciliation, and the agreement of a resolution between the victim and offender (Dandurand & Griffiths, 2006). According to Zehr (2014), a restorative perspective regarding crime and justice includes the following five principles:

1. Focus on the harms and consequent needs of the victims, as well as the communities' and the offenders';
2. Address the obligations that result from those harms (the obligations of the offenders as well as the communities' and societies');
3. Use inclusive, collaborative processes;

4. Involve those with a legitimate stake in the situation, including victims, offenders, community members, and society;
5. Seek to put right to the wrongs. (p. 45)

In North America, the concept of restorative justice is rooted in approaches to conflict resolution practiced by the Māori of New Zealand and Indigenous peoples in North America (Zehr, 2005). In general, the emphasis was on bringing victims, offenders, and communities together to address conflict. The first recognized case of restorative justice applied in Canada was documented in Elmira, Ontario, and was commonly referred to as the "Mennonite model" of Kitchener, Ontario (Gailly, 2003). In 1974, two young men pled guilty to 22 counts of property damage (Johnstone, 2011). The assigned probation officer, Mark Yantzi, and a Mennonite prison support worker, Dave Worth, received permission from the judge for the convicted pair to meet with the victims to determine if reparations could be made (Dandurand & Griffiths, 2006). The judge then ordered a one-month remand for the convicted young men to meet with the victims and assess the damage. Following meeting with the victims, the accused were able to better understand the impacts of their criminal behaviour. The judge later ordered for the accused to receive a term of probation that included the payment of a fine and restitution to the victims (Johnstone, 2011). In 1975, Yantzi and his colleagues refined their practice and developed the Victim/Offender Reconciliation Program (Johnstone, 2011). The program focuses on restitution and reconciliation between the victim and the community member in conflict with the law. Through this program, the community member develops a restitution plan with the victim. This program set the stage for much of the subsequent work in this area.

Sentencing circles are another aspect of restorative justice. In Canada, the courts are adopting the use of sentencing circles when addressing the sentencing of Indigenous persons. Sentencing circles are generally used when the person has been found guilty or has pled guilty to a criminal offence. A sentencing circle is arranged at the request of the accused. The request must be made voluntarily by the accused, and under no circumstance are they to be forced by the court or by the victim of the offence to participate in a sentencing circle. Participants in the sentencing circle may include the community member in conflict with the law, judge, Crown, defense, family members of the accused, community supports of the accused, and victim(s) of the offence. All participants of the sentencing circle participate voluntarily.

Participants of the sentencing circle are seated in the arrangement of a circle. The purpose of sitting in a circle implements the notion of equality. Each participant is to respect, listen, and provide insight into the resolution of the community member's court matter. Traditional Elders and Knowledge Keepers generally participate in circles to provide spiritual guidance and support to participants in the circle. Sentencing circles may be facilitated by Traditional Elders and Knowledge Keepers or trained sentencing circle facilitators. Circles are generally opened with a prayer followed by a smudge of participants in the circle. The Eagle Feather is passed around clockwise or counter-clockwise (depending on the First Nation of the accused). When a person is holding the Eagle Feather, they are allowed to speak and share their thoughts or feelings about the accused's circumstances and offence. While the person is holding the Eagle Feather, other participants in the circle are not to speak but to listen until they have received the Eagle Feather. Circles may take several hours to complete, as each participant may speak for an unrestricted amount of time. The purpose of the sentencing circle is for participants and the accused to collectively develop a resolution.

There are several beneficial aspects of participating in a sentencing circle. During the circle, the accused is held responsible through discussion of their actions and insight into their personal circumstances. Through the circles, family and community members (e.g., Elders, service providers) can collectively work together with the accused to identify a resolution for their court matter. Victims frequently want answers to questions they have regarding the offence, such as why it happened and what has happened since. This information is shared in a transparent manner within the circle and is not based on speculation or the legally constrained information from the trial or a plea agreement. The accused has the opportunity to experience their supports. At the closing of the circle, the court can decide to enforce the recommendations of that circle; however, applying the recommendations to the sentencing of the individual are at the discretion of the judge.

There are also challenges associated with implementing sentencing circles within the youth justice system. Sentencing circles are often conducted in a colonial traditional Western courtroom setting and not within the community. Unlike traditional circles, the judge is the ultimate decision-maker in the sentencing circle and not the collective body of the circle participants. Circles may not work in all criminal matters. For example, in cases involving sexual assault, victim participation in such a circle may increase the risk of being retraumatized by what is said in the circle.

While not directly a part of the youth justice system, it is worth noting that restorative justice circles, also known as alternative dispute resolution, can also be applied in family law matters that involve the issues of custody or apprehension of children and involvement in the child welfare system. Participants in the circle are encouraged to speak from their hearts in order to come to a realistic and appropriate resolution. This can present challenges if the parties participating in the circle have different agendas. For example, a mother may be fearful of sharing her personal circumstances or obstacles out of fear that child welfare will use this information against her.

With respect to addressing matters of family law, family group conferencing was first introduced in New Zealand through the *Children, Young Persons and Their Families Act* (1989) as a new method to address youth crime and child welfare issues (Johnstone, 2011). Family group conferences may include family members and professional caregivers of the youth. During family group conferences, youth involved with child welfare or in conflict with the law are invited to participate with their immediate and extended family members and professional caregivers in the development of their own plan (Liebmann, 2000). This includes time for the youth and their family members to meet privately in order to develop their own plan. In youth justice cases, young people can be referred to a family group conference when diversion is determined appropriate by police. Sometimes family group conferencing may include participation of the victim, where they can discuss how the offence impacted their life and ask the offender questions about the offence. Conference participants are expected to collectively work together to create a plan that addresses how the offender can repair the harm associated with the offence (Umbreit, 2000).

The Declaration of Principles of the *Youth Criminal Justice Act* (YCJA, 2002) provides that the court must consider all possible alternatives to custody for youth offenders, in which particular consideration must be given to the circumstances of young Indigenous offenders (Department of Justice Canada, 2013). However, underlying acts of discrimination and oppression continue to exist in the youth justice system, as Indigenous youth offenders are more likely to receive more severe charges and longer sentences than non-Indigenous youth offenders (Barker et al., 2015). Involvement in the youth justice system can complicate a youth's transition into adulthood, in which serving custodial sentences and having negative incarceration experiences may increase recidivism (Elman & Zinger, 2017).

In 1996, Parliament made changes to the *Criminal Code of Canada*, including section 718.2(e), which directs the court when sentencing an individual to consider alternatives to incarceration with special consideration to the circumstances of Indigenous persons (Department of Justice Canada, 2017). Pursuant to section 718.2(e), when an Indigenous person is in conflict with the law, the court must consider the colonial impacts of historical and contemporary realities on Indigenous persons, families, and communities, and alternatives to incarceration (Elman, 2016).

In 1999, Jamie Tanis Gladue, a Cree-Métis woman, and her lawyer appealed a sentencing decision in which the judge had determined that because Jamie did not reside on-reserve, special consideration to the circumstances of Indigenous persons pursuant to section 718.2(e) did not apply. In *R. v. Gladue (1999)*, the Supreme Court of Canada reviewed the sentencing decision and found the judge had erred (Department of Justice Canada, 2017). The Supreme Court recognized and determined that section 718.2(e) applies to all Indigenous persons regardless of whether they reside on- or off-reserve (Elman, 2016). In *R. v. Ipeelee (2012)*, the Supreme Court of Canada upheld the *R. v. Gladue (1999)* landmark decision and section 718.2(e), mandating courts to consider the impacts of colonialization, displacement from traditional territories and lands, and discriminatory legislation (including the Indian Residential School System) when sentencing Indigenous persons (Department of Justice Canada, 2017).

In order to address the Supreme Court of Canada's requirement, Gladue reports provide the court with systemic, historical, and contextual background factors, including the circumstances that led to an offence, and culturally grounded recommendations specific to the needs and circumstances of Indigenous persons being sentenced. Previously written Gladue reports may be considered for bail hearing decisions and sentencing decisions regarding Indigenous persons who have pled guilty or have been found guilty of a particular offence(s) in Canada. Although consideration of section 718.2(e) is mandated by the Supreme Court of Canada (Elman, 2016), there remains inconsistent recognition and implementation of its principles within justice systems across Canada. Despite consideration of section 718.2(e) being a human right for Indigenous individuals before the court, there are very low numbers of Indigenous youth who are able to exercise this right, often due to limited funding and time.

Indigenous children and youth (and their families and communities) continue to live through the detrimental effects of the Indian Residential School System that have been carried across generations. Specifically, for Indigenous youth involved in the system, the Truth and Reconciliation Commission of Canada (2015) explicitly calls "upon the federal, provincial, territorial, and Indigenous governments to commit to eliminating the overrepresentation of Indigenous youth in custody over the next decade" (p. 4). Principles of restorative justice and alternatives to custody when sentencing Indigenous youth are important steps in addressing their overrepresentation in the youth justice system.

ROLE OF CHILD AND YOUTH CARE WORKERS

The role of child and youth care workers can vary significantly within the youth justice system depending upon the context within which they are working. While not the primary profession employed in correctional facilities, child and youth care workers are hired to work in many different roles in the sector. By far, though, most who work with justice-involved youth are employed within programs associated with extrajudicial measures. This may involve working with restorative justice initiatives and other related services such as attendance centres and family support programs. In terms of this latter program, it is evident that young people who have parental involvement during their contact with the system tend to have better outcomes (Badali & Broeking, 2004). Child and youth care workers are involved in counselling and mental health services associated with the system or receive referrals regarding youth in contact with youth justice. Because of the higher likelihood that youth in care will be involved in the system, child and youth care workers are also more likely to have secondary connections with the youth justice system through young people in their care.

Child and youth care workers can have a role in terms of advocacy and prevention. Given the strong connection between oppression, poverty, trauma, and criminal activity, it is quite obvious that the best way to decrease youth involvement in the youth justice system is to address the issues that put youth at risk in the first place. This can involve advocating for measures and practices to decrease racism, structural oppression, and poverty. It can also include working in areas associated with prevention, such as family and parenting interventions and anti-violence initiatives. It can be argued that most child and youth care roles are directly or indirectly involved in some aspect of the youth justice system. Successful outcomes for young people in any service is likely to contribute to preventing youth from becoming involved in criminal activity and therefore keeping them out of the youth justice system.

Depending upon the settings and the circumstances, having relationship-based interactions can be quite challenging. It is one thing to build a relationship in an open setting and quite another to do so in a mandated service, especially if the young person is in a locked setting. While it can be argued that one of the functions of child and youth care, whether we like it or not, is about social control, we can often pretend that this is not what we are doing. However, this cannot be ignored in a locked or mandated program. The dynamics of our interactions with young people in an overtly social control setting is changed.

This is not to say that it is impossible to do relationship-based practice. It just makes it more difficult, not the least because the power differentiation between the practitioner and the young person is much more blatant and obvious. It becomes harder to balance the social control and the relationship aspects of the work. Whether it should be this way or not, the primary functions and therefore the expectations of the workplace are often on having a controlled and restrained environment, especially in custody settings. There can be less emphasis upon rehabilitation. Paradoxically, though, this means that it becomes even more important to focus on relationship. It becomes imperative that practitioners, while acknowledging the restrictions placed upon them in many settings, focus upon the humanizing and growth-promoting possibilities for young people in their care.

CONCLUSION

Child and youth care originated, in part, with staff who worked in the early youth justice system. While we are now less likely to be directly employed in the custodial aspect of the system, child and youth care still plays a significant role in programs directly involved with extrajudicial measures, such as restorative justice, and indirectly through other intervention, prevention, and advocacy initiatives. The justice system seeks to resolve social issues involving law, and it seems suitable that the profession of child and youth care, with our focus on relationships, strength-based practice, and trauma-informed practices, can play a major role in ensuring successful outcomes for young people, families, and communities.

REFERENCES

Badali, M. P., & Broeking, J. (2004). *Parents' involvement in youth justice proceedings: Perspectives of youth and parents.* Ottawa, ON: Justice Canada.

Barker, B., Alfred, G. T., Fleming, K., Nguyen, P., Wood, E., Kerr, T., & DeBeck, K. (2015). Aboriginal street-involved youth experience elevated risk of incarceration. *Public Health, 129*(12), 1662–1668.

Bennett, P. W. (1988). Taming "bad boys" of the "dangerous class": Child rescue and restraint at the Victoria Industrial School 1887–1935. *Histoire sociale/Social History, 21*(41), 71–96.

Carrigan, O. (1998). *Juvenile delinquency in Canada: A history.* Concord, ON: Irwin Press.

Cesaroni, C., Grol, C., & Fredericks, K. (2018). Overrepresentation of Indigenous youth in Canada's criminal justice system: Perspectives of Indigenous young people. *Australian & New Zealand Journal of Criminology, 52(1),* 111–128.

Charles, G. (2015). Doomed to repeat it: The selective and collective ignorance of the shadowy historical foundations of child and youth care. *International Child and Youth Care, 200,* 52–58.

Charles, G., & Gabor, P. (2006). An historical perspective on residential services for troubled and troubling youth in Canada revisited. *Relational Child and Youth Care Practice, 19(4),* 17–26.

Charles, G., & Garfat, T. (2013). Child and youth care practice in North America. In P. Share & K. Laror (Eds.), *Applied social care: An introduction for students in Ireland* (3rd ed., pp. 35–45). Dublin, Ireland: Gill & Macmillan.

Chartrand, L., & Horn, K. (2016). *A report on the relationship between restorative justice and Indigenous legal traditions in Canada.* Ottawa, ON: Justice Canada.

Corrado, R., Freedman, L., & Blatier, C. (2011). The over-representation of children in care in the youth criminal justice system in British Columbia: Theory and policy issues. *International Journal of Child, Youth and Family Studies, 2(1/2),* 99–118.

Dandurand, Y., & Griffiths, C. T. (2006). *Handbook of restorative justice programmes: Criminal justice handbook series.* New York, NY: United Nations Office on Drugs and Crime.

Demerson, V. (2004). *Incorrigible.* Waterloo, ON: Wilfred Laurier Press.

Department of Justice Canada. (2013). *The Youth Criminal Justice Act: Summary and background.* Ottawa, ON: Justice Canada.

Department of Justice Canada. (2017). *Spotlight on Gladue: Challenges, experiences, and possibilities in Canada's criminal justice system.* Ottawa, ON: Justice Canada.

Dowden, C. (2003). *The effectiveness of substance abuse treatment with young offenders.* Ottawa, ON: Justice Canada.

Elman, I. (2016). *Feathers of hope: Justice and juries—A First Nations youth action plan for justice.* Toronto, ON: Office of the Provincial Advocate for Children and Youth.

Elman, I., & Zinger, I. (2017). *Missed opportunities: The experience of young adults incarcerated in federal penitentiaries.* Toronto, ON: Provincial Advocate for Children and Youth.

Gailly, P. (2003). *Restorative justice in England and Wales.* Liège, Belgium: Actions Réparatrices, Prestations et Guidances Educatives (ARPEGE).

Gharabaghi, K. (2019). *A hard place to call home: A Canadian perspective on residential care and treatment for children and youth.* Toronto, ON: Canadian Scholars' Press.

Green, R. (2012). Explaining the *Youth Justice Act.* In J. Winterdyk & R. Smandych (Eds.), *Youth at risk and youth justice: A Canadian perspective* (pp. 54–79). Don Mills, ON: Oxford University Press.

Houston, S. E. (1972). Victorian origins of juvenile delinquency: A Canadian experience. *History of Education Quarterly, 2*(3), 254–280.

Johnstone, G. (2011). *Restorative justice: Ideas, values, debates* (2nd Ed.). New York: Routledge.

Kendall, P., & Turpel Lafond, M. E. (2009). *Kids, crime and care. Health and well-being of children in care: Youth justice experiences and outcomes.* Special Joint Report. Victoria, BC: Office of the British Columbia Representative for Children and Youth.

Kohli, M. (2003). *The golden bridge: Young immigrants to Canada, 1833–1939.* Toronto, ON: Dundurn Press.

Liebmann, M. (2000). *Mediation in context.* Philadelphia, PA: Jessica Kingsley Publishers.

Malakieh, J. (2018). *Adult and youth correctional statistics in Canada, 2016/2017.* Ottawa, ON: Statistics Canada Canadian Centre for Justice Statistics.

Marshall, T. F. (1996). The evolution of restorative justice in Britain. *European Journal on Criminal Policy and Research, 4*(4), 31–43.

Myers, T. (2006). *Caught: Montreal's modern girls and the law, 1869–1945.* Toronto, ON: University of Toronto Press.

Oudshoorn, J. (2015). *Trauma-informed youth justice in Canada: A new framework toward a kinder future.* Toronto, ON: Canadian Scholars' Press.

Pinchbeck, I., & Hewitt, M. (1973). *Children in English society* (Vol. 2). Toronto, ON: University of Toronto Press.

Rooke, P. T., & Schnell, R. L. (1983). *Discarding the asylum: From child rescue to the welfare state in English-Canada (1800–1950).* Lanham, MD: University Press of America.

Smandych, R. (2012). From "misguided children" to "criminal youth": Exploring historical and contemporary trends in Canadian youth justice. In R. Smandych & J. Winterdyk, *Youth at risk and youth justice: A Canadian overview* (pp. 3–25). Don Mills, ON: Oxford University Press.

Statistics Canada. (2018). *Adult and youth correctional statistics in Canada, 2016/2017.* Statistics Canada Catalogue No. 1209–6393. Ottawa, ON: Statistics Canada.

Truth and Reconciliation Commission of Canada (2015). *Calls to action.* Winnipeg, MB: Truth and Reconciliation Commission of Canada.

Umbreit, M. S. (2000). *Family group conferencing: Implications for crime victims.* Washington, DC: Office of Justice Programs, Office for Victims of Crime, US Department of Justice.

Verbrugge, P. (2003). *Fetal Alcohol Spectrum Disorder and the youth criminal justice system: A discussion paper.* Ottawa, ON: Justice Canada.

Wheatley, T. (2013). *"And neither do I have wings to fly": Labeled and locked up in Canada's oldest institution.* Toronto, ON: INANNA Publications.

Zehr, H. (2005). *Changing lenses: A new focus for crime and justice* (3rd ed.). Scottsdale, PA: Herald Press.

Zehr, H. (2014). *The little book of restorative justice.* New York, NY: Skyhorse Publishing.

CHAPTER 11

The Other, Forgotten, Hidden, Current, and Future Settings of Child and Youth Care Practice

Kiaras Gharabaghi and Grant Charles

INTRODUCTION

Child and youth care practice, in its narrow, professional designation or in its expanded, relational form, is ubiquitous. In both volume 1 and this volume, we have been able to feature many different sectors and contexts where child and youth care practice is present, established, or emerging, and where a particular way of being with young people, in the context of their families and communities, is relevant. Our initial ambition was to capture every sector and context where this might be the case. In some cases, it would be quite possible to produce a well-referenced chapter on specific service contexts. For example, Canada has produced several major researchers in the transitioning from care context doing their work from a child and youth care perspective; certainly Varda Mann-Feder comes to mind (Mann-Feder & Goyette, 2019; Mann-Feder, 2018; Mann-Feder, 2007). In other contexts, we learned quickly that this is not yet possible for at least two reasons. First, although child and youth care practice may be present and play a role in a particular sector or context, there is not yet enough of a presence to be able to write about it—at least not a whole chapter. Second, many sectors and contexts have evolved either without specific professional designations or with assumptions about specific expertise or skills that are not usually associated with child and youth care practice. And still, these are all sectors and contexts where being with young people in relational ways, in their life-space, and directed by their perspectives and experiences, is acutely relevant.

To this end, we are writing this final chapter to acknowledge the breadth of possibilities associated with child and youth care practice, and also the limitations associated with editing a book on this practice across sectors. In reality, we simply were not able to secure authors to ensure all the sectors and contexts of relevance are covered. We may not know a lot about how child and youth care practice is manifested in some of the contexts we will cover in this chapter, but our professional and academic experiences will suffice to at least briefly discuss areas of practice in which child and youth care practitioners have found opportunities to utilize their specific skills and values, and where child and youth care as "a way of being in the world" (Garfat, Freeman, Gharabaghi, & Fulcher, 2018) is making, or certainly could make, a significant difference. In total, we have identified 10 such sectors and contexts: policy and government, advocacy, international child and youth care practice, transition work, secure care, management and leadership, AfroFuturism, the Acquired Brain Injury sector, private practice, and addictions and harm reduction. We will discuss each of them briefly, and in some cases, we have asked our colleagues in the field to contribute their understanding and ways of thinking about a particular sector or context. What follows below, then, is a long list of possibilities and opportunities for our field, which range from private practice to international practice, and from leadership and management contexts to AfroFuturism. The structure of this chapter is somewhat *ad hoc*; by this we mean simply to say that as editors of the volume, we relied on partners and collaborators to provide a brief insight into other sectors and contexts reflecting their more in-depth involvement. We'll first present our contributions to this chapter, followed by a series of short insights into other sectors and contexts contributed by others.

THE POLICY AND GOVERNMENT SECTOR

Child and youth care practice is not necessarily front-line practice. This is, in and of itself, a bold statement, given that the field was really built on being with young people in their life-space, and using daily life events as a therapeutic, strength-based framework for guiding young people towards change (Garfat, Freeman, Gharabaghi, & Fulcher, 2018). Policy work, and more generally working for government, does not intuitively lend itself towards this way of being in the world. Quite the contrary, it is not infrequent that child and youth care practitioners find themselves working in resistance to policy and to government directions that appear to disadvantage young people involved with public systems of service. Yet, increasingly, we find that graduates from child and youth care programs enter government bureaucracies to work in policy development and policy analysis areas related to children, youth, families, and community. They do so in the hopes of changing policy approaches such that young people's life circumstances, their specific needs, and their voices become centred in bureaucratic decision-making. This is not without merit. It is, in fact, the case that government departments are constantly working to adjust legislative and regulatory aspects of child and youth services, sometimes without due consideration of the impacts of such changes to children and youth, their families, and their communities.

One area where a child and youth care perspective can, and has, made a difference is the residential care sector, where government policies impact everything from admission criteria to food services, and from case management approaches to the handling of serious occurrences. In Canada, residential care settings are subject to licensing processes carried out by government, and these processes do impact the everyday experience of young people placed in these settings. Child and youth care practitioners involved in the policy process are able to ensure that the inclusion of youth voice, for example, is more than just rhetoric, and work to include tangible and concrete procedural elements of residential care, such as complaint procedures and placement review processes, that centre youth voices. In the context of handling serious occurrences, child and youth care practitioners can work alongside other professionals and bureaucrats to ensure that the processes and the accountability embedded in serious occurrence reporting actually speak to the experiences of young people while such occurrences are unfolding. More generally across child welfare themes and processes, a child and youth care perspective can ensure that whatever policies may govern this sector, they take account of issues and themes that are integral to the well-being of young people and their families and communities, including avoiding policies that explicitly perpetuate the well-embedded racism of child welfare processes.

Policy and government work with child and youth care participation is not exclusive to the provincial or federal levels. Many child and youth care practitioners have taken on municipal-level positions in the policy area. In these positions, a child and youth care perspective informs policies and regulations pertaining to the youth homelessness sector, which in most jurisdictions in Canada falls under municipal oversight. Also relevant are policy areas related to housing, public transportation, recreational facilities, and child care services. These areas have a major impact on the young people typically encountered by child and youth care practitioners in service settings. For example, young women aging out of child welfare or child and youth mental health services often experience pregnancy and require access to child care in order to continue a pathway towards education and employment. The unique needs of homeless youth are often excluded from public transportation planning processes, and social housing is, of course, a core foundation for building more inclusive and healthier communities.

The need for child and youth care participation in policy processes and in government more generally is clear: almost everything that unfolds in public services unfolds without consideration of the unique needs and life circumstances of young people, their families, and their communities, with whom child and youth care practitioners engage across service sectors. When child and youth care practitioners do contribute to policy development processes, such processes unfold differently. In Ontario, we can cite the 2016 residential service review *Because Young People Matter* (Gharabaghi, Trocme, & Newman, 2016), as well as the 2018 coroner's review *Safe with Intervention* (Office of the Chief Coroner, 2018) as examples where child and youth care voices ensured that processes were taking account of the everyday realities faced by young people and the possible solutions to embedded problems emanating from the approaches and skill sets of child and youth care practitioners. Both these processes were led by or involved in significant ways child and youth care practitioners.

ADVOCACY

Child and youth care practice has been involved in advocacy work for decades. This is true across all sectors and contexts covered in this two-volume series. Although the field evolved as a direct practice profession, client-level advocacy activities have been part of the work from the beginning. This is at least in part because child and youth care practice has often been deployed to carry out direct service activities in support of case management and treatment coordination carried out by other professionals, often social workers, but also teachers, lawyers, psychologists, psychiatrists, doctors, and others. Not surprisingly, the perspectives of professionals who have only sporadic contact with young people, commonly in office settings, courtrooms, hospital rooms, or other professional settings, are often found to be incongruent with the observations of child and youth care practitioners who are with children and youth 24/7. Given the explicit focus on relationships embedded in child and youth care practice, the worker–client dyad frequently becomes a source of advocacy imperatives. Young people, according to child and youth care practitioners, far too often are not heard, not seen, and treated as if they were objects to be moved around. In these circumstances, practitioners become activated as advocates, and they serve this role particularly well when they advocate *with* young people rather than *for* them.

In spite of the long-standing connection between child and youth care practice and advocacy, there are limitations when we rely on practitioners employed by service organizations to advocate on behalf of or with young people served within those organizations. In reality, there are far too many political and organizational barriers to meaningfully address the problems and injustices characteristic of social and community services. Not all advocacy activities can meaningfully be carried out at the client level; often, systemic advocacy is necessary, particularly in the contexts of institutional racism and other forms of institutionalized oppression. Perhaps even more fundamentally, despite international and local articulations of child and youth rights through instruments such as the United Nations Convention on the Rights of the Child or provincial legislation related to child, youth, and family services, there are many instances when these well-articulated and clearly delineated rights are not observed. Such instances can relate to issues that affect all young people engaged with services (such as control of food in residential settings; see Gharabaghi & Charles, volume 1), or they can relate to particular groups of young people, such as Black Youth (see Hasford, Amponsah, Edwards, & Stephen, this volume; Batasar-Johnie & Gharabaghi, this volume), Indigenous young people and their communities (see de Finney et al., this volume; Ineese-Nash, this volume), Trans youth (see James, volume 1), or autistic youth (see Marshall, volume 1).

Systemic advocacy in the context of child and youth services has been professionalized across most provinces in Canada, and typically has been subject to a legitimation process through the establishment of independent child and youth advocacy offices[1] across the country (independent in the sense that these report to their respective provincial parliaments or assemblies rather than the government of the day). Provincial advocates have taken up systemic issues ranging from the ongoing oppression of Indigenous youth and their communities in child welfare systems, to the overrepresentation of Black Youth in coercive systems such as youth justice and child welfare in Ontario, to problems related to young people transitioning out of care. They have also tackled issues related to LGBTQ+ youth communities, Deaf youth communities, and youth with disabilities, amongst others. The work of advocacy at the system level is almost always informed by the voices of young people, and child and youth care practitioners are often employed to curate those voices. In fact, the relational context of child and youth care practice, both in interpersonal contexts as well as group contexts, has proven to be an effective framework within which the voices of young people involved in service systems find expression.

Perhaps one of the core areas of advocacy in child and youth care that is beginning to emerge more strongly and with greater assertiveness is that of anti-racism, notably anti-Black racism in Ontario, Quebec, and Nova Scotia and anti-Indigenous racism there and everywhere else. Anti-racism advocacy manifests itself through a duality: on the one hand, the specific experiences of Black Youth and Indigenous young people and their communities are centred in efforts to identify and resist deeply embedded institutional forms of racism; on the other hand, anti-racism advocates from within the field of child and youth care and others involved in youth care are clear on their critical perspectives of the field itself, which is seen as largely white in its ontological, epistemological, and practice-based manifestations (Vachon, 2018; Gharabaghi, 2016).

The fundamental premise of advocacy in child and youth care at any level is that ethical child and youth care praxis (White, 2007) requires not only an interpersonal connection with one young person, but an active and, if possible, revolutionary (Skott-Myhre, 2008) engagement with the social and political context in which such praxis unfolds.

INTERNATIONAL CHILD AND YOUTH CARE PRACTICE

While this two-volume series has focused on the Canadian context of child and youth care practice, there are in fact many Canadian child and youth care practitioners interested and already active in child and youth care practice in other countries around the world. Indeed, child and youth care practice, often known by different names, exists almost everywhere in the world. In Europe, much of what has been discussed across the two volumes of this series unfolds either under the umbrella of social pedagogy (especially in Central and Northern Europe) or psychoeducation (France and French-speaking countries). In some countries, notably the UK, but also Portugal and commonly Spain, child and youth care practice is a sub-discipline of social work. In South Africa, and increasingly in other African countries such as Kenya, Namibia, and Zambia, it is a recognized profession that is regulated through government-controlled qualification standards. In Australia and New Zealand, it is framed as community practice and either located within social work or as its own community service program in post-secondary institutions. In much of the rest of the world, child and youth care practice unfolds informally, through volunteers or employed people engaging children and youth on the streets, in marginalized neighbourhoods, and often also in schools. And international organizations such as UNICEF, Save the Children, Oxfam, and others employ people to do what we might recognize as informal child and youth care practice, at least in the sense that they are asked to be with young people wherever their lives unfold.

International child and youth care practice offers a world of opportunity for practitioners open to new experiences and different ways of thinking and doing things. On the one hand, institutional structures around the world often have similar features; residential care in Germany looks and feels quite similar to what we have in Canada, although the conversations about residential care can be substantially different, based on a strong orientation towards a subject–agency humanism embedded in social pedagogy. On the other hand, a great deal of youth work, broadly defined, unfolds in much less formal spaces, in rural areas, and on the streets. While some countries, such as South Africa and Israel, have highly organized professional structures, other countries, such as Brazil and India, do not, and yet youth work in all of these jurisdictions continues to value relationships, being in the moment, meeting young people where they are at, and maintaining strong orientations towards child and youth rights.

Professional opportunities to work with children and youth around the world are nearly endless. Canadian child and youth care practitioners interested in pursuing these need to be mindful of at least three core features of international practice: (1) you are impacting people's lives in the context of land, culture, language, and histories that are not yours—humility is therefore essential; (2) the conditions of work vary significantly across geographies, and often there are no regulations governing these conditions—flexibility and a very strong sense of self are required to manage these uncertainties; and (3) international work with children and youth often has transnational dimensions—it involves agencies and organizations that are global in scope, such as UNICEF, the Red Cross, Save the Children, and others, but it also involves young people whose identities and histories are often not limited to the land on which we encounter them. Many young people are products of colonialism, arbitrary movements, and forced migrations across borders. It is therefore essential to be led by young people even more so that one might be accustomed to in the relatively settled contexts of richer nations.

Finally, international child and youth care practice usually does not fit neatly into particular service sectors. The needs of young people and their communities are multidimensional and almost always include health care, legal, education, and survival and subsistence needs. This requires a much more fine-tuned capacity to work in teams with people able to think through the complexity of such multidimensional needs.

TRANSITION WORK

Much of the child and youth services sector involves young people transitioning; they may be transitioning from one service to another, or from a service to family or vice versa, or they may be transitioning to independence or to the adult systems of services. Transition work in child and youth care practice has emerged as a service sector in its own right largely because most child and youth serving services are not funded to support transitioning either into them or out of them. As a result, particularly in the contexts of residential care and child welfare services more generally, there have long been major problems associated with the abrupt ending of services and young people finding themselves alone and extremely vulnerable. Practical issues related to housing, employment, education, and health care further complicate this initial period of post-services, resulting in very negative outcomes for many young people (Mann-Feder & Goyette, 2019; Snow & Mann-Feder, 2013).

Transition work is a service context that is extremely congruent with child and youth care practice. Unfolding largely outside of institutional structures, transition work involves being present with young people as they encounter both the practical challenges and the emotional hardships of exiting systems that, for better or for worse, were their home for a period of time. This work involves virtually all of the sectors and service contexts covered in this series. There is the work related to "undoing" the reliance on structure and adult surveillance in residential or foster care; there is advocacy work in order to respond to landlords, principals, employers, and others who may wish to find reasons to exclude the young person and withhold their entitlements and access to opportunities. There may well be a need for anti-racism work, or for settlement work, or for in-home support work, depending on the circumstances of the young person. But perhaps most importantly, there is a great deal of work to be done to assist a young person to find comfort in being alone, to find social networks that are helpful, and to learn about ways of coping with hardship, loneliness, mental health concerns, and difficult relationships (Gharabaghi, 2016). In other words, transition work requires the capacity to bring the full complexity of child and youth care practice to the moment, and to enrich that practice with additional knowledge and skills related to child and youth rights, trauma-informed practices, family systems, and broader institutional and social structures and their affiliated racism and oppressive features.

What sets transition work apart from the more traditional child and youth care sectors such as residential care (see Gharabaghi & Charles, volume 1), foster care (see Modlin & Leggett, volume 1), or even the education sector (see Batasar-Johnie & Gharabaghi, this volume) is that the work unfolds outside of any surveillance systems. It requires risk management strategies that, in turn, rely on the decisions of the young person when they are alone and must rely on their instincts and good judgment. Transition work can be frustrating; neither the social environment nor the young people themselves are particularly cooperative in terms of "doing the right thing." Young people living on their own are subject to enormous stigma and are often mistrusted by others. At the same time, public systems are not equipped to deal with the practical needs of young people as these arise; chronic poverty, mental health crises, pregnancy and sexual exploitation, addictions, and other issues thus become ever-present. In this way, transition work is as much about prevention as it is about early intervention into emerging problems that may be life altering. And yet, it is an area of practice that requires the practitioner to let go of their need for control. Ultimately, the quality of life associated with transitions is a function of young people's choices and judgment. As a practitioner, we are there to support, to guide when possible, and to provide fair warning when we see things go in the wrong direction.

Child and youth care practitioners are increasingly finding employment specifically geared towards supporting transitions. In Ontario, designated transition workers are funded by the provincial government and work on a caseload basis under the supervision of community agencies. Across Canada, many agencies and organizations that provide residential and fostering services are building transition support into their standard processes and procedures. In some organizations, this means that child and youth workers are assigned to young people as they age out of service provision, and they are tasked with ensuring that whatever comes next for young people is engaged by young people with support and back-up plans.

SECURE CARE

Secure care can easily be understood as a sub-sector of residential care; in fact, on the surface at least, secure care is simply residential care in a locked setting. We believe, however, that a locked setting generates some significant particularities that are uncharacteristic of residential care more generally, and that, therefore, it makes sense to think about this service sector apart from more traditional and open residential services. Both the profile of young people admitted to secure care settings and the work culture in these settings are unique. Many provinces and territories in Canada do not have secure care settings at all, and in other jurisdictions they remain highly controversial.

The definition of *secure care* can vary significantly across jurisdictions, although in Canada it generally refers to two categories of residential interventions—secure care and secure treatment. Both are locked settings. Secure treatment tends to be of a longer duration than secure care. Secure care tends to last for up to 90 days. The purpose of both is to intervene with young people who are deemed to be in danger of harming themselves and/or others (Charles, 2016a).

Seven provinces have legislation allowing for secure care or treatment (Charles, 2016a). British Columbia, Prince Edward Island, Newfoundland and Labrador, and the three territories do not have such legislation; they try to provide short-term safe environments by placing young people in secure acute care mental health or youth justice settings. While this may provide some level of safety to the person in severe crisis, it also runs the danger of pathologizing or criminalizing young people. This can have longer-term and sometimes significant life consequences for young people because of the stigmatization associated with both systems.

While the legislation varies between jurisdictions, all have significant legal safeguards built into them to ensure that the human rights of the young people are respected, while at the same time presenting an avenue to provide for the safety of the young person (Charles, 2016a). All of the legislation acknowledges that young people have the same right as adults for the protection from inappropriate confinement. Appeal and review mechanisms are built into the legislation.

The primary focus of secure programming should be upon the safety and stabilization of the young person (Warshawski, Charles, & Warf, 2017; Warshawski, Charles, Vo, Moore, & Jassemi, 2019). Stabilization serves to provide the young person with a limited time in a safe environment so that they can regain control of their lives. It is meant to provide the young person with the structure and the time to access and enhance their emotional and psychological regulation while at the same time having their physical and medical needs met. It provides them with the opportunity to interact once again with their environment in a nonreactive manner. Secure care can also serve as an opportunity for the young person's family/caregivers and the involved professionals to have a time out from the impact of trying to help someone who is experiencing a significant and often long-term ongoing crisis.

Child and youth care practice in a locked setting requires additional skills compared to an open or community environment. There are a number of reasons for this, but the primary one is that a young person coming into a secure care program is often in severe crisis. They would generally not be placed in a secure program unless they have been deemed at risk to harm themselves or others. In concrete terms, this means that any interventions with the young person in at least the recent past have been ineffective. Less intrusive crisis interventions have failed. Given that we all work hard to cope in times of crisis, by the time someone is placed in a secure setting, they have reached a level of psychological, physical, and spiritual fatigue that creates a downward spiral of destructive behaviour. It also means that not only is the young person deeply exhausted, but so are their families and the professionals trying to help them. This is conceptually important to understand. While the young person is the one being placed in a secure setting, they are often not the only person in crisis. Intervention in a secure setting needs to focus on helping the young person restore their existing inner strengths and learn new coping strategies. It also should involve assisting other people involved with the young person to do the same.

Another dynamic often evident in a young person in severe crisis but rarely talked about is fear. Any crisis that exhausts us to the point where we are truly no longer coping involves a deep sense of being out of control. This feeling can be terrifying, and once we begin to experience it, the crisis can rapidly accelerate, increasing the likelihood that we could harm ourselves or others. The deeper the fear becomes, the more likely we are to strike out at others or hurt ourselves in an attempt to regain control of the situation. Interventions here need to focus on helping the young person experience a sense of safety. This can be achieved through creating a nurturing environment where the young person feels that they are not alone and where they feel they matter to others. Fear is counterbalanced by connection. This is not easy in a locked setting, but is essential to a positive outcome. A key way we can begin to access our own inner strengths again is through relationship with others.

The other dynamic that changes in a secure setting compared to other less intrusive interventions is the power differentiation between the staff and the young person. There can be no doubt that there is a significant power imbalance between staff and residents in a locked setting. Not only is the setting secure, with all of the ramifications that this brings, but the young people are in a highly vulnerable state regardless of how their behaviour may seem to others. This means that practitioners have to be acutely aware of the boundaries between themselves and young people. What may be considered appropriate boundaries in an open setting might feel far too intrusive in a locked setting, especially during the initial placement when the young person is still in acute crisis. It is also important that we accept that the power imbalance exists, and, as such, it is critical that we take the time to see how our actions may appear to the young person. It is important to remember that our intentions do not always match how the other person sees them.

Secure programs function most effectively when they are part of an integrated service network that includes programs meant to minimize the number of young people needing to be placed in locked settings (Charles, 2016b). Ideally, this includes family support, community crisis, and access to appropriate mental health and substance misuse services. While secure programs are a critical service in a well-structured service system, it is possible to decrease the need for them.

MANAGEMENT AND LEADERSHIP

by Ernie Hilton

It is not for everyone. Many times, those who desire to be "managers" are entirely unsuited, yet meet the simplistic criteria often associated with being promoted to a management position. A manager is generally tasked with duties and structural outputs, which become their measurement of proficiency and efficacy as experienced by subordinates and senior managers. Even language generally used to describe a manager sounds heartless and void of affect. Leadership, on the other hand, can be a self-appointed process because of such things as a title or a position. These titles or positions are recognized and located at the apex of an environment, such as the head of a classroom, front of a parade, whoever has written the most books, or an executive director/CEO/owner of a service delivery operation. These positions force followers to listen, read, watch, or endure their positional power, go elsewhere, or revolt. There is regularly much confusion about the concepts of leadership and management. However, there is more clarity about the negative connotations associated with being a manager and the prestige of being called a leader.

Leadership

Leadership is indisputably decided by one's ability to influence. Research into power relationships have taught us about five types of power: positional, coercive, referent, expert, and reward. In my own subjective observations inside a residential care setting, leadership is the result of an ability to influence another, the power of influence unattached to the other types of power. It appears a leader is able to trigger, some say inspire, in others a desire to attach themselves to or emulate the activities of the leader. The tell-tale sign of whether you are a leader, then, is if others will follow or emulate you without being oppressed by the above five types of power. Leadership is credibly communicating or validating ideas that influence other people's decisions. This is done by describing a goal, or through daily behaviours.

Whether someone is a good or bad leader remains subjective depending on the perspective of the followers or the protestors. My personal preference is influencing versus commanding as a more effective response in child and youth care (CYC), as it's closer to the characteristics associated with our defined relational approach. Followers initially create the first appearance and presence of a leader. I ask you this: What are the four or five remarkable qualities of that person you follow, and why have you chosen to follow them? If the answers are one of the five types of power, notice you are following and why it is a conscious choice. Be sure you have a goal to evolve past your current defined leader—do not simply imitate.

Both leadership and management exist to influence behaviour—one is not better than the other.

Management

All too often, the vacant position of a manager will attract a power-seeking individual versus an influence-seeking candidate. By power-seeking, I imply an unconscious desire to control the environment and be profoundly liked for doing so. It is almost always a nightmare process onboarding a new manager without a scaffolding of required developmental training to ease the potential manager into an accountable managerial role. I say *accountable* because it is different from responsible and especially from self-responsible. Sometimes, a new manager has a very inaccurate idea of what to expect as they enter the world of management. Basically, they expect to help others by doing what other managers were not able to do properly. Some might expect to receive adoration for their sacrifices, and that to be questioned about a decision is an abomination of their title. Others might begin their managerial journey with a perspective of a firefighter or an Avenger with hands on their hips as they enter the CYC unit exclaiming, "I have arrived!" . . . oh dear. Arrogance associated with positional power at any level of organizational functioning is detrimental to any service delivery model that supports relational practice.

Here is my truth, based on my 30 years as a manager. It is an appointed position that asks the incumbent to evolve to their highest level of capacity. More experienced managers must mitigate the potential havoc wreaked by new managers on "subordinates" or "direct reports" (managerial language is offensive but efficient) and the service model, including those who are intended to be served by the organization.

At first, managers need to learn to be responsible and "create contexts of safety" (Phelan, 2003). They must learn to explain *what* happened without blaming anyone or anything for their actions, similar to a CYC practitioner on the floor with youth. Their proficiency must evolve quickly to have a sense of accountability without blame and explain *what, why, and how* it happened. Finally, with the goal of becoming a "self-authored" manager as an end result, a manager evolves into being self-responsible in addition to being accountable (Modlin, 2017).

A service provider is accountable to multiple stakeholders, such as clients, employees, boards of directors, benefactors, donors, joint partnerships, governments for funding, and service-level agreements. Management has the responsibility to ensure there is focus on encouraging the best behaviours, not the right job titles, or risks losing it all. The needs of the many will always outweigh the needs of the few and the one. Management must have a focus on supporting and enforcing (yes, I am aware of what this implies) structures and behaviours that

- inspire others to act,
- model the way,
- share a vison,
- challenge the status quo,
- enable others to act, and
- encourage the heart.

If you have a need to be liked, never consider being a manager. If serving a purpose greater than yourself is your passion, sign up today—the CYC field needs you.

AFROFUTURISM

by Juanita Stephen

> Between fantasy and exact knowledge, between drama and technology, there is an intermediate station: that of magic. It was in magic that the

general conquest of the external environment was decisively instituted. For the magicians not only believed in marvels but audaciously sought to work them: by their straining after the exceptional, the natural philosophers who followed them were first given a clue to the regular.
—Lewis Mumford (1934, p. 149)

Both a philosophy of art and of history, AfroFuturism explores the themes and concerns of the diasporic peoples of Africa through technology, science fiction, and fantasy. In the spirit of the Akan tradition of Sankofa, AfroFuturism is centred on stories and images of a projected future that is grounded in an understanding of the past. AfroFuturistic scholar and founder of the Black Speculative Arts Movement, Reynaldo Anderson (2016), describes it in this way:

> Future-looking Black scholars, artists, and activists are not only reclaiming their right to tell their own stories, but also to critique the European/American digerati class of their narratives about cultural others, past, present and future and, challenging their presumed authority to be the sole interpreters of Black lives and Black futures. (p. 228)

In short, it is one means through which the African diaspora is reclaiming authority over their own stories and the possibilities for their own lives. As a genre, AfroFuturism embraces and celebrates the multi-dimensionality of Blackness, building on historical movements (such as Negritude and the Harlem Renaissance) and the works of academics such as W. E. B. Du Bois and Richard Wright, who have provided a critical lens to Black identity as it relates to speculative thought. AfroFuturism provides space for the voices of Black folks to establish and explore identities that are as closely tied to or distantly removed from Western constructs of gender and sexuality as they would like. It provides opportunities to define the meaning and value of transnational identities, to free Black bodies from the policing that they are subject to in the realities of the Western here and now. Technology, as a central tenet, offers the possibility of a barrier-free existence for differing abilities, and African spiritualities are not only normalized but honoured as an integral part of African ways of knowing. In many ways, AfroFuturism provides a much-needed vehicle to explore the nuanced complexities and fullness of personhoods that is not often afforded to African-descendant people living in the "West."

As the demand for a critical restructuring of child and youth care in Canada grows stronger—a restructuring that would engage critical race and critical feminist thought, that would pull from queer theory and critical disability studies, and that would integrate the scholarship of Indigenous and Black scholars—AfroFuturism offers an example of how the field and practitioners within it might begin to shift the default centre of existing narratives of care and capacity. This fantastical Afro-technological philosophy should not be understood as an escape from reality, but rather as a critical lens that can be used to challenge the status quo and as a potential avenue for the construction of a more culturally relevant profession that we have not yet had the courage to imagine.

THE ACQUIRED BRAIN INJURY (ABI) SECTOR

by Pat Gaughan

Although not a widely known or understood child and youth care practice area, the role of the rehabilitation support worker (RSW) came to fruition over 30 years ago, providing hospital-based, residential, and community support to individuals who have suffered an Acquired Brain Injury (ABI) as a result of a motor vehicle accident or other serious trauma. Given the behavioural issues associated with an ABI, it is no surprise that the first practitioners to provide support and treatment to those with ABIs were CYC practitioners, assuming the title and role of an RSW.

I recently read an article by Thom Garfat, James Freeman, Kiaras Gharabaghi, and Leon Fulcher (2018) titled "Characteristics of a Relational Child and Youth Care Approach Revisited" that, as these articles always do, triggered a number of thoughts about CYC practice and its continued evolution and the opportunities available to provide service across sectors. In the article, the authors argue that it was not long ago that the work of CYC practitioners was considered a sub-profession and the workers themselves were considered simply to be extensions of other helping professionals, but with the passage of time and the evolution of a distinct method of practice, CYC practitioners have come to be recognized as possessing a specific expertise and a unique approach to working with children, youth, and families. I would add adults and seniors to a CYC practitioner's expertise, given that their experience, education, and ongoing training are seamlessly transferred to older age groups. As for being an extension of other helping professions, I have never experienced this as a roadblock or a limitation to the profession. In fact, it is one of the greatest opportunities available to today's CYC practitioners, given their unique skills and abilities to incorporate different treatment modalities into their daily work with individuals of all ages, not to mention their comfort level in accepting oversight from other health care professionals when it is in the best interest of the individuals they support.

Although opportunities for CYC practitioners are available in both the public and private sector to support individuals with an ABI, my main focus is on the opportunities in the private, regulated sector, as limited funding in the public sector restricts families from accessing services and limits opportunities for experienced practitioners.

The role of the RSW in the brain injury sector focuses on providing community reintegration and transitional support, which includes assisting in the assessment of an individual's functional behaviour and cognitive skills and contributing to the design and delivery of treatment programs aimed at reducing the impact of impairments, promoting independence, and improving quality of life. Support may include personal and domestic activities of daily living, leisure/school/work integration, coaching, mentoring and training, and skill acquisition. Using a strength-based, relational approach, this service is almost always provided across all aspects of an individual's daily life, as well as across myriad life-spaces such as community, home, school, vocation, hospital, and residential settings. The main focus is to assist the individual to reach their maximum level of functional independence following their accident.

Given their strength-based approach and their ability to "do with" in the daily lives of their clients, CYC practitioners are an excellent match for the role of an RSW. Of equal importance, and one of the key roles of CYC practitioners working as RSWs, is not only their training but their comfort level in understanding and supporting individuals who are exhibiting moderate to severe behaviour, a common occurrence for individuals recovering from an ABI.

Circling back to CYC as an extension to other health care professionals, it is important to mention that in the private, regulated ABI sector, CYC practitioners in the role of a Rehabilitation Support Worker are unable to provide service unless a treatment plan is approved by a regulated health care professional, who, in turn, develops the goals and provides oversight to the service being provided. These regulated health care professionals are generally occupational therapists, speech and language therapists, psychologists, and social workers.

Although this may appear as a limitation to a CYC practitioner's practice, it actually creates a number of opportunities for them to not only provide their unique support but also to assist in the implementation of other health care professionals' treatment goals. Given their strength-based approach, relationship skills, and ability to work every day in a client's individual life-space, they often assist in the implementation of physiotherapy, occupational therapy, and social work goals and interventions.

Given that many of these regulated health care professionals have not received adequate training in supporting individuals exhibiting moderate to severe behaviour, the CYC practitioner is perfectly suited to implement these treatment goals, while at the same time having the expertise and training to recognize triggers and be comfortable understanding the behaviours associated with relearning skills following a brain injury. The CYC practitioner is able to assist in the implementation of the treatment plan on all levels, evaluate progress, provide feedback to the treatment team, and offer suggestions and revisions to the treatment plan and related goals. They are a perfect fit for this role.

Sadly, of all types of injuries, brain injury is the most likely to result in permanent disability, and given the fact that 30 percent of all brain injuries in Canada are suffered by children and youth (Brain Injury Society of Toronto, n.d.), causing physical, cognitive, emotional, and behavioural challenges, the assistance of a CYC in an individual's recovery and treatment is imperative.

Although there is training specific to ABI available through provincial brain injury associations and various universities, targeted curriculum in college- and university-level CYC/CYW programs would better prepare students who would like to specialize in this specific sector. Given their education and training, the CYC practitioner, going forward, has endless opportunities to work across sectors, giving them career options they can continue to practise for years to come.

PRIVATE PRACTICE

by Bill Carty, with Luke Carty

Private practice for unregulated life-space child and youth care practitioners is not an easy one to define. Private practice often refers to a wide range of regulated professionals who, for a variety of reasons, decide to offer their services directly to the public or to organizations as a single practitioner. Some practitioners occasionally join others to form a type of consortium that offers services as a group. This type of arrangement allows for more detailed and involved work to be taken on, as well as coverage for the practitioner to their clients, by a group member, when they are unavailable. There are also group and individual supervision options available as a member of a larger team of private practitioners.

Child and youth care practice, while not currently regulated, *is* provincially mandated in Ontario, so there are a wide range of educational programs that are governed at the provincial level. Training opportunities vary from province to province and geographically in each province, with urban centres having much more availability than rural settings. Another key differential in terms of practice is that each sector—health, education, social services, child welfare, and youth justice—have different expectations, standards, and procedures that child and youth care practitioners are required to meet and follow.

In the profession of child and youth care, certification is starting to be completed and recognized in some areas of the country, so that cost of services can be covered by insurance plans. Additionally, CYC-trained practitioners can offer their services as consultants, trainers, and practitioners to organizations and directly to the public and have their fees covered either by the contracted organization or by the consumer directly. Another alternative that has developed in child and youth care is the one where an organization is formed that contracts with other organizations in health, education, social service, and youth justice, as well as with families directly, and then contracts with practitioners to provide their professional service to the "customer." The practitioner is independent of the company and contracts with the company for agreed-upon services as well as professional fees to be received.

It should be noted that this third alternative has been exploited over the past few decades to the point where community organizations use this model, at times, to "contract out" service for financial savings rather than to enrich the service offerings in their organizations and agencies. Child and youth care practitioners in these situations are often exploited so that the price can be kept low and margins for the contracting company kept high so that the benefit, economically, goes to the agencies and organizations utilizing the service and to the contracting company for providing the workers. Clearly, in these situations, the losers are the CYC practitioners and, ultimately, the children, adolescents, and families receiving the services.

This writer suggests that ethical, professional, and effective child and youth care private practice can be provided directly to families, agencies, and to third-party organizations, as long as the practitioner

- has completed professional training in child and youth care;
- has a sense of control in the offering of their services;
- has set their prices for service in accordance to their professional standards;

- ensures that they participate in continuing education programs to stay current on acceptable and effective practices;
- has the required experiential base to allow for comfort and competence in providing their service as a private practitioner;
- is able to access consultation and/or supervision, as required, to ensure the quality of their services; and
- maintains a professional network to ensure other professional services that may be required by their clients can be accessed without undue delay.

The other factor that all CYC private practitioners must be acutely aware of is the need to practise within their own set of skills and experience. The range of mental health, developmental, and familial problems is very wide, and no individual practitioner would have the necessary skill or abilities to deal with the range of challenges that children and adolescents have, in all age groups.

There have been a number of trailblazers across Canada, who after many years of experience and after developing expertise in a particular area have set up a more traditional office-based private practice. These practitioners have used the format that many private practitioners in allied disciplines use, which is the clinical hour model. Within this model, these practitioners have used child and youth care philosophy, theory, strategies, and interventions to assist children and adolescents. Often these practitioners have additional specific training like art, play, or family therapy to attract clients requiring specifically trained practitioners. These practitioners are often recognized within their communities as competent practitioners and have a referral base from other professional groups to sustain their practice. Additionally, many of these practitioners have often worked or continue to work in academic settings that provide training in child and youth care.

Looking Forward

The continued evolution of the profession of child and youth care will undoubtedly result in formal recognition of the work that is provided by practitioners. Being a regulated health care profession could lead to the private practice model becoming a real option for practitioners who would then more closely resemble other professionals in health care. The work, it is predicted, will continue to be meeting children, adolescents, and youth where "they are at," in their homes, schools, hospitals, and communities rather than an office-based focus that is common in other professions.

What a regulated profession would mean for consumers—children, adolescents, and their families—would be an additional option to assist them in dealing with challenges that they are facing: an option that tends to be competency-based and non-medical, and that searches for the strengths in the family and individuals to move forward.

ADDICTIONS AND HARM REDUCTION

by Stephanie Griffin

"I don't plan to work with addicted youth"—a comment heard every year in our college substance abuse course. There is a belief that this is an isolated population, and while residential drug treatment and addictions counselling is certainly an independent sector within broader human services, CYC practitioners (CYCPs) have a strong and important role to play in addictions and harm reduction work. Working with young people and families renders encounters with addictions inevitable, even if CYCPs may not formally be employed as addiction counsellors. Many drug treatment programs operate from a medical model approach (which centres disease). In the medical model, funding is often tied to diagnosis because labelling a client as an addict or alcoholic provides them access to funded services. CYCPs work from a variety of perspectives and incorporate a bio-psycho-social lens to addiction treatment. Recognizing the influence of social and environmental factors, CYCPs employ prevention and intervention techniques that work to address contributors beyond the microsystem of the client. Drug and alcohol treatment is a sector of work that has not received a lot of attention in CYC literature. It requires some specialized training, knowledge, and expertise that is not present in many post-secondary education programs, yet there is congruence between common addiction approaches, harm reduction philosophy, and child and youth care practice.

As a concept and a practice, harm reduction is difficult to define, but there are common principles agreed upon by researchers and practitioners (British Columbia Centre for Disease Control, 2011). Harm reduction is "aimed at reducing negative consequences associated with drug use. Harm reduction is also a movement for social justice built on a belief in, and response for, the rights of people who use drugs" (Harm Reduction Coalition, n.d., para 1). Core principles of harm reduction include a pragmatic perspective on drug use, human rights, maximizing intervention options, prioritizing immediate goals, and direct involvement of the drug user (British Columbia Centre for Disease Control, 2011). When viewed against the characteristics of a relational child and youth care approach (Garfat, Freeman, Gharabaghi, & Fulcher, 2018), the parallels are evident.

A harm reduction approach recognizes that drug use is a complex, multifaceted issue. CYCPs examine context and seek to address the continuum of behaviours that clients exhibit. As previously discussed in this chapter, advocacy is a key aspect of child and youth care practice. An important harm reduction principle ensures that drug users have a voice in the services provided to them. CYCPs work with young people, community agencies, and government policymakers to advocate for the rights and needs of substance users. Harm reduction does not require abstinence and provides clients with alternatives and options for their use that decrease risk and improve quality of life while still using. CYCPs meet young people where they are at and foster relationships that will help move the client towards change.

Addictions work requires the CYCP to navigate and often embrace resistance. Hanging in is necessary, as clients often resist treatment or interventions aimed at exploring their use. Working in their life-space and employing harm reduction principles, CYCPs naturally work to develop a therapeutic relationship with clients. Working with drug and alcohol addiction with street-involved youth, I learned that motivation is an interpersonal process. Through attending to the relationship, I was able to help youth make meaning of their substance use. There are many approaches to substance use treatment, but one of the most common is motivational interviewing (MI) (Miller & Rollnick, 1991). MI originated in the field of addictions and operates from a strengths-based perspective. Child and youth care practitioners are ideally suited to using MI in their practice with young people because, instead of counselling, it is a style of communication designed to mobilize an individual's internal motivation for change (Centre for Substance Abuse Treatment, 2012). Motivational interviewing is a way of being with clients that evokes client autonomy over their substance use. A key aspect of effective addiction intervention is increasing the youth's sense of self-efficacy. Helping them set goals and develop action plans and providing referrals and support are all part of helping clients address their substance use.

The skill set of child and youth care practitioners aligns with intervention and addiction treatment practices regardless of the milieu in which they are working. Opportunities for CYCPs to expand their practice into substance use treatment are increasing as outpatient programs, concurrent disorder programs, and community after-care programs grow in Canada.

AN EVER-EXPANDING FIELD OF PRACTICE

In this chapter, we have explored a number of sectors and service contexts that hold relevance for child and youth care practice. In some of these, child and youth care practitioners are already active; they may or may not work under the title "child and youth care," but they are relationally engaged in the life-space of young people, making meaning with young people of everyday life events (Freeman & Garfat, 2014). In others, child and youth care practitioners may not yet have found a way of exercising their skills and unique approach to being with young people, but surely this will change. All of these sectors and service contexts have in common a simple reality—many of the approaches in use to make a difference aren't working, or are not working entirely. The expansion of child and youth care practice confirms that the formality of social and human service provision, although useful in many ways, is not in and of itself sufficient. Young people live their lives in multiple contexts and spaces, and the presence of child and youth care practitioners in those spaces turns out to be essential.

The risk, of course, is that child and youth care, much like other professions, becomes ambitious, and begins to seek out roles and functions beyond its fundamental purpose and impact. A strong sense of humility, combined with nuanced and well-defined skills in interprofessional practices, will ensure that our field continues to find relevance across sectors and service contexts.

Finally, it is worthwhile pointing out that the field of child and youth care, not unlike many other professions, has not adequately addressed its origins in colonial and oppressive systems and institutions (see de Finney et al., this volume; Ineese-Nash, this volume). While it is good and encouraging that practitioners are finding ways of connecting with young people, their families, and their communities across sectors and service contexts, it is important that the field develop its capacity to critically engage with its own troubled histories, including its complicity in the cultural genocide of Indigenous peoples, its perpetuation of disservices to Black Youth and African Canadian communities, and its silence and complacency with respect to many other social groups that have found public and private helping systems to be not particularly helpful (see James, volume 1; Erlich, volume 1; Hasford, Amponsah, Edwards, & Stephen, this volume). These challenges continue and are unlikely to be resolved any time soon.

NOTE

1. In Ontario, the Conservative government of Doug Ford abolished this office in 2019, not long after gaining power. Ontario is now the only province in Canada where young people do not have a provincially appointed advocate to turn to. A complaints-based process for responding to young people's concerns has been established in the Office of the Ombudsman, but this office has no investigative powers and cannot engage in system-level advocacy efforts.

REFERENCES

Anderson, R. (2016). Afrofuturism 2.0 & the Black speculative arts movement: Notes on a manifesto. *Obsidian: Literature & Arts in the African Diaspora, 42*(1–2), 228. Retrieved from https://search-proquest-com.ezproxy.lib.ryerson.ca/docview/1935243846/fulltextPDF/35BF3CE5D5ED406APQ/1?accountid=13631

Brain Injury Society of Toronto. (n.d.). *Brain injury facts*. Retrieved from www.bist.ca

British Columbia Centre for Disease Control. (2011). *Harm reduction training manual: A manual for frontline staff involved with harm reduction strategies and services*. Vancouver, BC: British Columbia Centre for Disease Control.

Centre for Substance Abuse Treatment. (2012). *Enhancing motivation for change in substance abuse treatment*. Treatment Improvement Protocol (TIP) Series, No. 35. Rockville, MD: Substance Abuse and Mental Health Services.

Charles, G. (2016a). *Secure care summary report (part one): Secure care legislation*. Vancouver, BC: School of Social Work and Division of Adolescent Health and Medicine, Department of Pediatrics, Faculty of Medicine, University of British Columbia.

Charles, G. (2016b). *Secure care summary report (part two): Secure care as a component of an integrated service network model*. Vancouver, BC: School of Social Work and Division of Adolescent Health and Medicine, Department of Pediatrics, Faculty of Medicine, University of British Columbia.

Freeman, J., & Garfat, T. (2014). Being, interpreting, doing: A framework for organizing the characteristics of a relational child and youth care approach. *CYC-Online, 179*, 23–27.

Garfat, T., Freeman, J., Gharabaghi, K., & Fulcher, L. (2018, October). Characteristics of a relational child and youth care approach revisited. *CYC-Online, 236*. Retrieved from https://www.cyc-net.org/cyc-online/oct2018.pdf

Gharabaghi, K. (2016). Networked transitions: Ensuring continuity of care for young people from intake to emerging adulthood. *Relational Child & Youth Care Practice, 29*(1), 51–60.

Gharabaghi, K., Trocme, N., & Newman, D. (2016). *Because young people matter.* Retrieved from http://www.children.gov.on.ca/htdocs/English/documents/childrensaid/residential-services-review-panel-report-feb2016.pdf

Harm Reduction Coalition. (n.d.). *Principles of harm reduction.* Retrieved from https://harmreduction.org/about-us/principles-of-harm-reduction

Mann-Feder, V. (2007). Transition or eviction: Youth exiting care for independent living. *New Directions for Youth Development, 113*, 151–162.

Mann-Feder, V. (2018). (You gotta have) friends: Careleaving, friendships and agency interventions. *International Journal of Child, Youth and Family Studies, 9*(1), 154–167.

Mann-Feder, V., & Goyette, M. (Eds.) (2019). *Leaving care and the transition to adulthood: International contributions to theory, research and practice.* New York, NY: Oxford University Press.

Miller, W. R., & Rollnick, S. (1991). *Motivational interviewing: Preparing people to change addictive behaviour.* New York, NY: Guilford Press.

Modlin, H. (2017). Developmental considerations in training for child and youth care workers in residential care. *RCYCP Journal, 30*(1), 7–22. Retrieved from http://www.rcycp.com/docs/RCYCP_Vol30-1_sample.pdf

Mumford, L. (1934). *Technics and civilization.* New York: Harcourt, Brace & Company.

Office of the Chief Coroner (Ontario). (2018). *Safe with intervention: Report of the expert panel on the deaths of children and youth in residential placements.* Retrieved from https://www.mcscs.jus.gov.on.ca/sites/default/files/content/mcscs/docs/Safe%20With%20Intervention%20Report%20Final.pdf

Phelan, J. (2003). Stages of child and youth care worker development. *CYC-Net.* Retrieved from http://www.cyc-net.org/phelanstages.html

Skott-Myhre, H. (2008). *Youth and sub-culture as creative force: Creating new spaces for radical youth work.* Toronto: University of Toronto Press.

Snow, K., & Mann-Feder, V. (2013). Peer-centered practice: A theoretical framework for intervention with young people in and from care. *Child Welfare, 92*(4), 75–93.

Vachon, W. (2018, June). Child and youth care fragility. *CYC-Online, 232.* Retrieved from https://www.cyc-net.org/cyc-online/june2018.pdf#page=14

Warshawski, T., Charles, G., Vo, D., Moore, E., & Jassemi, S. (2019). Secure care can help youth reduce imminent risk of serious harm and prevent unnecessary death. *Canadian Medical Association Journal, 191*(7), E197.

Warshawski, T., Charles, G., & Warf, C. (2017). *Secure care policy brief.* Vancouver, BC: British Columbia Pediatric Society.

White, J. (2007). Knowing, doing, and being in context: A praxis-oriented approach to child and youth care. *Child & Youth Care Forum, 36*(5), 225–244.

CONCLUSION

Expansion and Consolidation: Where to from Here?

Kiaras Gharabaghi and Grant Charles

Fifty years ago, this two-volume series on child and youth care sectors in Canada would have been brief; a massive chapter on residential care and treatment, and perhaps a shorter chapter on emerging practice settings, would have adequately captured the breadth of the field. Fifty years is not a very long time in the development of a professional field. The enormous expansion of child and youth care (CYC) practice into sectors and settings well beyond residential care and treatment, and well beyond young people experiencing emotional difficulties or the consequences of child abuse and neglect, is notable, exciting, somewhat adventurous, and, we reluctantly have to acknowledge, not always a happy story. Of course, 50 years ago, child and youth care practice even in residential care settings wasn't such a happy story either. Notwithstanding the strong theoretical and practical contributions of pre-CYC academic celebrities, including Redl, Bettelheim, Aichhorn, Addams, Maier, and others, this was still a time of labelling family as the problem; of overt racism and even segregation; of Indian Residential Schools; of ongoing institutional settings and cultures reflecting systems of surveillance and coercion; and even of experimenting with young people's emotions and states of mind through all manner of bio-chemical interventions. Child and youth care emerged, at least in part, in response to these dynamics. Young people cried out for care—being cared for, cared about, and in caring relationships. The systems offered to them did not always offer care, nor did these systems have much of a professional infrastructure to provide care. A profession built on the idea of care provision, and the integration of care into relationships, became necessary.

Child and youth care expanded based on its strengths—the focus on relationships, the nature of care and care practices, the centring of young people and their voices (which was more central prior to the 1980s before once again largely disappearing as a practice until it re-emerged in the early 2000s), and the integration of an understanding of mental health, family systems, and ecological systems into an everyday approach to being with young people. This, it turned out, was useful not only in residential care settings, but also in education, in health care, in community, and across major service sectors such as child welfare, child and youth mental health, and youth justice.

Child and youth care practitioners are often multi-skilled professionals with a capacity to adapt to a wide range of service contexts, and with a strong sense of fluidity in the operationalization of their concepts and practice approaches. As such, they are an invaluable resource to service systems that struggle to meet the needs of the people they encounter. The complexity of people's needs, individually and as social groups, almost always extends beyond the structured and routinized delivery of pre-programmed services. Someone is always left out, giving rise to a difficult dynamic whereby people (youth, their families, and their communities) have to fit the service system rather than the other way around. At least part of the expansion of child and youth care across service sectors can also be understood from an economic perspective. When standardized or structured and routinized services are not enough, child and youth care practitioners are a relatively affordable way of customizing service for young people, and sometimes families and their communities. Notwithstanding the frequent expressions of frustrations on the part of child and youth care practitioners with respect to employment terms, compensation, under-valuing, lack of professional regulation and legislation, and being left out of decision-making, there are vested interests operating at much higher levels of service systems, indeed of social governance, that benefit from the availability of an affordable but extremely flexible, adaptable, competent, well-trained, and ultimately reliable workforce ready for just about anything. This is why, we believe, child and youth care practitioners now find themselves in such a huge range of contexts. From implementing Applied Behavioural Analysis in autism and developmental services fields to extended outdoor adventure trips, and from supporting young people through the transition from care to taking part in suicide prevention programs in Indigenous communities, a strong child and youth care practitioner seems like a reasonable response when other programs, other services, and other professions either cannot provide meaningful responses or prefer not to do so because they see themselves as having evolved beyond direct care practice.

The impacts of this expansion have yielded mixed results. On the one hand, we are delighted to see an application of child and youth care values and approaches across so many different settings, and we believe that practitioners in all of these settings are providing valuable services to young people, their families, and their communities. On the other hand, child and youth care practice has developed as a professional field without much thought or discussion about issues of inclusion and equity, and also without engaging what has been apparent for a long time—the presence of exclusions, minimizing, dismissing, and othering child and youth care practices that fall outside of dominant approaches to delineating the field itself. In other words, while the expansion of the field has intensified discussions about professionalization and demands for a recognized, regulated, and legislated professional field along the lines of other human service professions such as social work, nursing, or, more recently, early childhood education, it has also resulted in the setting of boundaries of what is considered within the professional practice and what might be interesting but outside of it. Credentials play a major part and complete an almost impenetrable circle of exclusion. To be within the profession, one must demonstrate an early commitment to the professional field by signing up for formal post-secondary education in the field, and by identifying oneself with the literature, the professional gatherings, and the professional associations of the field. Increasingly, there is a demand for demonstrating competencies, based on a testing format developed to separate those who are placed in positions of child and youth care without qualifications from those who are the "real" practitioners, the ones who can demonstrate conformity to a particular framework, a particular set of values and practices, that are said to constitute child and youth care practice (in chapter 3 of this volume—Hasford, Amponsah, Edwards, & Stephen—questions are raised about the potential racism embedded in some of the competency testing formats).

At the same time that the field is tightening up on its framework for practice through competencies and even accreditation standards in post-secondary education programs, the demand from communities and organizations for the care-oriented child and youth care practice that predates the self-regulation imposed by the field is increasing. In many cases, such care-oriented practice is mixed with specific orientations, adoption of evidence, and trauma-informed sets of practice cultures and approaches that bear little resemblance to the competencies and accreditation standards being imposed by the field itself. In fact, now more than ever, child and youth care practitioners are reinventing themselves to meet the demands of employers and service settings that fall outside of any one professional orientation and that often unfold in settings and service contexts that transcend the field's traditional sectors.

In these two volumes, we have primarily focused on what constitutes the traditional service settings of child and youth care practice—residential care, foster care, shelters, schools, hospitals, day treatment—and then added to these a series of service contexts and settings that are less frequently discussed, that appear less frequently in child and youth care conference programs, or that are quite recent in their overt inclusion of child and youth care practice—outdoor adventure-based settings, Deaf communities, Trans youth contexts, immigration and settlement settings, Indigenous communities, and many others. In chapter 11 of volume 2, we have included brief discussions of settings, contexts, or simply themes that perhaps offer additional possibilities for thinking about child and youth care across sectors. AfroFuturism, private service and entrepreneurial activity, rehabilitation services, management and leadership, and advocacy are all examples of elements of child and youth care practice that may be impacted by the always strong identification with tradition in our field. As the two Indigenous-focused chapters, as well as the African-centred chapter, in volume 2 demonstrate, however, there are additional ways of thinking about being in community, being with people, and relational practices more generally that may help to enrich and perhaps even (post)modernize child and youth care practice. Whether we are encountering adult–youth groups focused on public arts, theatre groups based on relational practices, unpaid labour in Indigenous (and often in newcomer) communities, anti-racism advocacy with young people, or the many self-organized youth activities that draw on peer-led relational practices, advocacy, and programming, perhaps there is still more to be said about what CYC across sectors looks like.

As much as we have tried to be representative of child and youth care settings, cultures, communities, and contexts from across Canada, we have succeeded only in part, and only if one thinks of the provinces and territories as the markers of geographic representation. Many of the chapters across both volumes reflect our (the editors') home provinces of Ontario and British Columbia. Of course, there is much more to be done to even approach the richness and diversity of geographic contexts across this vast and highly differentiated country. We could focus much more explicitly on child and youth care practice in dense urban neighbourhoods, in rural settings, in a whole range of ethnic communities, in cities that face long-standing social and racial divisions (such as Saskatoon or Halifax-Dartmouth), or in fly-in communities across Canada's Northern territories. Moreover, notwithstanding two chapters focused on Indigenous contexts, the reality is that there are over 600 First Nations across Canada, each with its own set of histories, cultures, social and economic contexts, and relationships to settlers. And we certainly did not consider the uniqueness of particular communities, such as Brampton, Ontario, now a major city in which South Asian and Afro-Caribbean communities are the backbone of culture, history, and economic success, or Trois-Rivières in Quebec, a working-class French town with a proud history tied to the St. Lawrence River that is entirely unique in the country.

This is why we urge the reader to think of these two volumes as a strong beginning: one that provides a far more comprehensive exploration of the diverse settings and contexts of our field than any other attempt has managed, and one that hints at how the future of the field may develop. But, especially with respect to thinking about the future, we want to make sure everyone understands that these two volumes are not an adequate representation of what that future could be; for this reason, we may contemplate a third volume for the series, although this time with a targeted and specific focus on child and youth care practice that may not yet be recognized as such but that may come to define the field in much more inclusive ways.

VOLUME 3 AND BEYOND

What might such a future look like? If the field of child and youth care continues to focus substantively on young people living life outside of social and economic centres of power and privilege, then we have to take stock of who the profession is engaged with. We know that, across Canada, virtually all the core settings in which young people are served (once it becomes clear that mainstream institutions and processes won't work for them) are characterized by a significant overrepresentation of Indigenous youth; and where there are large African Canadian and Afro-Caribbean Canadian populations, such as in Ontario, Quebec, and Nova Scotia, there is also a significant overrepresentation of Black Youth across virtually all service sectors. But it is not only racial and cultural identities that are at the heart of many service contexts: it is also poverty, social alienation, mental health challenges, disability, gender fluidity, and other factors that render young people, their families, and their communities vulnerable to chronic exclusion from resources, opportunities, and social participation. Fundamentally, this means that the setting of the future is community, where the complex constellations and intersections of all of these factors emerge, evolve, and take shape. The task is not a quick fix or treatment, or even sustaining fragile family relationships or preventing child welfare involvement. Instead, the task is to find ways to create new spaces for young people to join, to find connection, to learn about themselves, others, and the world around them, and to find a sense of personal fulfillment and personal agency that facilitates a return to social participation, community association, and group well-being.

This will present new challenges to the field of child and youth care. Outside of traditional settings, the demand is for a relational practice that is not tied to the institutional or organizational norms and routines, that is not upheld by larger funding schemes and resource depots, and that is fluid, adaptable, and comfortable in the complexity of culture, identity, and the diverse rhythms of life. The tools of child and youth care will have to adapt as well: no more behaviour management, normatively pre-positioned values and ethics, and outcome-focused activities. Instead, the field will have to innovate and consider media for practice that have so far been largely excluded from the professional delineation of the field. The performing arts, visual arts, futurism, land-based practices, music, meditation, spiritual development, community peace activities, advocacy, and other types of activities and forms of engagement will serve as the fuel for relational practices. Such practice, moreover, will have to move well beyond the interpersonal relationship and become embedded in social movements, community engagements, and participatory structures and processes that take the mantra "You Matter" as the starting point of being with youth.

THE LAST POINT

We are proud of our field. Much has been accomplished, and the work of many thought leaders and practitioners has made an enormous difference in the lives of countless young people. Moving beyond what we have is not a rejection of what came before; we celebrate our field by opening the door for new ideas and new ways of thinking about child and youth care practice. Two volumes reflecting primarily the orthodoxy of the field—traditional settings and contexts—are probably enough, even if there are some settings and contexts, and certainly many geographic regions, that we were not able to include. If there is another volume, it will focus on the future—the emergent counter-movement—and solicit chapters that speak to child and youth care practice through the arts, through ideological diversity, and through a lens that is inclusive and in tune with the 21st century.

ABOUT THE CONTRIBUTORS

Chantal Adams completed her undergraduate degree in child and youth care (CYC) from the University of Victoria. She started writing about colonial injustices and violence when she was 14 years old. Chantal continues to pursue her passions of (re)centring her Indigenous ways of being into her writing and practice as a CYC worker.

Peter Amponsah is associate dean of the School of Community Studies within the Faculty of Applied Health and Community Studies (FAHCS) at Sheridan College. He previously taught in the Child and Youth Care program for six years. Peter holds a BSW and MSW with years of experience volunteering and working in the child and youth service sector in front-line, management, and governance roles. Peter is currently pursuing his PhD in Social Work at York University. Peter believes in the transformative potential for culturally based education. As his passion, Peter studies, performs, and facilitates Afro-diasporic drum teachings to youth groups in his community. Peter can be contacted at peter.amponsah@sheridancollege.ca.

Saira Batasar-Johnie graduated from Humber College in 2011 with an honours diploma in Child and Youth Work and furthered her education with a BA in Child and Youth Care and a MA in Child and Youth Care, at Ryerson University. Her graduate research focused on supervision for child and youth care practitioners working in the education sector. Saira has worked as a child and youth worker in residential settings with young people who have experienced abuse, trauma, or mental health challenges, in community programs for at-potential youth and women and children escaping violence, and in the education sector supporting students in kindergarten to grade 12, and is currently teaching and supporting students at the post-secondary level. Saira can be contacted at Saira.batasar@ryerson.ca.

Jessica Carriere graduated with honours from Humber College in Child and Youth Work. In the ensuing 14 years, Jessica has gained invaluable work and life experience in live-in-treatment programs and section 23 classrooms (day treatment) serving Simcoe County in Ontario. Jessica has worked for the past nine years as a school-based care and treatment worker in a section 23 classroom at

New Path Youth and Family Services. In this role, she had the pleasure of working alongside youth and providing mental health support and strength-building skills to enhance young people's academic pathways. Jessica's workplace passions involve facilitating advocacy between young people and school boards to best support the student's life-space in their education. Jessica can be contacted at jcarriere@newpath.ca.

Bill Carty has been involved in service delivery since 1972 when he first worked in children's mental health as a child and youth worker. He has been a practitioner, program supervisor, service manager, and service director in a variety of social service agencies in Ontario, Canada. He has also taught in a number of child and youth work programs and provided consultation services in the social service sector. He co-founded Bartimaeus in 1988 to respond to organizations and agencies in communities across Ontario who required experienced and skilled practitioners to assist with children, adolescents, and adults who have been identified as having special care and treatment needs due to behavioural, mental health, or developmental difficulties. Additionally, in the past decade, he established Improv Care Services for Children, Imagine That Family Care, and Brayden Supervision Services Inc., and he owns and operates Eldano Properties Inc. Bill can be contacted at billcarty@bartimaeus.com.

Luke Carty has over 15 years of experience in the field of child and youth care in a variety of roles and settings. He began his career as a child and youth worker at a leading children's mental health centre in its residential and school programs. In 2011, Luke founded Brayden Supervision Services Inc., a company focused on providing custody and access supervision services to children and families experiencing high-conflict separations. Luke holds a CYC diploma from Humber College and an MA in Child and Youth Care from Ryerson University. He has taught at several post-secondary institutions, including Sheridan College, Humber College, and Ryerson University. He is currently the Chief Operating Officer of Bartimaeus Inc. and can be reached at lcarty@bartimaeus.com.

Anna Chadwick worked collaboratively with rural school districts as a child and youth art therapist in northern British Columbia for 14 years. Currently, she works as a therapist in Victoria, BC, with children and youth who have experienced sexualized violence. Anna recently completed her graduate degree at the School of Child and Youth Care, University of Victoria.

Grant Charles is an associate professor in the School of Social Work and an affiliated faculty with the Division of Adolescent Health and Medicine in the Department of Pediatrics with the Faculty of Medicine. He holds an adjunct appointment with the School of Child and Youth Care at the University of Victoria. He is affiliated with the UBC Centre for Group Counselling and Trauma. He is a member of the UBC Cluster on Research Based Theatre. He is also a member of the Prato International Collaborative on Family Mental Health. He is a past editor of *Relational Child and Youth Care Practice*. Grant can be contacted at grant.charles@ubc.ca.

Sandrina de Finney (School of Child and Youth Care, University of Victoria) is a proud mother, auntie, and sister, and lead researcher for Sisters Rising: Honouring Indigenous Body and Land Sovereignty (sistersrising.uvic.ca), part of an international study that promotes Indigenous-led, youth-engaged, land- and water-based gender well-being and resurgence. Sandrina can be contacted at sdefinn@uvic.ca.

Travonne Edwards is a Social Work PhD student at the University of Toronto. He previously completed an advanced diploma, a bachelor's degree, and a master's degree in Child and Youth Care. Travonne has worked in various social services settings including child welfare, child protection, education, and supportive housing for youth experiencing homelessness. He has worked as a provincial research and evaluation specialist at York University's Youth Research Evaluation and Exchange (YouthREX) and numerous research projects related to the well-being of young people, race relations, child welfare, education, mental health, intersectional and interlocking oppressions, anti-Black racism, and community. He also teaches part-time in the Child and Youth Care program at Sheridan College in Ontario. Travonne can be contacted at travonne.edwards@mail.utoronto.ca.

Pat Gaughan is a child and youth care practitioner and is presently the president and CEO of Bartimaeus Rehabilitation Services and Bartimaeus Inc. He has spent the past 35 years in both front-line and management positions working in both the public and private sector, including mental health, addictions, and acquired brain injury, and has a particular interest in supporting individuals who are exhibiting moderate to severe behaviour. He has presented workshops and seminars at both national and international child and youth care conferences and has been published in the *Canadian Journal of Child and Youth Care*. Pat is a graduate of Ryerson University (CYC) and Cambrian College (CCW) and was recently the recipient of the Cambrian College Alumni Award and was nominated for the Ontario Premieres Award for outstanding Ontario College graduates. A strong believer in community involvement, Pat has provided leadership as board chair of the Reach Out Centre for Kids and the Ontario Rehab Alliance. He has served as a board member for the Ontario Association of Child and Youth Counsellors and for the Burlington Girls' Hockey Club. Pat can be contacted at pat@bartimaeusrehab.com.

Kiaras Gharabaghi is a professor and the director of the School of Child and Youth Care and the John C. Eaton Chair of Social Innovation & Entrepreneurship at Ryerson University. After a 25-year career working in child welfare, child and youth mental health, and youth homelessness, he was appointed as faculty at Ryerson. He has published over 200 articles and creative writings as well as eight books. His latest sole-authored book is *A Hard Place to Call Home: A Canadian Perspective on Residential Care and Treatment*, published by Canadian Scholars. Kiaras can be contacted at k.gharabaghi@ryerson.ca.

Stephanie Griffin has enjoyed over 25 years of work in the field. She is currently a CYC educator at the college and university level. Her front-line career primarily focused on youth community development in the community health sector, outdoor adventure programming, residential care, and work with street-involved youth. Stephanie began as a graduate of the Algonquin CYW program and went on to continue her education by completing a BA in Child and Youth Care through Ryerson University, a Master of Education, and a PhD in Child and Youth Care through the University of Victoria. Stephanie can be contacted at s6griffi@ryerson.ca.

Francis Hare is professor emeritus in the School of Child and Youth Care at Ryerson University. He moved to Canada in 1971 for graduate school and started at Ryerson in 1976 in the psychology department after completing his PhD at the University of Toronto. He was seconded to develop the Child and Youth Care program and served as founding director from 1989 to 2001. He also taught Research methods in and served as graduate program director of the MA program in Immigration and Settlement Studies, as well as teaching program evaluation research courses in MA programs in Early Childhood Studies and in Public Administration. His research interests reflected in his chapter in this volume are at the intersection of CYC practice and the issue of immigration. Francis can be contacted at francis.hare@ryerson.ca.

ABOUT THE CONTRIBUTORS

Julian Hasford is an assistant professor in the School of Child and Youth Care at Ryerson University. His research and advocacy seeks to promote equity, empowerment, and well-being through systems change and community engagement, with a particular focus on African Canadians. He holds a PhD in Community Psychology from Wilfrid Laurier University, and a MHSc in Health Promotion from the University of Toronto. Julian has led and contributed to a wide range of research and advocacy projects, including most recently the Cross-Over Youth Project for youth dually involved in child welfare and youth justice systems, and the Provincial Advisory Council for the Ontario Association of Children's Aid Societies's One Vision, One Voice initiative, which seeks to advance race equity through institutional change amongst the province's child welfare agencies. He has also been active in anti-racist child welfare advocacy in his home community of Peel Region, where he serves as co-chair of the Black Community Action Network, seeking to improve outcomes for vulnerable African Canadian families. He has over 18 years of experience as a youth worker in residential care and parks and recreation, including over 12 years with the City of Toronto where his role focused on engaging African Canadian youth in urban agriculture to promote environmental stewardship and employment. Julian can be contacted at jhasford@ryerson.ca.

Ernie Hilton, MSc CYCA, has been working in the field of CYC since 1985 in various roles: front-line caregiver in community-based and closed-custody settings, supervisor of programs, and director of operations/practice in the same organization for over 30 years. He is currently the executive director of HomeBridge Youth Society in Halifax, Nova Scotia, Canada. Ernie can be contacted at ehilton@homebridgeyouth.ca.

Nicole Ineese-Nash is an Indigenous research associate at Ryerson University. Her current work supports Indigenous community priorities in relation to holistic well-being, particularly with young people. Nicole holds a master's degree in Early Childhood Studies and is currently pursuing doctoral studies in Social Justice Education at the Ontario Institute for Studies in Education at the University of Toronto. In her dissertation work, she is exploring intergenerational land knowledge exchange as a mechanism for supporting youth leadership. Nicole is Anishinaabe (Oji-Cree) from Northern Ontario and is a member of Constance Lake First Nation in Treaty 9 territory. Nicole can be contacted at nicole.ineese-nash@ryerson.ca.

Sheldon Lane has been working with Key Assets Newfoundland and Labrador since March 2016, most recently as program supervisor overseeing two homes for young people. He has grown up and lived in Hopedale, Labrador, for most of his life and understands the importance of child care in the Nunatsiavut region, which is one of the reasons he had accepted a position within Key Assets. One of the great perks within this organization is the opportunity to take the young people out in boat or on skidoo to go hunting, go trapping, make trips to the cabin, or just make a connection with the land, which brings young people back to their roots and also keeps traditions alive. Sheldon practises this at home with his wife and three children. "Going off" (travelling on the land or water) is such a great way to practise self-care. He encourages more people to travel to more rural and isolated communities to get a chance to see the greatness in both the people and the land.

Heather Modlin has worked with young people in residential care for over 30 years. She is currently provincial director of Key Assets Newfoundland and Labrador. Heather is a board member of the International Child and Youth Care Network and a steering committee member for the Global Social Service Workforce Alliance. Heather has an MSc in Child and Youth Care Administration from Nova Southeastern University and a PhD in Child and Youth Care from the University of Victoria, where she is also a sessional instructor. In 2017, Heather received the YWCA Woman of Distinction Award for Community and Social Development in Newfoundland and Labrador; in 2018, was the Atlantic Canada nominee for the RBC Women of Influence Social Change Award; and in 2019, was one of six short-listed nominees in Canada for the Lynn Factor Stand Up for Kids Award. Heather can be contacted at heather.modlin@keyassetsnl.ca.

Shantelle Moreno, as a feminist and queer mixed-race woman of colour, believes that her work as a CYC practitioner, educator, research facilitator, and counsellor is inherently political. Her research interests include relationships of solidarity between Indigenous and racialized peoples, QTBIPOC (Queer and Trans Black, Indigenous, People of Colour) youth experiences in colonial institutions, and conceptualizations of decolonial love.

Jennifer Oliver, née Holwell, grew up in Nain, Newfoundland, raised by her parents Rex and Rosina Holwell. She graduated from Jens Haven Memorial School in 1997 and attended two semesters of university but, due to culture shock, moved back home. After living and working in Goose Bay for a few years and feeling a lack of belonging, she returned to school and graduated from the College of the North Atlantic in 2008 as a drill/blaster. In 2016, Jenny and her wife returned to Nain and she started work with the Nunatsiavut government's

Department of Health and Social Development as a family connections home visitor. In 2019, she graduated from Nova Scotia Community College via distant education with a CYC diploma (with honours). Her intention is to attain a bachelor's degree in Child and Youth Care with Mount Saint Vincent University in the near future. Jenny married the love of her life, Kim Oliver, in 2006 and they now have a son who is growing up in Nain.

Ashley Quinn is an assistant professor at the University of British Columbia, School of Social Work. Ashley's research has focused on participatory action research, First Nations' research ethics protocols, data analysis, and program evaluation, including projects related to First Nations' health; traditional Indigenous parenting programs for families mandated by the child welfare system; family homelessness; parent–worker engagement in child welfare and the impact on outcomes in child welfare; and experiences of First Nations communities with child welfare. Ashley can be contacted at ashely.quinn@ubc.ca.

Agnes Quittard is a contract lecturer at Ryerson University and a full-time child and youth counsellor at North York General Hospital where she works on the Child and Adolescent Mental Health Inpatient Unit. Her current scope of practice supports children and youth with mental health concerns and who are in crisis. Agnes is a life learner and has completed her master's degree in Child and Youth Studies through Strathclyde University. Her specialization is in clinical child and youth care with the primary focus on the practice of child and youth care in hospitals. Her dissertation explored the lack of role standardization of child and youth counsellors in hospital settings. Agnes can be contacted at aquittar@ryerson.ca.

Shezell-Rae Sam has a BCYC (UVic) and is currently an MA student at the School of Child and Youth Care at the University of Victoria. Her practice and research work with Indigenous children, youth, and families is focused on healing from lateral violence and promoting community-based resurgence. She is a research facilitator with Sisters Rising.

Angela Scott is an Ojibwe/Métis woman, Registered Clinical Counsellor (RCC), and child, youth, and family therapist at the Victoria Child Abuse Prevention and Counselling Centre. With a specialized focus on trauma and the child welfare system, Angela's educational background includes an MA in Child and Youth Care and a BA in Social Sciences (University of Victoria).

Kelly Shaw is currently core faculty at the Nova Scotia Community College in the Child and Youth Care diploma program. She has an MA in Child and Youth Study, holds Child and Youth Care certification from the CYC Certification Board, and is a PhD candidate in Educational Studies at Brock University. Prior to moving to pre-service CYC education, she spent a number of years working in a group treatment program that focused on family support and intervention and believes that family is always present. Kelly can be contacted at Kelly.shaw@nscc.ca.

Hans Skott-Myhre is a professor in the Social Work and Human Services department at Kennesaw State University. He is the author of *Youth Subcultures as Creative Force: Creating New Spaces for Radical Youth Work*, co-editor with Chris Richardson of *Habitus of the Hood*, co-editor with K. Gharabaghi and M. Krueger of *With Children and Youth*, with V. Pacini-Ketchabaw and K.S. Skott-Myhre of *Youth Work, Early Education and Psychology: Liminal Encounters*, as well as *Art as Revolt with David Fancy*. He has published multiple articles, reviews, and book chapters. Hans can be contacted at hskottmy@kennesaw.edu.

Juanita Stephen is CYC educator, a mother of a teenage son, and a PhD student at York University in Gender, Feminist and Women's Studies where her research is centred around Black theories and practices of care. She holds a master's degree in Child and Youth Care and has over 14 years of experience working with young people and families. As an educator, Juanita uses her classroom as a space to challenge students to (re)consider the way they think about justice, equity, identity, and power. Juanita can be contacted at Juanita.stephen@ryerson.ca.